International Perspectives on Pilgrimage Studies

Although research on contemporary pilgrimage has expanded considerably since the early 1990s, the conversation has largely been dominated by Anglophone researchers in anthropology, ethnology, sociology and religious studies from the U.K., the U.S., France and northern Europe. This volume challenges the hegemony of Anglophone scholarship by considering what can be learned from different national, linguistic, religious and disciplinary traditions, with the aim of fostering a global exchange of ideas. The chapters outline contributions made to the study of pilgrimage from a variety of international and methodological contexts and discuss what the 'metropolis' can learn from these diverse perspectives. While the Anglophone study of pilgrimage has largely been centred on and located within anthropological contexts, in many other linguistic and academic traditions, areas such as folk studies, ethnology and economics have been highly influential. Contributors show that in many traditions the study of 'folk' beliefs and practices (often marginalised within the Anglophone world) has been regarded as an important and central area which contributes widely to the understanding of religion, in general, and pilgrimage, specifically. As several chapters in this book indicate, 'folk'-based studies have played an important role in developing different methodological orientations in Russia, Poland, Germany, Japan, Hungary, and Italy, for example. With a highly international focus, this interdisciplinary volume aims to introduce new approaches to the study of pilgrimage and to transcend the boundary between centre and periphery in this emerging discipline.

Dionigi Albera is Director of Research in the CNRS and leads the Institute of Mediterranean, European and Comparative Ethnology at the University of Aix-Marseille, France.

John Eade is Professor of Sociology and Anthropology at the University of Roehampton; Research Fellow at the Department for the Study of Religion, University of Toronto; and co-founder of the *Routledge Religion, Travel and Tourism* series.

Routledge Studies in Religion, Travel, and Tourism

Edited by John Eade, Roehampton University; Ian Reader, Lancaster University; Alana Harris, University of Oxford and Ellen Badone, MacMaster University

1 **Pilgrimage to the National Parks**
Religion and Nature in the
United States
Lynn Ross-Bryant

2 **Pilgrimage in the Marketplace**
Ian Reader

3 **Christian Pilgrimage, Landscape and Heritage**
Journeying to the Sacred
Avril Maddrell, Veronica della Dora, Alessandro Scafi, and Heather Walton

4 **International Perspectives on Pilgrimage Studies**
Itineraries, Gaps and Obstacles
Edited by Dionigi Albera and John Eade

International Perspectives on Pilgrimage Studies
Itineraries, Gaps and Obstacles

**Edited by Dionigi Albera
and John Eade**

NEW YORK AND LONDON

First published 2015
by Routledge
711 Third Avenue, New York, NY 10017

and by Routledge
2 Park Square, Milton Park, Abingdon, Oxon OX14 4RN

First issued in paperback 2018

Routledge is an imprint of the Taylor & Francis Group, an informa business

© 2015 Taylor & Francis

The right of the editors to be identified as the authors of the editorial material, and of the authors for their individual chapters, has been asserted in accordance with sections 77 and 78 of the Copyright, Designs and Patents Act 1988.

All rights reserved. No part of this book may be reprinted or reproduced or utilised in any form or by any electronic, mechanical, or other means, now known or hereafter invented, including photocopying and recording, or in any information storage or retrieval system, without permission in writing from the publishers.

Trademark Notice: Product or corporate names may be trademarks or registered trademarks, and are used only for identification and explanation without intent to infringe.

Library of Congress Cataloging-in-Publication Data

   International perspectives on pilgrimage studies : itineraries, gaps, and obstacles / edited by Dionigi Albera and John Eade. — 1 [edition].
     pages cm. — (Routledge studies in religion, travel, and tourism ; 4)
   Includes index.
   1. Christian pilgrims and pilgrimages.   2. Pilgrims and pilgrimages.   I. Albera, Dionigi, editor.
   BV5067.I57 2015
   263'.041—dc23
   2014046178

ISBN 13: 978-1-138-05317-5 (pbk)
ISBN 13: 978-1-138-84035-5 (hbk)

Typeset in Sabon
by Apex CoVantage, LLC

To the memory of Michael Sallnow and
Michael Hollings

Contents

List of Figures	ix
Acknowledgements	xi

1   International Perspectives on Pilgrimage Studies:
Putting the Anglophone Contribution in Its Place   1
DIONIGI ALBERA AND JOHN EADE

2   Japanese Studies of Pilgrimage   23
IAN READER

3   Touching the Holy: Orthodox Christian
Pilgrimage Within Russia   47
STELLA ROCK

4   Old and New Paths of Polish Pilgrimages   69
ANNA NIEDŹWIEDŹ

5   Pilgrimages in Hungary: Ethnological and
Anthropological Approaches   95
GÁBOR BARNA

6   From Religious Folklore Studies to Research of Popular
Religiosity: Pilgrimage Studies in German-Speaking Europe   114
HELMUT EBERHART

7   Exploring Jewish Pilgrimage in Israel   134
NIMROD LUZ AND NOGA COLLINS-KREINER

8   Italian Studies on Pilgrimage: Beyond Folklore
Towards a National Anthropological Tradition and
the International Circulation of Ideas   152
ELENA ZAPPONI

viii *Contents*

9 **From Cryptic to Critique: Early and Contemporary French Contributions to the Study of Pilgrimage**   171
ANNA FEDELE AND CYRIL ISNART

Contributors   193
Index   197

Figures

2.1	Statue of Kōbō Daishi as a mendicant pilgrim in Shikoku.	26
2.2	Shikoku pilgrims: the writing on their shirts is an invocation to Kōbō Daishi and signifies his presence with them on pilgrimage.	31
2.3	Pilgrimage tour group climbing the steps up to a temple in Shikoku.	38
3.1	Pilgrims who have walked for three days in a procession of the cross to the Kirov region shrine of Velikoretskoe are blessed with holy water, June 2009. (Photo: Sandra Reddin)	62
4.1	'A company arriving to Częstochowa'. From the collection of The National Library of Poland, available through http://polona.pl, originally published in a Warsaw weekly, Kłosy, 1872, Vol. XIV, no. 363, p. 400.	73
4.2	Women from Klimontów near Kraków in their traditional attires, holding a local Marian image when welcoming the peregrinating image of 'Our Lady of Częstochowa', 2008. (Photo: Anna Niedźwiedź)	81
4.3	Members of a voluntary firemen unit in Klimontów village near Kraków, bringing a copy of the image of 'Our Lady of Częstochowa' to their parish church during a 'peregrination of the image', 2008. (Photo: Anna Niedźwiedź)	84
4.4	A 'Pilgrimage in the Footsteps of Karol Wojtyła the Worker', Kraków, 2013. On their way to a newly built shrine dedicated to John Paul II, pilgrims visit an old quarry where Wojtyła used to work during the Nazi occupation of Poland. (Photo: Anna Niedźwiedź)	90
5.1	Map of important pilgrimage sites in Hungary in the eighteenth through twentieth centuries.	101
5.2	New state borders after the Trianon Peace Treaty, 4 June 1920. Map of the Central Statistical Office of Hungary, Census 1920 VI.	107

x *Figures*

7.1 Praying at the Wailing Wall—Jerusalem, Israel.
(Photo: Guy Raivitz)   139
7.2 Pilgrims at the Baba Sali annual festivities—Netivot, Israel.
(Photo: Guy Raivitz)   141
7.3 Women at Rachel's Tomb—Jerusalem/Bethlehem, Israel.
(Photo: Guy Raivitz)   144

Acknowledgements

This volume has emerged from a variety of workshops held in both England and France over a number of years. The first interdisciplinary meeting took place at the University of Surrey in 2010, supported by CRONEM, where John Eade was Executive Director, and its administrator, Mirela Dumic. The success of this event led to two similar workshops at University College London in 2011 and 2012, where John Eade was Visiting Professor at the Migration Research Unit (MRU). These two events benefitted from the support of the Department of Geography, especially Claire Dwyer (Co-Director of the MRU), European Institute at UCL and the Centre for the Study of Christianity and Culture, University of York, led by Dee Dyas, who also invited us to contribute to two conferences at her centre during 2013 and 2014.

The intellectual engagements and personal friendships, which were forged at these events, encouraged Dionigi Albera to convene a three-day workshop during October 2013 in the Musée des civilisations de l'Europe et de Méditerrannée, overlooking Marseille's old harbour. We are very grateful to the financial and administrative support liberally provided by LabexMed, based at Aix-Marseille University (AMU), IDEMEC, and the MuCEM, Marseille. Besides those included in this volume we would like to thank the very helpful contributions made by Michel Boivin, Katia Boissevain, Marion Bowman, Mathieu Claveyrolas, Simon Coleman, Premakumara De Silva, Lena Gemzoe, Steve Sangren and Galia Valtchinova. Marion Bowpman was particularly helpful in discussions of the folklore studies tradition and in recruiting Gábor Barna for this volume. We benefitted a great deal from the comments concerning the volume proposal, which we received from the anonymous reviewers and the series editors.

We have also enjoyed our collaboration with our Routledge partners—Nancy Chen, Margo Irvin and Laura Stearns.

1 International Perspectives on Pilgrimage Studies
Putting the Anglophone Contribution in Its Place

Dionigi Albera and John Eade

INTRODUCTION

During the last twenty years 'pilgrimage studies' has frequently been used to describe the expanding Anglophone research on contemporary pilgrimage. However, in global terms what really exists is a highly variegated range of empirical studies influenced by different disciplinary and linguistic traditions as well as by changing theoretical debates within the social sciences. These traditions and theoretical debates are shaped by two key processes—deeply embedded national structures of knowledge production and an increasingly globalised economy of academic publication dominated by Anglophone universities and publishing houses (such as the publisher of this volume!).

These processes intersect, to some extent, through the flows of knowledge and academic networks encouraged by the status of English as a global medium of communication. Indeed, a range of edited volumes on pilgrimage have been published in English since the 1970s, which work across national and disciplinary boundaries (see, for example, the recent publications by Margry 2008, Hermkens, Jansen and Notermans 2009, Bowman 2012, Hyndman-Rizk 2012, Eade and Katić 2014). However, the global dominance of Anglophone literary production means that when it comes to communication between Anglophone and non-Anglophone scholars, the links are far weaker (see Yamashita, Bosco and Eades 2004 and Hann 2011 for related discussions). Anglophone awareness of pilgrimage research undertaken in other languages usually depends on the limited cases where studies are translated into English, mainly from French and German sources.

The international flow of knowledge and ideas is seriously hampered by this Anglophone hegemony and the pervasive assumption among Anglophone scholars that 'pilgrimage studies' refers to research published in English and what has permeated across the linguistic boundary through translation. This volume seeks, therefore, to work against this hegemony and to start closing the gaps and overcoming obstacles, which it has created by introducing Anglophone readers to the wide range of pilgrimage research developed by non-Anglophone linguistic and disciplinary traditions. By bringing together chapters on pilgrimage research in Japan, Russia, Poland, Hungary,

2 Dionigi Albera and John Eade

German-speaking countries, Italy, France and Israel, we can help Anglophone readers to look beyond the boundaries of the English-speaking world and introduce them to the rich history of research in this wider world. We hope that our volume will encourage further exploration across linguistic and disciplinary boundaries and generate itineraries where those involved in different traditions can engage in creative dialogue.

DISCIPLINARY AND LINGUISTIC BOUNDARIES: THE EMERGENCE OF THE ANGLOPHONE STUDY OF CONTEMPORARY PILGRIMAGE

As we will see later, compared with research undertaken in other linguistic and disciplinary traditions Anglophone pilgrimage studies is a late arrival. It emerged during the 1960s and 1970s, with historians taking the lead and then social scientists, especially social anthropologists. Not surprisingly, the historians focussed largely on mediaeval European society and Christianity (see, for example, Ladner 1967, Christian 1973, Sumption 1975, Zacher 1976, Finucane 1977, Howard 1980, Davies 1988).[1] Interest among social scientists was minimal. Those studying contemporary religion in the highly industrialised societies of W. Europe and N. America, for example, were preoccupied with the secularisation paradigm and debates concerning religious beliefs and formal institutional structures. Anglophone anthropologists focussed primarily on the intensive study of small, non-Western face-to-face communities, making it difficult to study ritual activities that operated across geographical and ethnic frontiers. Even those Anglophone pioneers of the study of rural society in W. Europe during the 1950s and 1960s ignored pilgrimage, despite the millions travelling back and forth to European shrines.

During the late 1970s and 1980s interest in contemporary pilgrimage among Anglophone anthropologists and other social scientists quickened with the publication of studies on pilgrimage in various areas of the world and religious traditions (Marx 1977, Turner 1973, Turner and Turner 1978, Pfaffenberger 1979, Sallnow 1981, Morinis 1984, Neville 1987, Bhardwaj and Rinschede 1988, Nolan and Nolan 1989, Eickelman and Piscatori 1990). The influence of Victor Turner, one of the leading figures of twentieth-century Anglophone anthropology, played a key part in this development. During the 1950s he had pursued a conventional path as a British social anthropologist by studying the Ndembu in Northern Rhodesia (Zambia) and the part played by ritual in resolving episodes of endemic conflict. Like other social anthropologists he was influenced by Francophone scholars, especially Arnold van Gennep's seminal text *Rites de passage* (1909). His move to the US in 1961 led eventually to the University of Chicago (1968) where he turned towards world religions and pilgrimage, in particular.

International Perspectives on Pilgrimage Studies 3

Several theoretical interests displayed in his previous publications, such as the study of social processes, anti-structure and ritual symbols, converged now in his analysis of pilgrimage. In his view, pilgrimages were liminal phenomena, characterised by *communitas*, which enables them to celebrate a universal humanity and freedom from structural divisions. (Although he distinguished between three types of *communitas*, subsequent debate has focussed on 'normative *communitas*'; see Coleman 2002.) Besides this structural approach, he also suggested that pilgrimages could also be examined in terms of the extended-case history method, studying pilgrims' personal experiences and isolating sequences of social dramas (1974: 167).

The subsequent book, *Image and Pilgrimage in Christian Culture* (1978), written with his wife, Edith Turner, represents the first, fascinating materialisation of this research programme. However, we see here a reduction in the scope of the enterprise sketched some years before. The Turners observed that their 'original intention was to compare the pilgrimage systems of several major historical religions, but it soon became apparent that the study of Christian pilgrimage alone is an awesome task' (1978: 15). They presented, therefore, a comparative analysis of several major pilgrimages in Europe and America, which are seen as representative of a broader 'Christian culture'.

Even from a methodological point of view, there was a narrowing of the research span. The authors focussed on what they define as 'institutional structures' and 'implicational meanings'. Borrowing some categories from F. Allan Hanson (1975), they distinguished between 'institutional questions', which are concerned with the structure of values, norms, symbols, customs, roles, relationships and the 'individual questions', which inquire into the nature of the drives, reasons, intentions and needs that people manifest in their behaviour. Yet only the first type of investigation was pursued in the book as they sought 'to map and frame some of the institutional "territories" within which pilgrimage processes circulate, and to suggest how institutional changes within pilgrimage may be linked to changes outside it' (1978: XV).

The publication of *Image and Pilgrimage in Christian Culture* is generally seen as a ground-breaking study, which combines a highly influential theoretical agenda with the authors' own research on major pilgrimage shrines in both the Americas and Western Europe. They showed how anthropologists could fruitfully study large-scale, urbanised shrines which attracted pilgrims from diverse social and cultural backgrounds. The *communitas* model reaffirmed the sacred/profane binary, explored earlier by Emile Durkheim, because pilgrims are seen to move to and from a sacred place where the universal humanity and freedom from structural divisions can be ritually celebrated. Although the Turners acknowledged that, in practice, the mundane world of the secular surrounds this sacred space—they noted, for example, Lourdes' busy shops and cafes—the *essential* character of pilgrimage was established by the boundary between sacred and profane.

4 Dionigi Albera and John Eade

Turner's approach was followed by a number of studies, which tried to test the relevance of the *communitas* thesis in various ethnographic contexts. Brian Pfaffenberger carried out fieldwork on the Hindu pilgrimage centre of Kataragama, Sri Lanka, inspired largely by Turner's paradigm. However, in his 1977 PhD thesis and a subsequent article (1979) he concluded that, at this pilgrimage site at least, the pilgrims did not experience *communitas*. William LaFleur (1979) followed up Pfaffenberger's critique by suggesting ways in which his work could be interpreted to fit Turner's model. More generally, LaFleur sought to demonstrate that Turner's theory on pilgrimage was 'a valuable tool, which students of Asia can use with profit' (1979: 272). He further underlined this point by presenting an 'analysis of an Asian pilgrimage that supports Turner's theory' through summarising four essays published between 1974 and 1978 by the Japanese scholar Eiki Hoshino, who had studied pilgrimage on the island of Shikoku, drawing on the *communitas* model (LaFleur 1979; see also Ian Reader's chapter in this volume).[2]

The debate was continued by Alan Morinis (1984), who investigated Hindu pilgrimage in another part of the Indian subcontinent (West Bengal). He accepted that *communitas* feelings were an aspect of the pilgrims' performances, but they had no exclusivity because they coexisted with other components of the ritual behaviour, which were at least of equivalent significance (1984: 274). Donald Messerschmidt and Jyoti Sharma (1981) went further and proposed a critical assessment of anti-structure and *communitas* theory, drawing on their research on another Hindu pilgrimage site in Northern Nepal. They concluded that their data refuted 'the *communitas* hypothesis; this pilgrimage is fundamentally and unequivocally a structure-affirming occasion' (1981: 572). They suggested an alternative hypothesis to Turner's broad cross-cultural generalisation, which emphasised the cultural autonomy of each religious system. They posited that a pilgrimage serves to highlight 'the principal themes *idiosyncratic* to a religious system' (1981: 572). Thus, within the hierarchical system of Hinduism, it is reasonable to presume a structure-affirming behaviour. In Christianity, on the other hand, with its emphasis on brotherly love, *communitas* may be a reasonable expectation (Ibid.).

Researchers working on Chinese pilgrimage also engaged with the Turnerian approach. A book edited by Susan Naquin and Chün-Fang Yü, *Pilgrims and Sacred Sites in China* (1992), sought to contribute to the general literature on pilgrimage by drawing on several case studies which were 'scarcely mentioned in comparative works' (1992: 7). They acknowledged that 'Turner had done a great service by distilling a general model from the confusion of a vast variety of pilgrimages' (Ibid.), but the Chinese examples suggested that 'it may be time to reconsider the chaos of pilgrimage and to listen again to the cacophony' (1992: 7). In another religious and regional context—pilgrimage (*ziyarat*) to a Muslim shrine in Morocco—Dale Eickelman (1976) also engaged with Turner's model and concluded that while pilgrims to Mecca might be involved in *communitas*, at the

Moroccan shrine 'there is no free comingling of pilgrims from different social groups' and 'the inequalities implicit in everyday social relations are preserved' (1976: 173).

A more radical critique was proposed by Bawa Yamba (1990). He studied Africa pilgrims to Mecca who stop halfway in Sudan, where they reside in enclaves, sometimes as fourth- and fifth-generation immigrants. Yet they still see themselves as pilgrims and consider their villages as temporary stations on their way to Mecca. In this case, 'pilgrimage must be regarded not as something that occurs outside of life daily lived, breaking the regular flow, but rather as something that is part of everyday life itself' (1990: 12). Yamba also criticised Turner's approach in more general terms:

> Anthropologists who embark on the study of pilgrimage almost all start out debating with the pronouncements of Victor Turner, whose framework they invariably employ as a point of departure, but beyond whose initial formulations and questions never venture. . . . The problem of the anthropologist, therefore, arises from inhibitions derived from Turner himself, whose own varied and complex pronouncements on pilgrimage, provide what amounts to an uncomfortable yardstick for every prospective analysis of the phenomenon (1990: 8–9).

Yet it was within the emerging study of contemporary Christian pilgrimage that the critique of the Turnerian paradigm was elaborated more forcefully. The claim that *communitas* provided ritual and ontological space for the expression of human commonality was challenged not by someone who, like the Turners, focussed primarily on large-scale, urbanised shrines but by an anthropologist—Michael Sallnow—who focussed on a remote rural Peruvian community. In a 1981 article he observed:

> My debt to Turner's seminal writings on pilgrimage will be readily apparent. I shall argue, however, that ultimately the concept of communitas is dispensable from understanding of the phenomenon, and that in fact it tends to inhibit an appreciation of the contradiction and emergent processes in Andean regional devotions. (1981: 164)

Although Sallnow referred to Robert Hertz's pioneering work on the tensions inherent to the St Besse pilgrimage (1913) in his subsequent *magnum opus*, *Pilgrims of the Andes: Regional Cults in Cusco* (1987), his critique of the *communitas* paradigm drew mainly on the discussion of regional cults by the American anthropologist (and former colleague of Victor Turner at Manchester University), Richard Werbner:

> As Werbner has argued, the weakness of Turner's model is that 'like other ideal typologies . . . it tends to represent as mutually exclusive alternatives . . . what are in fact *aspects* which combine in a surprising

6 *Dionigi Albera and John Eade*

variety of ways within a range of actual cases' (1977, xiii, emphasis in the original [1987: 9])

Sallnow proceeds to suggest that in 'examining Andean pilgrimage cults from this perspective, the most helpful, preanalytic image to hold in mind is of a tangle of contradictions, a cluster of coincident opposites' (Ibid.).

This critique of the *communitas* paradigm was developed further in a book edited with John Eade, devoted to a comparative analysis of Christian pilgrimage—*Contesting the Sacred: The Anthropology of Christian Pilgrimage* (1991). In the introduction the authors accepted that 'some of the features and conditions glossed by the term *"communitas"* will not be found in some cases' (1991: 5). Yet they noted that the theoretical critiques, which had already greeted *Image and Pilgrimage*, had demonstrated that

> it is the determinism of the model which limits its usefulness, for the necessary alignment of pilgrimage and anti-structure not only prejudges the complex character of the phenomenon but also imposes a spurious homogeneity on the practice of pilgrimage in widely different historical and cultural settings. (Ibid.)

In many ways the Turnerian model could be seen as 'representative of a particular discourse *about* pilgrimage rather than as an empirical description *of* it' (Ibid., emphasis in the original). Hence, rather than pursuing dichotomies based on structuralist foundations (Turnerian, functionalist, Marxist), researchers should approach pilgrimage 'not merely as a field of social relations but also as a *realm of competing discourses*' (Ibid., emphasis in the original). Their focus should be on the manifold ways in which individuals and groups pursued different and often competing understandings of person, place and text.

Contesting the Sacred helped to expand the field of Anglophone pilgrimage research through explorations of contestation in a variety of contexts—not just with regard to religious pilgrimage but also the variety of non-religious pilgrimages described as spiritual, secular, alternative, etc. (see, for example, Reader and Walter 1993, Bowman 1993, Duijzings 2000, Ivakhiv 2001, Digance 2003, Bowman 2008, Margry 2008, Hermkens et al. 2009, Jansen and Notermans 2012, Fedele 2013, Badone 2014). Furthermore, researchers began to define pilgrimage more broadly and moved beyond the preoccupation with religious pilgrimage to explore a particularly important relationship—that between pilgrimage and tourism. An extensive literature emerged, which uncovered the complex intersections and overlaps between the two (see, for example, Eade 1992, Vukonic 1992, Rinschede 1992, Jackowski 2000, Badone and Roseman 2004, Timothy and Olsen 2006, Raj and Morpeth 2007, Collins-Kreiner 2010, Stausberg 2011, Fedele 2014).

Although the two theoretical perspectives have often been interpreted as opposing one another, Eade and Sallnow readily acknowledged what others have subsequently confirmed—*communitas* and contestation are both empirically discernible (Coleman 2002). It also became clear that the contestation approach encouraged the exploration of the complex relationships among religious, spiritual, political and economic processes. These relationships were studied from other disciplinary perspectives too. Working across the boundaries of history and sociology, Kaufman (2005), for example, demonstrated the vital role played by mass consumption in the development of Europe's most popular Marian shrine—Lourdes—and the ways in which visitors (pilgrims/tourists/travellers) embraced the artefacts sold in Lourdes's multitudinous shops and frequented its cafes and bars and other modern attractions (see also Eade 1992 and Reader's more general analysis, *Pilgrimage in the Marketplace* 2014).

The *communitas*/contestation debate has given some theoretical shape to the expanding field of Anglophone pilgrimage research. It is also partially unified by a common intellectual genealogy because some scholars share a bibliography, ancestors and the memory of debates and controversies. As shown by the abundance of books whose title refers to the study *of* pilgrimage, it is possible to see a Turnerian legacy through the distinct and more distant approaches that focus on pilgrimage *per se*. Moreover, this legacy also implies a perpetuation of the Turners' 'institutional' questions, principally concerned with the structure of values, norms, symbols, customs, roles and relationships.

MOVING ON: THE EMERGENCE OF A MORE DIVERSE FIELD OF STUDIES

From the early 1990s theoretical debates in social science more generally have moved on from structuralist to postmodern enquiries, and researchers have continued the expansion and diversification of Anglophone pilgrimage research. This development can be seen in the wide range of issues and themes, which have been studied from diverse disciplinary perspectives, e.g. mobility and globalisation, dwelling and crossing, gender, ethnicity, political processes, performativity, landscape and nonreligious pilgrimage and the relationship between pilgrimage and tourism (see, for example, Reader and Walter 1993, Dubisch 1995, Christian 1996, Coleman and Elsner 1998, Vasquez and Marquardt 2000, 2003, Swatos 2002, Tomasi 2002, Coleman and Eade 2004, Tweed 1997, 2006, Campo 1998, Blackwell 2007, Margry 2008, Post 2011, Albera and Coroucli 2012, Ross-Bryant 2013, Eade and Katić 2014, Maddrell 2014).[3] At a theoretical level, this expansion and diversification has been informed by various 'turns' within Anglophone social science, such as the 'cultural turn', 'mobility turn' and 'spatial turn' (see, for example, Vasquez and Marquardt 2003, Coleman and Eade 2004,

8 *Dionigi Albera and John Eade*

Tweed 2006, Knott 2009). A growing body of literature has also focussed on 'individual' questions and is more sensitive to the drives, needs and fears of people who engage in pilgrimages. Moreover, for some authors pilgrimage seems a strategic context for the study of related issues renouncing an explicit theorisation of pilgrimage *per se* (see Coleman's distinction (2002) between the anthropology *of* and *through* pilgrimage).

Recently, some have called for a radical break with the notion of coherent, bounded (collective or individual) ontologies, which has long underpinned social scientific research. Huff and Stallins (2013), for example, have suggested moving beyond ontology towards ontogenesis, defined by Dodge and Kitchen as a dynamic process of '"continually bringing into existence"' (2013: 99). This questioning is particularly suggestive in terms of the popular distinction between nature and society, where Rob Shields (1991), Tim Ingold (1995) and Nigel Thrift (2008), in particular, have challenged the dominant representational approach. Ross-Bryant in a recent analysis of pilgrimage in the context of American national parks (2013), draws on their phenomenological-hermeneutic approach to challenge conventional binaries between sacred/profane, nature/culture, subject/object, individual/community to explore 'the many different threads that weave together to make up an experience' (Ibid. 2013: 13). She argues that we need to avoid both labelling 'some things part of the pilgrimage experience and others outside of it' and encourages us to explore 'unexpected elements that would otherwise be ignored as irrelevant (Ibid.: 13–14). We should focus, therefore, on 'emotional geographies' and other ways through which we interact with other people, material objects and our environment through bodily practices.

These developments by Anglophone social scientists have opened up new avenues in pilgrimage research. A recent example is provided by the volume produced by Avril Maddrell and her colleagues (Maddrell 2014), which examines the relationship between pilgrims and landscape from different disciplinary perspectives. Maddrell contends that 'landscape and its landforms are . . . not mere blank canvasses passively imprinted with meanings'; rather, they are 'complex textures', which are 'speaking back' to those 'staring at or traversing' the landscape (2015: 7). She argues that: 'It is thus through this two-way dialogue, between the land and the subject, between matter and meaning, that geographical imaginations are articulated' (Ibid.).

As we noted at the beginning of this chapter, the study of pilgrimage was initially dominated by historians. The expansion and diversification of research has tended to put the continuing contribution by historians in the shade, so it is important to note not only their individual research but also their recent collaboration with those working in other disciplines. Research on the Marian shrine at Lourdes and the pilgrimage routes to Santiago de Compostela illustrate this trend (see Harris 2010, 2103), while the building of international networks between multidisciplinary research centres provides another example, e.g. the Institute for Pilgrimage at William and Mary

College, US, and the Centre for Pilgrimage Studies at the University of York, UK. These developments have encouraged social scientists to locate contemporary pilgrimage within a longer historical perspective. Furthermore, historical attention to the rigorous analysis of a wide range of textual material across time serves as a reminder that the relationship between person, place and text (see Eade and Sallnow 1991) has still been insufficiently examined.

A MORE GLOBAL APPROACH: WORKING ACROSS BOUNDARIES

Although the flow of knowledge and the generation of creative debate is still constrained by the structures of national universities, networks, conferences, funding and publishing regimes, some Anglophone publications demonstrate the effectiveness of working across national boundaries (see Coleman and Eade 2004, Badone and Roseman 2004, Dubisch and Winkelman 2005, Hermkens et al. 2009, Bowman 2012, Hyndman-Rizk 2012, Crumrine and Morinis 1991). Collaboration has been most intense among those undertaking research in Europe and N. America, but networks are also being forged with Anglophone scholars working in other regions of the globe, such as S. Asia, the Asia Pacific and S. America. Furthermore, a more equal dialogue is emerging as Western preoccupations and definitions of religion are questioned (see Petersen, Vasquez and Williams 2001, Vasquez and Marquardt 2003, Reader 2007, 2014, Vasquez 2011).

Global labour migration has also encouraged researchers in particular regions of the world to look across and beyond religious boundaries. In the European region attention is beginning to be paid to the creation of non-Christian pilgrimages (see Eade 2013) and the increasing cultural diversity of those visiting Christian shrines (see Weibel 2005, Notermans 2012). Old Christian shrines are being revived and reinterpreted together with pilgrimage routes, and European scholars are analysing these developments by working together across national and disciplinary borders (see Margry 2008, Hermkens, Jansen and Notermans 2009, Eade and Katić 2014).

The issue of mobility reminds us to examine not just the ways in which places become sacred but also how routes are sacralised. The revival of mediaeval routes in Europe highlights this process, but it also has encouraged scholars to make comparisons with non-Christian traditions, e.g. Shinto and Buddhist routes in Japan and Hindu pilgrimage in India (see Sax 1991, 2006 and Reader's chapter in this volume). Ian Reader (2014) develops this comparison further in his global analysis of pilgrimage, which builds on Kaufman's historical study of Lourdes mentioned above. Pilgrimage routes and shrines are increasingly being shared by those inspired by differing religious and nonreligious interests. The expanding research on the *camino* to Santiago de Compostela illustrates this plurality and 'postmodern' mingling of religious, 'spiritual', 'New Age', touristic impulses and the

10 *Dionigi Albera and John Eade*

political and economic interests encouraging the flow of travellers along the *camino* (see Murray and Graham 1997, Frey 1998, Gonzalez and Medina 2003, Zapponi 2011, Gonzalez 2013). This plurality is not just evident on the open road—the modern historian Alana Harris (2013) shows how similar processes have developed since the 1960s at a specific place (Lourdes).

Mobility is not just evident among those engaged in pilgrimage, however broadly defined, but also among those studying pilgrimage. Flows of knowledge and people across national boundaries in the European region have also been encouraged by the collapse of the 'Iron Curtain' and the concomitant strengthening of ties between researchers working on pilgrimage across the region. This process has been promoted politically through the expansion of European Union after 2004 and the associated expansion of the EU Erasmus academic exchange scheme, the growth of European conferences and collaborative research programmes. Research centres in former socialist countries have further contributed to European academic collaboration, such as the Max Planck Institute for Social Anthropology at Halle/Saale, even if dialogue is still constrained by academic prejudices/assumptions (see Hann and Goltz 2010, Hann 2011).

Anglophone influence has been strengthened by these developments as scholars in central and Eastern Europe have sought to adapt to the power of Anglophone universities and the academic publishing industry in an increasingly globalised market. As a result the historic role of German-speaking universities, in particular, as an important conduit for the dissemination of East European research, has declined. International conferences on the sociology and anthropology of religion, ethnology and folklore across central and Eastern Europe are acknowledging this shift in linguistic power by using English as the prime means of communication (Eade and Katić 2014), a practice which has long been established in some West European countries, such as the Netherlands.

The dominance of English in pilgrimage research has been accompanied by the strong focus on Christian pilgrimage, especially shrines and routes associated with Roman Catholicism. Turner's example is prototypical also in this respect. During the 1970s he oscillated between a study of the pilgrimage as a universal phenomenon (or at least in the great historical religions) and the study of the pilgrimage as a manifestation of Christian culture. Even in the 1978 book, the references to non-Christian experience are recurrent. The gestation process of *Contesting the Sacred* offers some parallels. At the conference in London, where papers dealing with many religions were presented, only those by anthropologists concerning the Christian world were finally assembled in the edited volume. Indeed, both publications reveal a synecdoche, where the whole (Christianity) stands for a part (Catholicism), which is the book's real subject, thereby neglecting other Christian traditions (see, for example, Tweed 2000, Coleman 2004, Hann 2011).

An unbalanced state of the affairs also characterises the relationships with other religious systems. As we have seen, Turner's proposals were tested

International Perspectives on Pilgrimage Studies 11

in various contexts (Hinduism, Buddhism, Taoism and Islam). A specialist of India, Alan Morinis, was a leading figure in the exploration of a general anthropology of the pilgrimage and edited several collective books oriented in this perspective. Yet despite the growth of research in South Asia, South-East Asia and the Pacific Rim on non-Christian pilgrimage and the relationship between pilgrimage and tourism published in a variety of languages including English, Anglophone studies on Catholic pilgrimage in the West and related theoretical debates still attract far more attention. One can mention, for example, how the important study of Chinese pilgrimage by Naquin and Yu (1992) cited earlier has been largely ignored in the Anglophone arena, apart from by scholars working on East Asia.

NON-ANGLOPHONE CONTRIBUTIONS: FRENCH AND ITALIAN EXAMPLES

So it is difficult for research undertaken in other traditions, obeying different intellectual agenda and written in other languages to become visible given the power and dynamism of Anglophone research and its strong focus on Roman Catholic pilgrimage in W. Europe and the Americas. The central field of pilgrimage research represents the visible part of an iceberg, protected by an imperial self-assurance underpinned by English monolingualism. The cross-fertilisation of theories and debates is seriously hampered by this Anglophone hegemony.

This volume will introduce the reader to the rich traditions of pilgrimage research lying beyond the Anglophone boundary. Here we just want to refer to Francophone scholarship because Anglophone social science has been deeply influenced by Francophone theoretical debates since the late nineteenth century and, to some extent, a similar colonial experience.[4] It might be assumed, therefore, that Anglophone awareness of Francophone pilgrimage research was keen. In fact, very few Anglophone scholars know about one of France's most important students of pilgrimage, Alphonse Dupront. As Chapter 7 in this volume shows, although his academic reputation in France largely rests on his monumental study on the Crusades (1987), he also undertook a fascinating study on Lourdes (1958) and organised wide-ranging surveys on contemporary pilgrimages and sanctuaries across France and Italy. Furthermore, he proposed a general, somewhat phenomenological, perspective on pilgrimage (with some arguments that independently correspond with Turner's vision) that has been highly influential in France and has also inspired Peter Brown's (1981) study of Christian shrines in Late Antiquity (see Dupront 1987). Other influential attempts to delineate a general approach to pilgrimage came from the leading sociologist Freddy Raphaël (1973) and several historians, such as Jean Chélini and Henri Branthomme (1982, 1987, 2004) and Philippe Boutry, Pierre-Antoine Fabre and Dominique Julia (2000a, 2000b).

12   Dionigi Albera and John Eade

French research on pilgrimage also includes several studies that examined pilgrimage processes without seeking to establish a theoretical model or propose an explicit and comprehensive theory of pilgrimage *in itself*. Although these works are generally neglected in the Anglophone field, they offer important insights. Arnold van Gennep, for example, not only influenced Turner's theory on ritual but also undertook pioneering ethnographic research on pilgrimage in France and Algeria. Furthermore, it is only recently that the seminal essay by Robert Hertz on St Besse (1913), which anticipated the contestation approach, reached an international audience (see MacClancy 1994). In the last decades several important anthropological studies on pilgrimage in different regions have been published in France, e.g. Claverie 2003, Mayeur-Jaouen 2004, 2005, Boissevain 2006, Aubin-Boltanski 2007, but once again their international impact has been restricted by linguistic barriers.

Despite its richness, Italian pilgrimage scholarship has had an even more limited impact. Ernesto De Martino, the leading figure in Italian anthropology after the Second World War, was keenly interested in the traditional rituals associated with tarantism and healing in southern Italy. These rituals were often linked to pilgrimages at shrines reputed for their therapeutic qualities. To explore the multifaceted character of religious beliefs and practices in this setting, De Martino brought together interdisciplinary teams, including psychiatrists, musicologists, photographers and filmmakers (1961). His approach demonstrates what Simon Coleman describes as anthropology through pilgrimage rather than anthropology of pilgrimage. Indeed, De Martino was not so interested in pilgrimage *per se*, and generally he prefers to refer to the people under study as 'devotes' instead than 'pilgrims'. However, in building on his contribution, several of his disciples have developed a more explicit focus on pilgrimage across the country (see Rossi 1969, Gallini 1971 and Chapter 8 in this volume).

DEVELOPING A MORE DIVERSE LANDSCAPE: THEMES EMERGING FROM THIS VOLUME

i)   Relativising Anglophone Pilgrimage Research

We seek, therefore, to develop a more plural landscape in pilgrimage research, by encouraging itineraries where intellectual internationalism engages with research traditions, which have been less influential in the global arena. Although some English-speaking scholars are aware of pilgrimage research undertaken in other languages, there is a general ignorance about the rich history of research on pilgrimage outside the Anglophone arena. Furthermore, Anglophone discussions of pilgrimage tend to start with the 'West' (often meaning, in effect, N. America and Britain) and Christianity (predominantly, Roman Catholicism).

International Perspectives on Pilgrimage Studies   13

We challenge this powerful tendency by starting in Japan and moving across Eurasia towards central and West Europe before ending in France. We also bring together scholars from different disciplines, such as ethnology, religious studies, geography, history and anthropology, to reveal the rich national traditions, theoretical approaches and wealth of data concerning pilgrimage, which have been confined to a narrow range of audiences until now. While the contributors approach these traditions in different ways, two clear, related themes have emerged. They not only describe what might be termed distinctive 'brands' of scholarship associated with particular countries or linguistic regions but also introduce us, in varying degrees, to the ways in which pilgrimage has been performed at particular sacred places (predominantly religious) and through journeys to and from those places.

The development of an international perspective entails the relativising of the theoretical and substantive debates, which have emerged in Anglophone academic circles since the 1980s. The Turnerian paradigm continues to attract researchers because it offers both a universal model of pilgrimage and a focus on powerful interpretations of what pilgrimage should involve, which both religious officials and the pilgrims themselves embrace. However, this is only part of a much more complex picture, as we have argued above. As Ian Reader's chapter on the Japanese context shows, a strong, multidisciplinary field can emerge in a particular country without recourse to 'any overarching paradigms or "must refer to" scholarly names and theories'. Although the lack of engagement with 'Western theories and scholarship' could be seen as an indication of Japanese insularity, it also calls into question Western assumptions about both the centrality of 'Western agendas' and Christian pilgrimage.[5]

ii)   Linguistic Difference and 'Pilgrimage as a Universal Category'

Relativising Anglophone pilgrimage studies also involves paying close attention to linguistic difference. As the chapters on research in Japan, Russia, Poland and Israel in particular point out, the categories used to classify different types of pilgrimage are shaped by specific linguistic cultures so that we must be careful about using the English word 'pilgrimage' as a universal category. Dubisch (1995), Reader and Swanson (1997) and Reader (2005), for example, have illustrated the variety of terms used in Greece and Japan to describe the different types of journeys which people make to shrines. This terminological diversity tends to be ignored in Anglophone research, where 'pilgrimage' can be used simplistically as a 'catchall' term. While 'pilgrimage' is still useful for the pursuit of comparative, cross-cultural discussion—we are not advocating a hard form of relativism here—we need to be alert to the nuances in the term's use within different linguistic contexts.

14   *Dionigi Albera and John Eade*

iii)   Learning From Others

Although we have criticised the hegemonic status which Anglophone scholarship has established in pilgrimage research, we still have to communicate in a particular language. The current role of English as the global *lingua franca* justifies, therefore, the medium of communication we have chosen for this volume. Yet while the economics of Anglophone academic publishing means that a large segment of our readership is located in N. America, it is crucial that curious readers look beyond this region's borders. The same is true for those wanting to learn more about pilgrimage in other regions, of course. If we look at how pilgrimage research has developed since the late nineteenth century through this wider lens, we can learn that the study of modern pilgrimage did not begin with the Turners and the *communitas* paradigm, for example! As Anna Niedźwiedź notes in Chapter 4, during the late 1930s Stefan Czarnowski in Poland was already discussing the immersion of individual pilgrims within the group and hierarchical organisation of the 'companies' as they travelled to and from shrines. We have also noted above how Dupront was developing similar arguments to Turner since the 1950s.

Given the multiplicity of linguistic and disciplinary traditions across the European region, the engagement with boundaries, gaps and obstacles is even more pressing than in N. America. As the contributors to this volume demonstrate only too clearly, to gain a more comprehensive and deeply rooted understanding of contemporary pilgrimage research we need to look beyond the last forty years and W. Europe. Hence, most chapters begin their discussion in the late nineteenth and early twentieth centuries and introduce us not only to the pioneering studies by Arnold van Gennep, Robert Hertz and Giuseppe Pitrè in France and Italy but also to the contributions by Władysław Reymont and Sándor Bálint in Poland and Hungary.

iv)   Political and Ideological Change

This deeper understanding involves not just an intellectual journey—it also leads us towards the long-established relationship between research and wider political and ideological movements. The chapters in this volume focus primarily on religious pilgrimage and the dominant religious institutions in particular countries because they were heavily engaged in political and ideological movements bound up with emerging secular nation-states, urbanisation and the turbulence of war and revolution, in particular. Religion was frequently the object of suspicion or hostility among secular nationalists, and after the 1917 revolution in Russia this hostility was accompanied by repression. Many studying pilgrimage before the Second World War were influenced by secular nationalist discourses and the assumption that institutional religion and its associated practices, including pilgrimage, would retreat in the face of secular modernity, however interpreted (liberal-democratic or Marxist, for example). The chapters here on French, Italian and Israeli research show the influence of these assumptions very clearly.

Yet religion could also be embraced by other models of the nation. As the chapters on Japan and Poland demonstrate, nationalism was also informed by romanticist ideas, which saw 'folk' customs as the cultural foundations of the new or emerging nation. During the early twentieth century the study of folklore emerged as a respected academic discipline in Japan and countries across central and Eastern Europe through various versions of ethnology. These disciplinary traditions fostered the careful academic study of the religious life of the 'people' and peasants, in particular. Hence, in the newly independent Polish republic of the 1920s and 1930s Polish researchers saw pilgrimage as an expression of the 'folk religiosity', which the peasantry sustained within the close embrace between Polish nationalism and Roman Catholicism. A similar development emerged in Japan at the same time as *minzokugaku* ('folk studies'/'folk ethnography'/'native ethnology') emerged as a prominent academic field, which supported more general beliefs in the distinctiveness and superiority of Japanese culture and religious practices including pilgrimage. In these and other romanticist interpretations there was no gulf between past and present/tradition and modernity/religious and secular worlds.

The contributors to this volume largely consider the research undertaken on religious majorities in their particular countries or linguistic areas. However, the less extensive research on religious minorities has demonstrated the crucial impact which the intimate relationship between nationalism and dominant religious groups had on those minorities and their own pilgrimage practices. This impact involved in some countries periods of repression and even extermination (see, for example, Chapter 5 in this volume, where Gabór Barna discusses Jewish pilgrimage in Hungary, and Eade 2012, Eade and Katić 2014).

v) Global Trends after 1989

The intimate relationship between academic and political worlds was dramatically illustrated by the collapse of Communist regimes across Eurasia. Because institutional religion was repressed in the USSR, it is not surprising that Stella Rock begins her chapter on Russian pilgrimage research in the 1990s. Pilgrimage research was also stymied in Poland and Hungary between the 1950s and 1970s, although studies of what Anglophone scholars call 'material religion' were undertaken during the 1970s in Hungary, for example, while an historical and ethnological survey of Hungarian pilgrimage was completed before the collapse of the Communist regime.

Since 1989 pilgrimage research in former Communist countries has expanded and become more open to Western influences. Although historic intellectual and linguistic ties with Germany and France, in particular, have

16 *Dionigi Albera and John Eade*

survived and even strengthened, the younger generation have largely been attracted to the Anglophone world. While Japanese scholars are still largely self-reliant, the pressures of academic globalisation have encouraged government support for elite universities, where links with Anglophone universities can be forged and/or strengthened through student exchanges and scholarly collaboration, for example.

These developments have both increased the global reach of Anglophone pilgrimage research and enabled Anglophone scholars to learn about other disciplinary traditions, theoretical debates and empirical research. The Marseille workshop in October 2013, from which this volume has emerged, was partly a product of the links forged through these exchanges, serendipitous meetings at conferences and recommendations from trusted colleagues. This collaboration has led us not only to learn about the fascinating empirical research undertaken across Eurasia but also to explore the rich history of pilgrimage studies across that vast area shaped by the diverse disciplinary traditions, such as ethnology and folk studies, and theoretical perspectives inspired by broader philosophical debates, which are particularly evident in Chapter 6 on research in German-speaking countries. Where this learning will take us remains to be seen, but this volume's starting point is to establish a base from which a truly informed dialogue between Anglophone and non-Anglophone researchers can take place.

FINAL COMMENT

We do not claim to provide a comprehensive review of pilgrimage research even in Europe, and we are well aware of the excellent work undertaken in countries beyond this collection's boundaries. Space and time have prevented us from including chapters on different religious traditions and their related pilgrimages in the Americas, South and South-East Asia, Africa and China, for example. Even within Europe and the Near East we have only touched on the rich research undertaken on Eastern Christianity and on shared shrines. Despite these inevitable constraints, we have sought as much as possible to refer to research and publications generated by scholars around the world.

Hopefully, this volume will encourage others to generate new itineraries so that an even more global perspective can be generated through the closing of gaps and the surmounting of obstacles. We have made a start through bringing together chapters which range across Eurasia and by displaying the wealth of research available outside the limits of Anglophone pilgrimage studies.

ACKNOWLEDGEMENTS

We are grateful for the comments from the participants of the October 2013 Marseille workshop and from the four reviewers of the book proposal. Ian

Reader provided very helpful advice during the final stages of writing the chapter.

NOTES

1. An interesting and provocative analysis across the history of Christianity up to the 1980s was provided by Perry and Echeverria (1988).
2. Hoshino was one of Victor Turner's students and the articles cited by LaFleur were written during Hoshino's early *communitas* phase (personal communication from Ian Reader).
3. The relationship between pilgrimage and tourism had been explored during the 1970s and 1980s (see Graburn 1977, for example), but from the 1990s the complexity of the relationship was examined in greater depth and was influenced by postmodern perspectives.
4. This similarity raises the ambiguous relationship between anthropology and colonialism. See D. Mills (2008).
5. Ian Reader has been particularly helpful in the construction of this subsection.

REFERENCES

Albera, D. and Couroucli, M. (eds.) (2012) *Sharing Sacred Spaces in the Mediterranean: Christians, Muslims and Jews at Shrines and Sanctuaries*, Bloomington and Indianapolis: Indiana University Press.

Aubin-Boltanski, E. (2007) *Pèlerinage et nationalisme en Palestine. Prophètes, Héros et Ancêtres*, Paris: Éditions de l'ÉHESS.

Badone, E. (2014) 'Conventional and unconventional pilgrimages: conceptualizing sacred travel in the twenty-first century', in A. Pazos (ed.) *Redefining Pilgrimage: New Perspectives on Historical and Contemporary Pilgrimages*, Farnham, UK, and Burlington, VT: Ashgate.

———. and Roseman, S. (eds.) (2004) *Intersecting Journeys: The Anthropology of Pilgrimage and Tourism*, Champaign, IL: University of Illinois Press.

Bhardwaj, S. and Rinschede, G. (1988) *Pilgrimage in World Religions*, Berlin: D. Reimer Verlag.

Blackwell, R. (2007) 'Motivations for religious tourism, pilgrimage, festivals and events', in R. Raj and N. Morpeth (eds.) *Religious Tourism and Pilgrimage Festivals Management: An International Perspective*, Cambridge, MA, and Wallingford, UK: CAB International.

Boissevain, K. (2006) *Sainte parmi les saints: Sayyda Mannûbiya ou les recompositions culturelles dans la Tunisie contemporaine*, Paris: Maisonneuve and Larose.

Boutry, P., Fabre, P.-A. and Julia, D. (eds.) (2000a) *Pèlerins et pèlerinages dans l'Europe Moderne*, Rome: Ecole française de Rome.

———. (eds.) (2000b) *Rendre ses voeux. Les identities pelerines dans l'Europe modern (XVIe–XVIIIe siècle)*, Paris: Editions de l' l'ÉHESS.

Bowman, G. (1993) 'Nationalizing the sacred: shrines and shifting identities in the Israeli-occupied territories', *Man*, 9 (1): 431–460.

———. (ed.) (2012) *Sharing the Sacra: The Politics and Pragmatics of Intercommunal Relations Around Holy Places*, New York and Oxford: Berghahn Books.

Bowman, M. (2008) 'Going with the flow: contemporary pilgrimage in Glastonbury', in Margry, op. cit.

Brown, P. (1981) *The Cult of the Saints: Its Rise and Function in Latin Christianity*, Chicago: University of Chicago Press.

18   Dionigi Albera and John Eade

Campo, J. (1998) 'American pilgrimage landscapes', *The Annals of the American Academy of Political and Social Science*, 558 (1): 40–56.

Chélini, J. and Branthomme, H. (eds.) (1982) *Les chemins de Dieu. Histoire des pèlerinages chrétiens des origines à nos jours*, Paris: Hachette.

——. (eds.) (1987) *Histoire des pèlerinages non-chrétiens. Entre magique et sacré: le chemin des dieux*, Paris: Hachette.

——. (2004) *Les pèlerinages dans le monde. A travers le tempest l'espace*, Paris: Hachette.

Christian, W., Jr. (1996) *Visionaries: The Spanish Republic and the Reign of Christ*, Berkeley: University of California Press.

——. (1973) 'Holy people in peasant Europe', *Comparative Studies in Society and History*, 15 (1): 106–114.

Claverie, E. (2003) *Les guerres de la Vierge. Une anthropologie des apparitions*, Paris: Gallimard.

Coleman, S. (2004) 'Pilgrimage to "England's Nazareth": landscapes of myth and memory at Walsingham', in Badone and Roseman, op. cit.

——. (2002) 'Do you believe in pilgrimage? Communitas, contestation and beyond', *Anthropological Theory*, 2 (3): 355–368.

——. and Eade, J. (2004) *Reframing Pilgrimage: Cultures in Motion*, London and New York: Routledge.

——. and Elsner, J. (1998) 'Performing pilgrimage: Walsingham and the ritual construction of irony', in F. Hughes-Freeland (ed.) *Ritual, Performance, Media*, London and New York: Routledge.

Collins-Kreiner, N. (2010) 'Researching pilgrimage: continuity and transformations', *Annals of Tourism Research*, 37 (2): 440–456.

Crumrine, N. Ross and Morinis, A. (1991) *Pilgrimage in Latin America*, Westport, CT: Greenwood Press.

Davies, J. (1988) *Pilgrimage Yesterday and Today*, London: SCM Press.

De Martino, E. (1961) *La Terra del Rimorso. Contributo a una storia religiosa del Sud*, Milan: Il Saggiatore.

Digance, J. (2003) 'Pilgrimage at contested sites', *Annals of Tourism Research*, 30 (1): 143–159.

Dodge, M. and Kitchen, R. (2005) 'Code and the transduction of space', *Annals of the Association of American Geographers*, 95: 162–180.

Dubisch, J. (1995) *In a Different Place: Place, Pilgrimage and Politics at a Greek Island Shrine*, Princeton, NJ: Princeton University Press.

——. and Winkelman, M. (eds.) (2005) *Pilgrimage and Healing*, Tucson: University of Arizona Press.

Duijzings, G. (2000) *Religion and the Politics of Identity in Kosovo*, London: Hurst.

Dupront, A. (1958) 'Lourdes. Perspectives d'une sociologie du sacré', *La Table ronde*, 125: 74–96.

——. (1987) *Du sacré. Croisades et pèlerinages. Images et langages*, Paris: Gallimard.

Eade, J. (1992) 'Pilgrimage and tourism at Lourdes, France', *Annals of Tourism Research*, 19 (1): 18–32.

——. (2012) 'Pilgrimage, the Assumptionists and Catholic evangelisation in a changing Europe: Lourdes and Plovdiv', *Cargo*, 10 (2): 29–48.

——. (2013) 'Identitarian pilgrimage and multicultural society', in A. Pazos (ed.) *Pilgrims and Pilgrimages as Peacemakers in Christianity, Judaism and Islam* Farnham UK and Burlington VT: Ashgate.

——. and Katić, M. (2014) *Pilgrimage, Politics and Place Making in Eastern Europe: Crossing the Borders*, Farnham, UK, and Burlington, VT: Ashgate.

——. and Sallnow, M. (1991) *Contesting the Sacred: The Anthropology of Christian Pilgrimage*, London and New York: Routledge.

Eickelman, D. (1976) *Moroccan Islam: Tradition and Society in a Pilgrimage Center*, Austin, TX, and London, UK: University of Texas Press.

International Perspectives on Pilgrimage Studies 19

——. and Piscatori, J. (eds.) (1990) *Muslim Travellers: Pilgrimage, Migration and the Religious Imagination*, London: Routledge.

Fedele, A. (2013) *Looking for Mary Magdalene: Alternative Pilgrimage and Ritual Creativity at Catholic Shrines in France*, Oxford and New York: Oxford University Press.

——. (2014) 'Energy and transformation in alternative pilgrimages to Catholic shrines: deconstructing the tourist/pilgrim divide', *Journal of Tourism and Cultural Change*, 12 (2): 150–165.

Finucane, R. (1977) *Miracles & Pilgrims: Popular Beliefs in Medieval England*, London, Melbourne, and Toronto: J.M. Dent and Sons.

Frey, N. (1998) *Pilgrim Stories: On and Off the Road to Santiago*, Berkeley and Los Angeles: University of California Press.

Gallini, C. (1971) *Il consumo del sacro. Feste lunghe in Sardegna*, Bari: Laterza.

Gonzalez, R. (2013) 'The Camino de Santiago and its contemporary renewal: pilgrims, tourists and territorial identities', *Culture and Religion*, 14 (1): 8–22.

——. and Medina, J. (2003) 'Cultural tourism and urban management in northwestern Spain: the pilgrimage to Santiago de Compostela', *Tourism Geographies*, 5 (4): 446–460.

Graburn, N. (1977) 'Tourism: the sacred journey', in V. Smith (ed.) *Hosts and Guests*, Philadelphia: University of Pennsylvania Press.

Hann, C. (2011) *Eastern Christianity and Western Social Theory*, Erfurt: Erfurt University.

——. and Goltz, H. (eds.) (2010) *Eastern Christians in Anthropological Perspective*, Berkeley: University of California Press.

Hanson, F. (1975) *Meaning in Culture*, London: Routledge and Kegan Paul.

Harris, A. (2010) 'A place to grow spiritually and socially: the experiences of young pilgrims to Lourdes', in S. Collins-Mayo and B. Dandelion (eds.) *Religion and Youth*, Farnham, UK, and Burlington, VT: Ashgate.

——. (2013) 'Lourdes and holistic spirituality: contemporary Catholicism, the therapeutic and religious thermalism', *Culture and Religion*, 14 (1): 23–43.

Hermkens, A.-M., Jansen, W. and Notermans, C. (eds.) (2009) *Moved by Mary: The Power of Pilgrimage in the Modern World*, Farnham, UK, and Burlington, VT: Ashgate.

Hertz, R. (1913) 'Saint Besse. Étude d'un culte alpestre', *Revue de l'histoire des religions*, 67 (2): 115–180 (English translation in S. Wilson (ed.) (1983) *Saints and Their Cults: Studies in Religious Sociology, Folklore and History*, Cambridge: Cambridge University Press).

Howard, D. (1980) *Writers and Pilgrims*, Berkeley: University of California Press.

Huff, B. and Stallins, J. (2013) 'Beyond binaries: conservative Catholic visions and real estate in Ave Maria, FL', *Culture and Religion*, 14 (1): 94–110.

Hyndman-Rizk, N. (2012) *Pilgrimage in the Age of Globalisation: Constructions of the Sacred and Secular in Late Modernity*, Newcastle, UK: Cambridge Scholars.

Ingold, T. (1995) 'Building, dwelling, living: how animals and people make themselves at home in the world', in M. Strathern (ed.) *Shifting Contexts*, London and New York: Routledge.

Ivakhiv, A. (2001) *Claiming Sacred Ground: Pilgrims and Politics at Glastonbury and Sedona*, Bloomington: Indiana University Press.

Jackowski, A. (2000) 'Religious tourism—problems with terminology', in A. Jackowski (ed.) *Peregrinus Cracoviensis*, Cracow: Publishing Unit, Dept. of Geography, Jagiellonian University.

Jansen, W. and Notermans, C. (eds.) (2012) *Gender, Nation and Religion in European Pilgrimage*, Farnham, UK, and Burlington, VT: Ashgate.

Kaufman, S. (2005) *Consuming Visions: Mass Culture and the Lourdes Shrine*, Ithaca and London: Cornell University Press.

20 Dionigi Albera and John Eade

Knott, K. (2009) 'From locality to location and back again: a spatial journey in the study of religion', *Religion*, 39: 154–160.

Ladner, G. (1967) '*Homo Viator*: medieval ideas of alienation and order', *Speculum*, 42: 232–259.

LaFleur, W. (1979) 'Points of departure: comments on religious pilgrimage in Sri Lanka and Japan', *Journal of Asian Studies*, 38 (2): 271–281.

MacClancy, J. (1994) 'The construction of anthropological genealogies: Robert Hertz, Victor Turner and the study of pilgrimage', *Journal of the Anthropological Society of Oxford*, 25 (1): 31–40.

Maddrell, A., della Dora, V., Scafi, A. and Walton, H. (2015) *Journeying to the Sacred: Christian Pilgrimage, Landscape and Heritage,* London and New York: Routledge.

Margry, P. (ed.) (2008) *Shrines and Pilgrimage in the Modern World: New Itineraries Into the Sacred,* Amsterdam: Amsterdam University Press.

Marx, E. (1977) 'Communal and individual pilgrimage: the region of saints' tombs in South Sinai', in R. Werbner (ed.) *Regional Cults,* London: Academic Press.

Mayeur-Jaouen, C. (2004) *Histoire d'un pèlerinage légendaire en islam. Le mouled de Tantā du xiiie siècle à nos jours,* Paris: Aubier.

———. (2005) *Pèlerinages d'Égypte. Histoire de la piété copte et musulmane, xve–xxe siècles,* Paris: ÉHESS.

Messerschmidt, D. and Sharma, J. (1981) 'Hindu pilgrimage in the Nepal Himalayas', *Current Anthropology*, 22 (5): 571–572.

Mills, D. (2008) *Difficult Folk? A Political History of Social Anthropology,* New York and Oxford: Berghahn Books.

Morinis, A. (1984) *Pilgrimage in the Hindu Tradition: A Case Study of West Bengal,* Delhi: Oxford University Press.

Murray, M. and Graham, G. (1997) 'Exploring the dialectics of route-based tourism: The Camino de Santiago', *Tourism Management*, 18 (8): 513–524.

Naquin, S. and Yü, C.-F. (eds.) (1992) *Pilgrims and Sacred Sites in China,* Berkeley and Los Angeles: University of California Press.

Neville, G. (1987) *Kinship and Pilgrimage: Rituals of Reunion in American Protestant Culture,* New York and Oxford: Oxford University Press.

Nolan, M. and Nolan, S. (1989) *Christian Pilgrimage in Modern Western Europe,* Chapel Hill, NC, and London: University of N. Carolina.

Notermans, C. (2012) 'Interconnected and gendered mobilities: African migrants on pilgrimage to Our Lady of Lourdes in France', in Jansen and Notermans, op. cit.

Perry, N. and Echeverria, L. (1988) *Under the Heel of Mary,* London and New York: Routledge.

Petersen, A., Vasquez, M. and Williams, P. (eds.) (2001) *Christianity, Social Change and Globalization in the Americas,* Baltimore, NJ: Rutgers University Press.

Pfaffenberger, B. (1979) 'The Kataragama pilgrimage: Hindu-Buddhist interaction and its significance in Sri Lanka's polyethnic social system', *Journal of Asian Studies*, 38 (2): 253–270.

Post, P. (2011) 'Profiles of pilgrimage: on identities of religion and ritual in the European public domain', *Studia liturgica*, 41 (2): 129–155.

Raj, R. and Morpeth, N. (eds.) (2007) *Religious Tourism and Pilgrimage Festivals Management: An International Perspective,* Cambridge, MA, and Wallingford, UK: CAB International.

Raphaël, F. (ed.) (1973) *Les Pèlerinages: de l'Antiquité biblique et classique à l'Occident médiéval (Études d'histoire des religions),* Paris: Geuthner.

Reader, I. (2005) *Making Pilgrimages: Meaning and Practice in Shikoku,* Honolulu: University of Hawaii Press.

———. (2007) 'Pilgrimage growth in the modern world: meanings and implications', *Religion,* 37 (3): 210–229.

International Perspectives on Pilgrimage Studies 21

——. (2014) *Pilgrimage in the Marketplace*, Abingdon, UK, and New York: Routledge.

——. and Swanson, P. (1997) 'Editors' introduction: pilgrimage in the Japanese pilgrimage tradition', *Japanese Journal of Religious Studies*, 24 (3/4): 225–270.

——. and Walter, T. (eds.) (1993) *Pilgrimage in Popular Culture*, Basingstoke: Macmillan.

Rinschede, G. (1992) 'Forms of religious tourism', *Annals of Tourism Research*, 19 (1): 51–67.

Ross-Bryant, L. (2013) *Pilgrimage to the National Parks: Religion and Nature in the United States*, London and New York: Routledge.

Rossi, A. (1969) *Le feste dei poveri*, Bari: Laterza.

Sallnow, M. (1981) 'Communitas reconsidered: the sociology of Andean pilgrimage', *Man*, New Series, 16 (2): 163–182.

——. (1987) *Pilgrims of the Andes: Regional Cults in Cusco*, Washington, DC: Smithsonian Institution Press.

Sax, W. (1991) *Mountain Goddess: Gender and Politics in the Himalayan Pilgrimage*, London and New York: Oxford University Press.

——. (2006) 'A divine identity-crisis', in K.-P. Köpping, B. Leistle and M. Rudolph (eds.) *Performative Practices as Effective Transformations of Social Reality?*, Münster: LIT Verlag Münster.

Shields, R. (1991) *Places on the Margin: Alternative Geographies of Modernity*, London and New York: Routledge.

Stausberg, M. (2011) *Religion and Tourism: Crossroads, Destinations and Encounters*, Abingdon, UK, and New York: Routledge.

Sumption, J. (1975) *Pilgrimage*, Totowa, NJ: Rowman and Littlefield.

Swatos, W. (2002) *From Medieval Pilgrimage to Religious Tourism: The Social and Cultural Economics of Piety*, Westport, CT: Praeger.

Thrift, N. (2008) *Non-Representational Theory: Space, Politics, Affect*, Abingdon, UK, and New York: Routledge.

Timothy, D. and Olsen, D. (eds.) (2006) *Tourism, Religion and Spiritual Journeys*, London and New York: Routledge.

Tomasi, L. (2002) '*Homo Viator*: from pilgrimage to religious tourism via the journey', in Swatos, op. cit.

Turner, V. (1973) 'The center out there: pilgrim's goal', *History of Religions*, 12 (3): 191–230.

——. (1974) *Dramas, Fields, and Metaphors. Symbolic Action in Human Society*, Ithaca and London: Cornell University Press.

——. and E. Turner (1978) *Image and Pilgrimage in Christian Culture*, New York: Columbia University Press.

Tweed, T. (1997) *Our Lady of the Exile: Diasporic Religion at a Cuban Catholic Shrine in Miami*, New York: Oxford University Press.

——. (2000) 'John Wesley slept here: American shrines and American Methodists', *Numen*, 47 (1): 41–68.

——. (2006) *Crossing and Dwelling: A Theory of Religion*, Cambridge, MA: Harvard University Press.

Vasquez, M. (2000) 'Globalizing the rainbow Madonna: old time religion in the present age', *Theory, Culture & Society*, 17 (4): 119–143.

——. (2011) *More Than Belief: A Materialist Theory of Religion*, New York: Oxford University Press.

——. and Marquardt, M. (2003) *Globalizing the Sacred: Religion Across the Americas*, Baltimore: Rutgers University Press.

Vukonic, B. (1992) 'Medjugorje's religion and tourism connection', *Annals of Tourism Research*, 19 (1): 79–91.

Weibel, D. (2005) Of consciousness changes and fortified faith: creativist and Catholic pilgrimage at French Catholic shrines', in Dubisch and Winkelman, op. cit.

22 *Dionigi Albera and John Eade*

Yamashita, S, Bosco, J. and Eades, J. (eds.) (2004) *The Making of Anthropology in East and Southeast Asia,* New York and Oxford: Berghahn Books.

Yamba, B. (1995) *Permanent Pilgrims: An Anthropological Study of the Role of Pilgrimage in the Lives of West African Muslims in Sudan,* Edinburgh: Edinburgh University Press.

Zacher, C. (1976) *Curiosity and Pilgrimage: The Literature of Discovery in Fourteenth Century England,* Baltimore, MD: Johns Hopkins University Press.

Zapponi, E. (2011) *Marcher vers Compostelle. Ethnographie d'une pratique pèlerine,* Paris: L'Harmattan/AFSR.

2 Japanese Studies of Pilgrimage

Ian Reader

INTRODUCTION

Japan has both a highly developed network of pilgrimages and a rich academic tradition of studying them. Throughout the country there are hundreds of pilgrimages of different types, along with a complex set of vocabularies to describe them. Pilgrimage has also played a significant role in the expansion and development of Buddhism, Shinto and the Japanese new religions, all of which have constructed sacred geographies as a way of expanding their clienteles and public standings. Pilgrimage and associated practices—including mountain religious traditions, itinerancy and legends associated with wandering holy figures—are deeply embedded in the religious and folklore structures of Japan. These are all areas that have been important for cultural debates about Japanese identity and the formation of Japanese academic disciplines as Japan emerged as a modern nation-state (Josephson 2012, Christy 2012).

Such a complex and rich pilgrimage culture has also produced an appropriately rich Japanese scholastic tradition of studying pilgrimages. This tradition spans a number of disciplinary areas, from folk studies (*minzokugaku*, regarded as an important academic discipline in Japan) to religious studies and Buddhist Studies (the latter also a recognised disciplinary area in Japan), to anthropological, historical, sociological, economic and regional studies. In this chapter I focus specifically on the areas of study and the thematic issues that have been predominant in the Japanese academic and linguistic milieu, rather than on the nature, dynamics and structures of Japanese pilgrimage culture and its specific pilgrimages, about which an accessible literature now exists in languages such as English and French.[1]

In Japanese academic contexts pilgrimage has been examined not so much as a free-standing entity (as in 'pilgrimage studies') or as a topic subsumed largely within anthropology but as an intrinsic element in fields such as folk studies and religious studies, as well as being important in historical studies, linked to social and economic development. Pilgrimage has thus been viewed not as a marginal activity but—in line with its significance in Japanese religious terms, in general—as a very central element in Japanese

24   Ian Reader

social, religious and historical contexts and widely studied across a number of Japanese academic disciplinary areas.

This multidisciplinary field has not been dominated by any overarching paradigms or 'must refer to' scholarly names and theories, unlike in the English-language arena where there appears to be an almost obligatory need to refer to certain names and theories. Certainly, there are some major Japanese scholars whose work is prominent within particular disciplinary areas and whose influence has impacted on the wider field. Perhaps the most notable figure here has been Shinjō Tsunezō, whose work on the historical development and social and economic context of religious travel and pilgrimage in Japan up to the mid-nineteenth century has provided much of the background for later studies. Others include Shinno Toshikazu, whose work is grounded in Japanese ethnology and draws on legends, folk studies, oral traditions and historical examinations of ascetics and religious travellers, and Hoshino Eiki, who is the foremost Japanese scholar in the anthropological study of pilgrimage.

I will refer again to these figures and disciplinary areas later but first should make two important points for the wider study of pilgrimage. The first is that Japanese studies of pilgrimage have been somewhat insular and have focussed very much on Japan, with studies of non-Japanese pilgrimages carried out by Japanese academics being comparatively rare. Indeed, when non-Japanese pilgrimages are studied to any degree, it has, at least until very recently, been primarily as a foil for the more vital task (to Japanese scholars) of examining the Japanese pilgrimage tradition.[2] This is not surprising, given the tendency of scholastic communities to focus predominantly within their own cultural sphere and also given the rich Japanese pilgrimage milieu, which provides such scope for study.

However, it does alert us to a second point, which is that Japanese studies of pilgrimage have produced a rich array of publications with little recourse to or apparent need for reference to Western theories and scholarship.[3] While this is, on one level, a sign of insularity, it is also a reminder that what is sometimes taken for granted in Western scholastic contexts—that Western agendas set the paradigms and serve as the 'universal' for the field—needs to be reconsidered. Western academic studies of pilgrimage have tended to treat pilgrimage largely as a Western-centric phenomenon and to pay little heed to pilgrimage contexts and studies beyond the Western. Scholars working on Japan have rightly criticised this tendency.[4]

Furthermore, many of the theories that have guided Western studies have been developed around Christian pilgrimages, which are treated as if they reflect the universal dimensions of pilgrimage and are the key filter through which all studies of pilgrimage should flow. Yet this itself displays a degree of insularity that mirrors Japanese scholarship in its tendency to treat all other traditions and studies as secondary or marginal. Viewed from a Japan-centred perspective, Christianity is very much a marginal area in pilgrimage terms. It is perhaps unsurprising, then, that Western theories developed around Christian pilgrimage have had little purchase in the Japanese scholastic context, which provides a good example of how studies of a seminal topic such as pilgrimage can develop a very rich vein in other parts of the world and in other languages without needing to place discussions of Western theories and Christian pilgrimages at their centre.

BACKGROUND: THE IMPORTANCE OF PILGRIMAGE IN JAPAN

The folklore specialist and historian Shinno Toshikazu has argued that pilgrimage was one of the main pillars of Japanese religion (Shinno 1980, 1991a: 19, 1991b; see also Miyake 1980). As Shinjō Tsunezō (1960: 1) has commented, for premodern Japanese people, travel meant going on pilgrimage to shrines and temples. Strict government controls in the Tokugawa period (1600–1868) regulated travel to the extent that the only reason that the feudal population could get permits to travel was to make pilgrimages to distant religious sites such as the shrines of Ise or the temples of Shikoku and Saikoku. Restrictions on travelling beyond feudal borders also stimulated the development of intra-domain pilgrimages, contributing massively to a highly developed localised pilgrimage culture (Shinjō 1982, Reader 1988, Shinno 1996).

Pilgrimage was also used as a Buddhist strategy of expansion, promoted by priests, who sacralised landscapes and geographies where physical locations were projected as gateways to or earthly embodiments of higher spiritual realms. The priests also developed the cultic popularity of Buddhist figures of worship in order to extend their remit throughout the country (e.g., Shinno 1991b).

Hence, historians of religion and specialists in Buddhist studies, such as Hayami Tasuku, have examined the historical development of Buddhist popular faith in Japan through studies of figures such as Kannon, one of the most prominent figures of worship in Japanese Buddhism. As Hayami (1980, 1983) has shown, one way Buddhism in Japan built itself into a powerful tradition appealing to all strata of society was through the promotion of pilgrimage cults centred around popular figures of worship such as Kannon and around places where prominent Buddhist holy figures lived. From around the twelfth century onwards, temples promoted themselves as centres of reverence and worship able to grant wishes to supplicants, and stories emphasising these facets of holy places were promoted far and wide by wandering Buddhist figures known as *hijiri* (wandering holy men), who encouraged people to visit such temples, thereby helping to develop a culture of pilgrimage. *Hijiri* were also involved in promoting the cult of Kōbō Daishi, a Buddhist figure depicted in popular lore as a wandering pilgrim, around whom a pilgrimage tradition especially manifested in the Shikoku pilgrimage, which was developed from the twelfth century onwards (see below and also Hinonishi 1988).

Figure 2.1 Statue of Kōbō Daishi as a mendicant pilgrim in Shikoku.
Photograph by Ian Reader, from the Photo Archives of the Nanzan Institute for Religion and Culture, Nagoya, Japan.

Pilgrimages, indeed, were created (mainly involving circuits of temples) in order to attract such visits. This was a strategy designed not just to enhance Buddhism's remit but also to address the changing economic conditions that Buddhist temples (and Shinto shrines) encountered by the twelfth century. During the Heian era (794–1185) temples and shrines had been heavily supported by the land-owning aristocracy, but subsequent economic and political power shifts weakened the aristocracy so that temples could no longer rely on them for patronage or political support. They needed to develop new clienteles and support structures, and many turned to pilgrimage and the development of popular faith cults around figures such as Kannon, whose attributes included offering worldly benefits, miraculous healing and salvation to supplicants. In such ways, as Hayami and others have shown, pilgrimage was integral to Buddhist expansion among the common people. In this context, too, wandering religious figures such as *hijiri* and related figures, such as *furaibō* (wandering monks), *oshi* and *sendatsu* (pilgrimage promoters and guides), were important, and scholars have seen them as seminal formative agents in the structure of Japanese religion (see Shinno 1991a, 1991b, Gorai 1975, 1984).

Pilgrimage has also been examined as intrinsic to Shugendō, the Japanese mountain religious tradition, widely regarded as one of the formative elements in Japanese religious history and structure (Miyake 1971, 1978, 1988, 1992, 2000). Shugendō developed as an amalgam of Buddhist, folk, Taoist and Shinto ideas and practices, and its practitioners, known as *yamabushi*, engage in ascetic practices including mountain pilgrimages and rituals centred on mountain veneration. The tradition incorporates beliefs in mountain deities and regards mountains as the dwelling places of spiritual entities and an 'other' world to that of the inhabited world. The mountain, also, serves as a blueprint for the journey to enlightenment, with pilgrimage ascents serving as metaphorical spiritual journeys and symbolically passing through different realms of existence to reach the mountain peak/enlightenment. Mountains have also been seen as the setting for the creation of sacred geographies and itineraries of holy places linked together by pilgrimage routes.

Mountain religious traditions, therefore, have not only been seen as highly formative in Japanese religious structures but have also been a major focus of academic research, much of which incorporates studies of pilgrimage. Careful attention has been paid to the figure of the *yamabushi*, who often occupies a very similar position to that of the above-mentioned *hijiri*, as inspirational in creating sacred geographies and mediating between the world of the gods and that of humans (e.g., Gorai 1975, 1991, Miyake 1971, 1978, 1988, 1992, 2000, 2002).[5]

Individual figures such as *sendatsu*, *hijiri* and *yamabushi* are relevant beyond the Japanese context because they show how devotion to them has assisted in the creation and promotion of pilgrimages. Furthermore, they indicate that pilgrimages may structurally develop as practices grounded

28   *Ian Reader*

in, and as replications of, the spiritual journeys of charismatic and inspirational figures in whose footsteps later pilgrims follow. This focus on the role of charismatic and inspirational figures in the construction, development and promotion of pilgrimage is an area perhaps less well explored in Western (and notably Anglophone) studies of pilgrimages than in the Japanese pilgrimage context and Japanese scholarship. It suggests an area where Japanese scholarship has much to offer to those studying pilgrimage in the West.

It should also be noted that the *hijiri* and other such inspirational guiding figures have been discussed not just as formative agents of pilgrimage but also as exemplars of the charismatic religious tradition in Japan—a tradition which, in modern times, has given rise to religious activists, such as the founders/leaders of Japanese new religions, whose roots have been traced back to the Shugendō tradition (see, for example, Numata 1988). Hence, by paying attention to itinerant mendicants and charismatic proselytisers, the study of pilgrimage links directly to areas, which are seen as important in modern religious developments in Japan: i.e., charisma and the new religions, in particular. Although new religions have developed their own pilgrimage traditions, these have not been studied in the wider context of pilgrimage, so there is an important opportunity for pilgrimage scholars here.[6]

MINZOKUGAKU (NATIVE ETHNOLOGY/FOLK STUDIES), OUTSIDERS AND PILGRIMAGE

The section above indicates the significance of pilgrimage in Japanese religious contexts, showing why pilgrimage has never been treated as a marginal academic topic of study, why studies of pilgrimage have been embedded within wider studies of religion and social history and why itinerant figures such as *hijiri* have been seen as of central importance. A further reason has been the development of the academic field known as *minzokugaku*, translated variously as 'folk studies', 'folk ethnography' and 'native ethnology', which developed from the early twentieth century to become one of Japan's most prominent academic fields. *Minzokugaku* has focussed quite specifically on Japanese customs, practices and local legends and beliefs—an ethnic focus which has been influential also in the extent to which Japanese academia focusses on Japan above all else.

The ways in which *minzokugaku* developed in Japan, along with a sub-branch focussed on 'folk religion' (*minkan shinkō* or *minzoku shūkyō*), cannot be discussed here (see Christy 2012, Reader 2005b). The significant point is that *minzokugaku* has developed as a respected disciplinary area, different from such fields as history, anthropology and religious studies, and with a specific focus on Japanese customs, culture and identity. It has developed its own academic departments, societies and journals and acquired a wide readership, both academically and in the popular domain, inspiring also numerous local ethnology and history societies.

'Folk' customs and beliefs came, in the first decades of the twentieth century, to be seen as critical elements in Japan's social and psychic makeup, and hence worthy of special academic attention. *Minzokugaku* encouraged the belief that Japan possessed a culture, which was distinct from and superior to other cultures as well as deeply rooted in antiquity. As this field of study developed and gained leverage within the university system, it promoted the study of such topics as itinerancy and pilgrimage, which the Meiji government (1868–1912) had sought at one point to ban as anti-modern practices that might undermine Japan's economic growth and turned them into key subjects of academic enquiry associated with Japan's national identity, history and social cohesion.[7]

The development of *minzokugaku* also influenced studies of religion, by paying great attention to folk practices, customs and beliefs associated with spirits, veneration of popular figures of worship and practices related to itinerancy. This, in turn, helped make these topics important subject areas in the Japanese study of religion and encouraged Japanese scholars to move beyond the normative patterns of the field more quickly than in the West, where scholars primarily focussed on belief and doctrine and historical traditions and institutions.

Minzokugaku was empathetic towards travellers and pilgrimage not just because figures such as *hijiri* were seminal in developing a grassroots religious tradition but also because of how the discipline itself developed. Its early pioneers, such as Yanagita Kunio (1875–1962) and Orikuchi Shinobu (1887–1953), were initially unsure what their discipline was and what fieldwork, methodologies and theoretical frameworks they should use. They were also avid travellers, who were often unsettled in their daily lives, and who found solace 'on the road' doing fieldwork. As the title of Alan Christy's (2012) study indicates, *minzokugaku* was a discipline, which developed 'on foot' and whose protagonists worked out the methodological and theoretical problems that confronted them as they went far and wide in Japan collecting field data, interviewing subjects and observing practices in remote corners of the country.

It is thus unsurprising that pilgrimage and legends of wandering and itinerant religious figures played an important part in their studies and the theories they developed. Orikuchi's theory of the *marebito* (an outsider, usually a divine or otherwise spiritually charged figure) was particularly influential. There are numerous stories in Japanese folklore associated with outsiders (often wandering deities or ascetics), who visit villages bringing spiritual and worldly benefits to the local populace. In Orikuchi's view, such stories were foundational to Japanese religious beliefs and structures. While Japanese rural society may have been sedentary, it was linked to wider cultural trends and patterns through the visits of outsiders and itinerants, whose influences shaped the nature of the localised practices of the villagers. Such

30   *Ian Reader*

ideas were developed further by later folklore/ethnology scholars, for whom the image of the spiritually potent wanderer as central to religious structures and thought led them to focus on these figures as well as on pilgrimage, which was thus located at the core of Japanese religion.

These ideas also fed into typological analyses of pilgrimage by scholars such as Gorai Shigeru, who drew on Orikuchi's theories in his studies of itinerancy, *hijiri* and other such figures. Gorai wrote extensively about pilgrimages in Japan, along with studies of itinerant Buddhist wanderers, expressing ideas best encapsulated by the title of his 1989 book *Yugyō to junrei: Nihonjin no tabi to shinkō no genten* 'Ascetic Wandering and Pilgrimage: The Roots of Japanese Faith and Travel'. While Gorai's studies were located within phenomenology and native ethnology, they also tended to veer towards the mystical, stressing those aspects of *minzokugaku* that emphasised the special nature of Japanese concepts and practices and endowing them with an almost reverent dimension. This tendency was also demonstrated by Yamaori Tetsuo, who has published widely on religious itinerancy and pilgrimage in Japan (e.g., 1986), and who has developed a sizeable following as a popular writer on religion in Japan.

Movement as a core theme in popular faith has also been the focus of numerous other folk/ethnological studies, including Matsuzaki Kenzō's (1985) volume *Meguri no fōkuroa: yugyōbutsu no kenkyū* ('The Folklore of Pilgrimage: Studies of Itinerant Buddhas'), which examines folk practices where statues of Buddhist figures of worship, such as Jizō, are carried in ritual processions during festivals, along with local Kōbō Daishi–related pilgrimage practices. This links into a prominent strand in Japanese pilgrimage development, namely, pilgrimages centred around Kōbō Daishi, whose legendary travels are central to the Shikoku pilgrimage and who is believed to accompany and protect each pilgrim. Some studies of this pilgrimage focus on folktales associated with Kōbō Daishi and portray the pilgrimage as a projection of Shikoku's folk tradition (e.g., Takeda 1972, 1987).

Sociological studies of local Shikoku communities have also indicated that faith in Kōbō Daishi is the predominant strand in local religious structures. Thus, Kaneko Satoru's (1991) study of Buddhist temple parishioners belonging to the Pure Land tradition in Shikoku shows that their dominant religious orientation is not to Pure Land Buddhism (their official affiliation) but to the local tradition of Kōbō Daishi faith and the Shikoku pilgrimage. The pilgrimage is, therefore, both a dominant faith tradition and a mainstay of local culture and belonging.

Such studies also indicate that pilgrimages, while nationally and internationally famous, may also be very local affairs, embedded in local beliefs and customs and supported by local people. This theme, evident also in Shinjō's work, has been developed in historical terms in Western language contexts by the French scholar Natalie Kouamé (1998, 2001). Sociological surveys (e.g., Maeda 1971, Satō 2004), studies of pilgrim provenance in

Figure 2.2 Shikoku pilgrims: the writing on their shirts is an invocation to Kōbō Daishi and signifies his presence with them on pilgrimage.

earlier eras based on local historical records (see Shinjō 1982) and records of those staying at pilgrim lodges in Shikoku (Hoshino 2001: 264) have further drawn attention to this localised dimension of the pilgrimage.

This research has shown how problematic are assumptions that pilgrimage predominantly involves travel to distant places. This, again, is an area where Japanese pilgrimage studies, enriched greatly by the importance placed on folk studies and examinations of the local, offer some lessons for wider studies of pilgrimage, especially those undertaken in the West.

Mention should be made also of Shinno Toshikazu (1991a, 1991b, 1996), one of the most prominent figures in the study of 'folk religion',[8] whose work combines ethnological studies, examinations of oral traditions and historical research into textual materials and analyses pilgrimage legends and miracle stories and their role in creating support structures for pilgrims at local levels. He is one of several scholars who pay attention to how such stories help shape perceptions of the landscape and contribute to concepts of sacred geographies, where the physical realms are enhanced by legendary stories, associated with *marebito*-style outsiders, that endow the 'real' landscape with mystical dimensions. The physical journey through these landscapes, therefore, is transformed into a spiritual one.

32 Ian Reader

Shinno also draws attention to the role of ascetics (*hijiri*) in constructing and promoting pilgrimages and how they used pilgrimage to promote the causes of great temples and institutions. As with other scholars previously discussed, Shinno locates pilgrimage and itinerancy at the centre of Japanese religious structures, while showing how it serves to connect ordinary people with sacred and charismatic figures, in whose footsteps (whether in legend, like Kōbō Daishi, or in reality, such as the *hijiri*) later generations can follow.

Crucial also to Shinno's analysis is the argument that Japanese religion contains a dual structure of folk faith, associated with legends and popular localised practices, and organised traditions, such as Buddhism, centred on specific institutions, i.e., temples, and doctrinal systems. For Shinno, pilgrimage serves as a unifying link and arena where these two parts of the structure meet, a point he makes with regard to the Shikoku pilgrimage (1991a: 91). This is not a theory of contest between the two poles of established religious orthodoxy and folk faith (i.e., between conflicting interest groups of priests and pilgrims) but about how pilgrimage provides common ground within which different spheres can be accommodated without overt contest.

Another significant influence of *minzokugaku* scholars on pilgrimage studies in Japan was their formulation of a specifically Japanese-centred field of study that researched and collected data on Japanese ethnic practices and rural customs. They saw the rural and agrarian as the core of Japanese culture and viewed urbanisation and modernity as external intrusions that were eroding the essence of Japan. Consequently, they also strove to collect materials in order to preserve (even if in museums and archives) this 'native' essence before it disappeared entirely. They promoted the formation of local societies to study local traditions, collect and preserve legends and to publish studies conducted at local levels (Christy 2012). The upshot has been a vibrant culture of local histories and ethnographies that remains extremely valuable in terms of preserving materials and historical evidence about local pilgrimages that, while generally descriptive and lacking theoretical focus, have been invaluable sources of knowledge. These local histories enabled me, for example, to develop a general analysis of the patterns of formation of local and replica pilgrimages in Japan (Reader 1988).

TYPOLOGIES OF PILGRIMAGE

Japanese scholars have developed some broad definitional/theoretical typologies for analysing pilgrimage in Japan. Here one should note that, as with other linguistic contexts elsewhere (e.g., Greek, as discussed by Dubisch 1995), there are several Japanese terms that may be translated by the English word 'pilgrimage' (see Reader and Swanson 1997, Ambros 2005) while containing within them different nuances of meaning. In Japan one critical typological framework in the terminology of pilgrimage and in its structural manifestations is the distinction between linear and circuit pilgrimages. Pilgrimage has often been assumed to be a linear process, as in notions of the 'centre out there' and ideas of linear progression to a goal. Such forms of pilgrimage exist in Japan along with specific terms (*mairi, mōde, sankei*) for them; the pilgrimage to the Shinto shrines of Ise is the *Ise mairi* or *Ise sangū* (with *sangū* specific to Ise pilgrimage alone) and that to the mountainous region of Kumano and its shrines is the *Kumano mōde*. There are also circuit pilgrimages, especially prominent in Buddhist contexts, such as the thirty-three-stage Saikoku pilgrimage centred on Kannon and the eighty-eight-stage Shikoku pilgrimage. These two pilgrimages provide the template for many regional versions, while there are several other numerical pilgrimage forms, such as pilgrimages to seven shrines and temples each enshrining one of the Seven Gods of Good Fortune.

Terms such as *junrei* and *junpai* (both meaning going around and worshipping) indicate pilgrimages, which have no single goal but involve a journey whose aim is to complete a circuit while visiting a linked group of sites. Just as some linear pilgrimage terms are location specific so are some circuit-related terms. While the Shikoku pilgrimage may be referred to as a *junrei* because it entails going round the island of Shikoku and involves eighty-eight temples, it is usually referred to as the Shikoku *henro*, a term specific to this pilgrimage and its replicas, which centre on Kōbō Daishi and a circuit of eighty-eight sites.

Circuit pilgrimages have been differentiated typologically by Japanese scholars through the concepts of *honzon* and *seiseki* pilgrimages. *Honzon* pilgrimages (*honzon junrei*) are pilgrimages focussed on a main image of worship (*honzon*) shared by all the sites in a circuit. Hence, the Saikoku pilgrimage is a *honzon junrei* because the thirty-three temples linked by the pilgrimage route share a core unitary focus on the bodhisattva, Kannon, who is a main image of worship at each of the temples visited. The other category, *seiseki*, refers to the traces or presence of a holy figure or group of holy figures that unite temples on a route Thus, the Shikoku pilgrimage is a *seiseki* pilgrimage because, while the main devotional focus for pilgrims is Kōbō Daishi, he is not the main image of worship at the temples visited. Each Shikoku temple has a hall of worship to Kōbō Daishi, but this is never the main hall of worship at the temples; they each have a main hall enshrining the temple's *honzon*, who is one of the various Buddha and bodhisattva figures in the Buddhist tradition. What unites the temples, therefore, is not their disparate main figures of worship but the itinerant figure of Kōbō Daishi, whose traces permeate the island, route and temples (Kojima 1987, Hoshino 2001: 57).

The *honzon-seiseki* categorisation model is, in much Japanese scholarship, supplemented by two related subcategories. One distinguishes between different levels of importance for pilgrimages, between major pilgrimages (a category thatwhich centres on Shikoku and Saikoku but also usually

34 Ian Reader

includes two historically prominent regional pilgrimages—Chichibu and Bandō, both in the region around Tokyo—which follow the Saikoku thirty-three-temple model) and numerous smaller-scale and regional pilgrimages, many of which use the Shikoku or Saikoku model of eighty-eight sites and a focus on Kōbō Daishi or thirty-three temples centred on Kannon.

The second subcategory relates more specifically to the copies of Saikoku and Shikoku, which are found in vast numbers throughout Japan at regional or local levels, even at times so small that they fit within a temple courtyard or within a special room within a temple. These regional pilgrimages are designated by various terms including *utsushi junrei* (copied pilgrimages) and even recently (using foreign loan words) *mini junrei*. The development of these pilgrimages has led to debates about the spatial and geographical dimensions of replication in pilgrimage. Tanaka Hiroshi (1983), for example, compared a Shikoku replica pilgrimage in western Japan with pilgrimage on Shikoku Island and claimed that replicas are primarily modelled on the actual spatial structures of the 'original' pilgrimage. His claim has been countered particularly by Oda Masayuki (1996), who examined the eighty-eight-stage Kōbō Daishi Shōdoshima pilgrimage in conjunction with Shikoku to argue that local political and historical factors play a greater part in the structural layout of replicated pilgrimages than the wish to represent exactly the spatial and geographical features of the 'main' pilgrimage.

These categorical and typological differentiations are best seen in the three-volume set edited by Shinno Toshikazu in 1996, which brought together some of the most important essays and book chapters or extracts on pilgrimage from Japanese scholarship of past decades. The three-volume set replicates the prevalent typologies of the field: one volume focusses on *honzon*, one on *seiseki* and one on regional and 'replicated' pilgrimages (Shinno 1996).

Through the development of typological classificatory structures (*honzon, seiseki, utsushi*), using concepts such as linear and circuit pilgrimages and drawing on the rich terminology of Japanese words associated with and translatable by the word 'pilgrimage', Japanese academic studies of pilgrimage encourages us to think more deeply about pilgrimage classifications and typologies—an area which has, perhaps, not been so deeply explored by Anglophone studies of pilgrimage.

HISTORICAL STUDIES AND ECONOMICS AND SOCIAL (IM)MOBILITY

Pilgrimages have also been widely studied by historians, who identify travel in general and pilgrimage, more specifically, as factors in the social and economic development of Japan in the Tokugawa era (1600–1868). This was a period when many of the foundations of Japan's initial development as a modern nation were laid, even as Japan remained feudal. Japanese scholars have shown how important pilgrimage and travel, including the *sankin kōtai* system, which obliged feudal lords to make regular processional journeys from their domains to spend periods of time at the Shogun's court in Edo (Tokyo), were to the structure of Japan during this period.

The Tokugawa regime strictly controlled mobility and, worried that mobility would bring about social disorder, did not normally allow people to leave their feudal domains. An exception was made in the case of religion because the regime relied on the support of religious institutions and feared upsetting the gods and buddhas. It was, therefore, reluctant to stop people travelling to prominent religious centres. Indeed, to some extent, it encouraged such travel in order to boost a public sense of identity and cultural belonging. Pilgrimages to the Shinto shrines of Ise (associated with the imperial lineage and with myths of Japan's founding as a divine country) and to the famed temples of Saikoku, which had deep cultural and historical associations with Japan's past, were seen as especially important in this context.

Hence, pilgrimage was the only way ordinary people could gain travel permits to leave their feudal domains. Because local Buddhist temples served as civil offices that could grant permits to travel for religious purposes, this helped to promote a massive tourist/pilgrimage market during the Tokugawa period—one that was boosted by the social harmony, which the regime established, and by economic development. Moreover, the heavily bureaucratic system used to ensure that only *bona fide* pilgrims were travelling, and the barrier system of control gates where they had to present their permits to enter and exit feudal domains, have provided immense historical resources for scholars to examine. Thus, pilgrimage has featured significantly in research by economic historians, who have paid particular attention to the role of travel in expanding economic markets and developing economic infrastructures throughout Japan. The records, which economic and social historians have examined, provide comprehensive data about the way in which pilgrimage changed from a largely ascetic exercise for small numbers of itinerants into a mass activity. This is another area which Japanese studies has explored more intensely than in the Anglophone world, where the part played by economic factors has been less appreciated, especially in the study of contemporary pilgrimage.

The work of scholars such as Shinjō Tsunezō, the preeminent scholar in this field, is significant here. Among his publications (1960, 1964, 1971 and 1982), the book produced in 1982 is very much the gold standard in the field; it is a key reference point for subsequent studies and an expanded version of his 1964 publication. His work brings together research on historical developments surrounding temples, shrines, pilgrimage routes and figures associated with pilgrimage (such as *oshi* and *sendatsu*, professional guides and promoters/organisers of pilgrimage itineraries in premodern Japan) with depictions of economic flows in Japanese society and how they impacted on and shaped pilgrimage patterns, and an examination of local, regional and national politics and their role in pilgrimage development.

36 *Ian Reader*

Shinjō also traces the historical development of pilgrimages from early travels by ascetics, who, from the Heian era onwards, opened up routes that later generations of pilgrims followed. These early religious itinerants then became guides leading those with the wherewithal and social status to travel, i.e., aristocrats and members of the Imperial court, to sacred places to seek the benefits and graces of their holy figures. Subsequently, as Shinjō shows, pilgrimage became popularised through the development of routes and infrastructures that catered to these early pilgrims and, thereafter, to growing numbers of people from other social strata.

In investigating how, as potential markets grew, more and more places sought to attract pilgrims, Shinjō and the social and economic historians who followed him have shown the importance of 'nonreligious' factors in the shaping of pilgrimage. This research, especially Shinjō's, has served as an important corrective to the strong tendency to focus on the seemingly 'sacred' and 'religious' dimensions of pilgrimage (including legends, miracles and concepts associated with sacred figures and places). Those working in Japanese religious studies clearly show this tendency, but the existence of an extensive corpus of Japanese social and economic historical work has helped scholars to avoid the trap of thinking that pilgrimage is only about such things and has alerted them of the need to pay attention to surrounding contextual factors.

Hence, several scholars have paid close attention to the links between markets and religious travel. They have examined, for example, the extent to which pilgrimage helped in constructing better infrastructures and highways during the Tokugawa period and played a significant role in the movement of capital and the building of a national economic structure. These and other studies have also shown how the support structures, emerging around pilgrimage sites, contributed to an increasingly touristic dimension in religious travel. Scholars such as Kanzaki Noritake (1990) have pursued this matter further by focussing their attention on the development of tourism in Japan, by showing how tourism emerged from pilgrimage and how pilgrimage guides to places such as Ise created package tour pilgrimages in the premodern era. Recently, too, a new wave of scholarship in Japan has further focussed attention on the links between religion, pilgrimage and tourism and explored 'religious tourism' (*shūkyō kankōgaku*), an area of growing interest at present in Japan (Yamanaka 2012, Kadota 2013).

Japanese social and economic historians have also shown the intimate link between fluctuations in pilgrim numbers and economic flows. This is a recurrent theme in Shinjō's work. While he demonstrates that pilgrimage generally became an increasingly popular practice over the centuries, enabling artisans, merchants and then, in Tokugawa times, peasants and even, to an extent, women, to travel, he also shows that this process was not regular and continuous. At different periods within the Tokugawa era, for example, there were periods of pilgrimage growth and times of decline, which reflected the prevailing economic conditions of the time. Hence, periods of economic

Japanese Studies of Pilgrimage   37

growth gave rise to better facilities, e.g., through the building of bridges and the provision of ferries across rivers and inlets, and enabled more people to have the money to travel, thereby increasing the supply of inns, services and guidebooks. During the two and half centuries of Tokugawa rule the Genroku (1688–1704), Hōreki (1751–1763) and Bunka (1804–1818) periods were identified by Shinjō and subsequent historians as particular periods of growth. By contrast, economic decline produced the opposite effect. Shinjō also shows (as do later sociologists) how different pilgrimages attracted different clienteles, a point I will discuss below.

SOCIOLOGICAL STUDIES

These studies by social and economic historians also revealed how different pilgrimages might attract different clienteles. Saikoku in the Tokugawa period, for example, attracted a better-off clientele and built a sophisticated infrastructure of guidebooks, facilities and places for pilgrims to spend their money. Shikoku, on the other hand, remained largely a pilgrimage of the poor, where many people were outcasts, fugitives from the law or sufferers of diseases, such as leprosy, which caused them to be driven from their villages.

Sociologists have also explored the provenance and social standing of pilgrims. Maeda Takashi made a notable contribution through a pioneering study on Saikoku and Shikoku pilgrims in the Tokugawa period (1971), which was followed by research undertaken by his former graduate student, Satō Hisamitsu (1989, 1990a, 1990b, 2004) and by scholars such as Osada Kōichi and Sakata Masaaki. Maeda's 1971 study, for example, provides detailed evidence of where pilgrims from the 1700s to the 1960s came from, what ages and genders they were and what they sought from their pilgrimages. Its sociological data reinforces the point made above about how different pilgrimages within the same cultural arena can attract different clienteles and how different eras and economic conditions can create fluctuations within pilgrimages.

Satō Hisamitsu's more recent research (notably Satō 2004) further develops these themes in the modern period and shows how the success of one pilgrimage does not necessarily indicate a general pilgrimage 'boom'. While Shikoku pilgrim numbers, for example, grew during the late 1990s and early 2000s, the Saikoku and Chichibu pilgrimages—both seen as among Japan's major pilgrimages—have suffered falling numbers.

The studies by Maeda and Satō have also been augmented by a group of sociologists at Waseda University headed by Osada Kōichi and Sakata Masaaki, along with Seki Mitsuo, whose studies of several pilgrimages including Shikoku provide the most detailed profiles of Japanese pilgrimage clienteles and their motivations since the 1990s.[9] The Waseda group has examined different pilgrimages in Japan through sociological surveys,

38 Ian Reader

extensive questionnaires, the gathering of empirical data on pilgrim numbers and the like and several qualitative studies based on interviews with pilgrims.

Their studies have largely focussed on narrative accounts and reports rather than the analysis of pilgrimage theories. While those involved in the Waseda project have visited pilgrimage sites elsewhere (I accompanied one of its leaders to Walsingham in 2004) and are aware of wider theoretical debates, their main interest has been in developing datasets that provide a narrative of pilgrimage development and the state of pilgrimage in modern Japan. In this respect they have made a significant contribution by showing how the development of pilgrimage infrastructures and support systems impacts on and changes the profiles of the pilgrim community. Shinjō and Maeda have both shown that premodern pilgrimages largely centred on individual and predominantly younger males, while Shikoku's clientele tended to be mostly among the poorer sections of society. The Waseda studies have also revealed how these profiles have changed and how transport developments have speeded up and altered pilgrimage patterns. The gradual development of bus tour pilgrimages in Shikoku from the mid-1950s onwards, for example, has made this pilgrimage more accessible to wider circles of people and has produced a shift away from poorer, mendicant-oriented younger males, towards older female pilgrims with an average age of around sixty (Osada, Sakata and Seki 2003).

Figure 2.3 Pilgrimage tour group climbing the steps up to a temple in Shikoku.

Japanese sociological studies thus provide us with some of the richest material available anywhere on changing patterns of pilgrimage, while adding to earlier historical studies which demonstrate that the success of some pilgrimages in any given era need not indicate that pilgrimage *per se* is flourishing. As Satō (2004), for example, shows, and as the various Waseda studies also indicate, the growth of some pilgrimages may well be at the expense of others in the same cultural region, country or religious tradition. They show that it is important to be aware of competition between pilgrimages and of how social and economic changes constantly reshape the pilgrimage market. Their studies have also been reinforced by the work of Mori Masato (2005), a social geographer and historian. His study of the Shikoku pilgrimage in twentieth- and early twenty-first-century Japan emphasises how transport and other concerns have shaped the pilgrimage and its clientele more than seemingly 'religious' factors, while showing how mass media interests and representations play a significant role in this process.

The relationship between the media and pilgrimage in Japan has attracted considerable attention among both Japanese and Western scholars (see Reader 2011, 2014 and Shultz 2011a, 2011b). Key here is the impact of mass media influences (including the Internet) on the projection, construction and public representation of pilgrimages, as well as the ways in which this affects pilgrimage practice and clienteles. Again this is an area which has been relatively unexplored by pilgrimage scholars in the West.

ANTHROPOLOGICAL STUDIES

While anthropology has been in the vanguard of Western pilgrimage studies and the main arena from which theoretical notions have developed, this is less so in Japan. Many Japanese scholars, who study their own traditions in ethnographic/ethnological terms, locate themselves within *minzokugaku* and/or may work in a department of that nature. To many Japanese scholars (at least until recently) anthropology was seen as concerned with other places and other ethnic and linguistic cultures. Furthermore, even when engaging in qualitative, interview-oriented fieldwork, scholars continue to use other labels to describe themselves. The Waseda study group, for example, conducted extensive field interviews and incorporated a great deal of ethnographic material in their work but considered themselves sociologists. Moreover, they focussed primarily on collecting and analysing quantitative data; the qualitative materials they gleaned from fieldwork were viewed as subsidiary to and support for their sociological work.

There are, however, a few scholars who have pursued anthropological perspectives. The most significant is Hoshino Eiki, a Shingon Buddhist priest and academic, who undertook postgraduate work at Chicago with

40 Ian Reader

Victor Turner in the 1970s and has written widely about the Shikoku pilgrimage (Hoshino 2001, Hoshino and Asakawa 2011), about structural studies of Japanese pilgrimage (1981, 1986) and about regional pilgrimages (1979). Hoshino can be seen as the main proponent in Japan of the anthropological and comparative study of pilgrimage. He has drawn on Western studies, made field trips to sites beyond Japan and cited examples drawn from a variety of contexts besides the Japanese, to inform his studies of Japanese pilgrimages (see Hoshino 1997, translated by Reader, for an example of his work). He has also developed a modified Turnerian approach to the study of pilgrimage, where he discusses *communitas* in terms of the interaction between pilgrims and locals in Shikoku (Hoshino 1979). He shows how pilgrims and locals established a bond together in protest against established political hierarchies and the regulations imposed by feudal authorities.

Hoshino has also, in his most comprehensive study of the Shikoku pilgrimage (2001), paid attention to competing fields of influence in the pilgrimage. He examines how priests and temple authorities, with their roots in the Shingon Buddhist tradition, sought to create a religious orthodoxy in pilgrimage in order to promote their sectarian agendas. In so doing, they sought to domesticate the popular folkloric Kōbō Daishi and reinforce an image of him as an arbiter and representation of Shingon Buddhist orthodoxy. However, as Hoshino indicates, such attempts at creating a pilgrimage orthodoxy centred on institutions and doctrines have little purchase compared to the folk orientations of most pilgrims. He also discusses how pilgrim attitudes change, focussing particularly on contemporary Japanese, who walk the Shikoku pilgrimage. As Hoshino indicates, they have increasingly manifested attitudes, which accord not with the earlier Buddhist orientations of the pilgrimage but with 'New Age' ideas. They search for self-discovery free from any religious set of beliefs or affiliation; they are detached from overt religious expressions and seek to get fit and challenge themselves (Hoshino 2001).

These points have also been expressed in various forms through the studies mentioned earlier by the Waseda group and by Mori (2005). They point not only to further changes and segmentations in the Japanese pilgrimage community but also, as Hoshino (2001) suggests, to parallels with the walkers who follow the *camino* to Santiago de Compostela. These travellers similarly appear to be less oriented towards religion and more influenced by New Age ideas of personal discovery and challenge.

More recently, Asakawa Yasuhiro (2008), who studied with Osada and Sakata at Waseda, and who comes from Shikoku, has examined the Shikoku pilgrimage from the perspective of the local custom of almsgiving. He has also collaborated with Hoshino, who was himself involved in some of the Waseda group projects, to draw attention to the contemporary attitudes of pilgrims in Japan, and especially of those who go on foot in Shikoku. Asakawa reinforces some of the points made by Hoshino about the prevalence of 'New Age' attitudes among Shikoku foot pilgrims. He also joins Hoshino in attending to the influence of mass media on Japanese pilgrimage, thereby reinforcing the work of Mori Masato mentioned earlier. He focusses, in particular, on how mass media has helped pilgrimage to be projected as a symbol of cultural heritage (Hoshino and Asakawa 2011).

CONCLUDING COMMENTS

Japanese studies of pilgrimage are rich and variegated in nature, spanning a variety of fields—notably, native ethnology/folk studies, religious studies, social and economic history, sociology, anthropology and social geography. Of these, native ethnology/folk studies has been particularly important in theorising about the nature of the Japanese people and their identity and, thereby, incorporating examinations of religious travel within this theoretical framework.

Religious studies, together with native ethnology, has contributed to understandings of pilgrimage through an emphasis on the role of the wanderer and the interactions of popular/folk ideas with organised social and religious structures. Likewise, social and economic studies of pilgrimage have offered significant insights into how economic changes impact on pilgrimages, while such studies, especially in historical contexts and drawing on sociologically based quantitative research, have shown how different pilgrimages within the same wider tradition and era may attract different socio-economic clienteles.

More generally, studies of Japanese pilgrimage have shown how the practice and its relationship with particular figures of worship has been integral to Japanese religious development. Far from being on the margins, pilgrimage occupies a central position within religious structures at popular, folk and institutional levels. Japanese pilgrimage studies also offer significant contributions to more general typological studies of pilgrimage through their discussion of 'main' (*hon*) and 'copied/localised' pilgrimages, as well as their differentiation between pilgrimages centred on place/region and holy figures (*seiseki*), on the one hand, and the main images of worship at linked sites (*honzon*), on the other.

There have, nonetheless, been problems with the field. Japanese studies have tended to be insular, rarely engaging with wider studies in the field and eschewing much contact with or use of theoretical concerns discussed elsewhere. The language issue has also been a serious problem. Japanese scholars have unsurprisingly written in Japanese, and this has made one of the most important bodies of literature in the field unavailable to most of the international scholastic community. The field beyond Japan has relied on

42 *Ian Reader*

the work of Western scholars, such as Ambros 2005 and myself, who have drawn attention to aspects of the Japanese field or have translated specific works into English. The language barrier has operated the other way, too, because most Japanese academics have had little access to Western sources and writings. The lack of engagement with (Western-based) theories can be seen as a form of Japanese insularity on one level, but it is also a reflection of the extent to which Japanese pilgrimage culture is so rich and diverse, and tied in to deeper issues of national identity, history and development, that scholars find plenty to examine and analyse within that culture without recourse to Western studies.

A wider knowledge about Japanese studies of pilgrimage and the field of pilgrimage in Japan itself would encourage Western scholars to learn more about the topic in non-Western contexts. If pilgrimage is to be considered as a truly universal phenomenon, then this naturally requires a properly universal analytical approach, which is inclusive both in terms of geography and religious tradition. The Japanese case shows us that theories of pilgrimage need not be based around Western examples nor be grounded in a standard 'from the West to the rest' format. Western studies of pilgrimage need to break out of their ghetto and take much more note of the non-Western world—just as Japanese studies could benefit from opening up more to studies of pilgrimage beyond Japan.

NOTES

1. See, for example, the special double of the *Japanese Journal of Religious Studies* (1997: Vol. 24, Nos. 3–4), which focussed on pilgrimage in Japan. It included articles by Western scholars, translations of important work by Japanese scholars and an extensive introduction by Reader and Swanson (1997) that outlined terminologies associated with pilgrimage and some of its main practices. Various book-length studies (e.g., Reader [2005] on Shikoku, Ambros [2008] on Ōyama, Thal [2005] on Konpira and Moerman [2005] on Kumano) discuss major pilgrimages either in modern times or historically and provide broader overviews of pilgrimage in Japan, in general. There are also a number of studies in French, mainly focussing on historical issues prior to the twentieth century, such as the studies by Kouamé, studies of how local populations interacted with and provided support for pilgrims in Shikoku between the seventeenth and nineteenth centuries (Kouamé 1998, 2001) and Barbaro's (2013) doctoral study of pilgrimage guidebooks in premodern times.
2. In November 2009, for example, I was invited to speak at a conference at Ehime University, Matsuyama, Japan, titled *Sekai no Junrei no Naka no Shikoku Henro* ('the Shikoku pilgrimage in the context of world pilgrimages'). All of the presentations including my own (Reader 2009) used Shikoku as a core theme and framing device, even when examining other pilgrimages. A few Japanese edited volumes examine pilgrimages around the world (e.g., Seishin Joshi Dai Kirisutokyō Kyōka Kenkyūjo 1987), but these tend to use Japan as the lens through which to compare and analyse pilgrimages elsewhere. Very recently, with the growth in interest in religion and tourism as a field of study (see later in this chapter) there have been a few more studies of non-Japanese pilgrimages, but they remain comparatively rare.

Japanese Studies of Pilgrimage   43

3. As I indicate later, Turner's work has been introduced to Japanese audiences through the work of Hoshino Eiki (e.g., 2001), which refers to a number of Western scholastic studies of pilgrimage, but he is a rare case. My work (because it focusses on Japanese pilgrimages) has been reviewed in Japanese academic publications and is referred to in some studies of Shikoku (e.g., Asakawa 2008, Hoshino and Asakawa 2011), and I have been invited to write for Japanese academic publications on the topic of pilgrimage (see Reader 2005a), but, again, these are comparatively rare examples.

4. Paolo Barbaro (2013: 46) strongly criticises Western pilgrimage studies for its failure to take note even of Western-language studies of Japanese pilgrimages— and he notes that the same criticisms were made by Reader and Swanson (1997) sixteen years earlier; in the ensuing years very little has changed.

5. Mention should also be made of the eighteen-volume series *Sangaku shūkyōshi kenkyū shōsho* ('collected writings on research into the religious history of mountains') published by Meicho Shuppan, many of whose volumes were edited by Gorai or Miyake.

6. In English Ellwood (1982) examined Tenrikyō, a nineteenth-century new religion that created a new sacred centre to which followers were expected to make pilgrimages, as a 'pilgrimage faith'. Japanese studies of the new religions have generally discussed pilgrimage to the sacred centres of these movements as a facet of their religious practice rather than examining them in the context of pilgrimage studies.

7. For a full discussion of the development of *minzokugaku*, see Christy (2012). This valorisation of pilgrimage also led, by the early twentieth century, to newspapers and magazines running positive features about Japanese pilgrimages, thereby adding to their appeal (Mori 2005).

8. For more on these issues and the terminology and academic developments within 'folk religion', see Reader (2005b), where I discuss Shinno amongst others, plus my review of Shinno (1991a), available at http://nirc.nanzan-u.ac.jp/nfile/2476.

9. The group has published around a dozen quantitative reports on different pilgrimages in Japan, plus one major book based on data collected in Shikoku (Osada, Sakata and Seki 2003).

REFERENCES

Japanese-Language Sources and References Cited

Asakawa, Y. (2008) *Junrei no bunkajinruigakuteki kenkyū: Shikoku henro no settaibunka*, Tokyo: Kokon Shoin.

Gorai, S. (1975) *Kōya hijiri*, Tokyo: Kadokawa Sensho.

———. (1984) *Bukkyō to minzoku*, Tokyo: Kadokawa Sensho.

———. (1989) *Yugyō to junrei: Nihonjin no tabi to shinkō no genten*, Tokyo: Kadokawa Shuppan.

———. (1991) *Yama no shūkyō: Shugendō kōgi*, Tokyo: Kadokawa Sensho.

———. and Miyake Hitoshi et al. (1975–1984) *Sangaku shūkyōshi kenkyū shōsho* ('Collected Writings on Research into the Religious History of Mountains'), eighteen volume series, Tokyo: Meicho Shuppan.

Hayami, T. (1980) 'Kannon shinkō to minzoku: Kannon junrei no hattatsu o chūshin ni', in S. Gorai and T. Sakurai (eds.) *Nihon no minzokushūkyō 2: Bukkyōminzokugaku*, Tokyo: Kōbundō.

———. (1983) *Kannon shinkō*, Tokyo: Hanawa Shobō.

Hinonishi, S. (ed.) (1988) *Kōbō Daishi shinkō*, Tokyo: Yūzankaku.

44 Ian Reader

Hoshino, E. (1979) 'Shikoku henro to sangakushinkō', in H. Miyake (ed.) *Daisen. Ishizuchi to Saikoku shugendō* (Vol. 12 of the Sanshūkyōshi kenkyū series), Tokyo: Meicho Shuppan.

———. (1981) *Junrei: sei to zoku no genshōgaku*, Tokyo: Kōdansha Gendaishinsho.

———. (1986) 'Aruki to mawari no shūkyōsei', in T. Yamaori (ed.) *Yugyō to hyōhaku* (Taikei Bukkyō to Nihonjin Vol. 6), Tokyo: Shunjūsha. (Available in English translation by I. Reader as E. Hoshino (1997), 'Pilgrimage and peregrination: contextualising the Saikoku junrei and the Shikoku henro', *Japanese Journal of Religious Studies*, 24 (3–4): 271–300.)

———. (2001) *Shikoku henro no shūkyōgakuteki kenkyū*, Kyoto: Hōzōkan.

———. and Y. Asakawa (2011) *Shikoku henro: samazamana inori no sekai*, Tokyo: Furukawa Kōbunkan.

Kadota, T. (2013) *Junrei tsūrizumu no minzokushi*, Tokyo: Shinwasha.

Kaneko, S. (1991) *Shinshū shinkō to minzoku shinkō*, Kyoto: Nagata Bunshōdō.

Kanzaki, N. (1990) *Kankō minzokugaku e no tabi*, Tokyo: Kawade Shobō.

Kojima, H. (1987) 'Junrei.henro', in F. Tamamuro et al. (eds.) *Minkan shinkō chōsa seiri handobukku* Vol. 1, Tokyo: Yuzankaku.

Matsuzaki, K. (1985) *Meguri no fōkuroa: yugyōbutsu no kenkyū*, Tokyo: Meichi Shuppan.

Miyake, H. (1971) *Shugendō girei no kenkyū*, Tokyo: Shunjūsha.

———. (1978) *Shugendō: Yamabushi no rekishi to shisō*, Tokyo: Kyōikusha.

———. (1980) *Seikatsu no naka no shūkyō*, Tokyo: Nihon Hōsō Shuppan.

———. (1988) *Ōmine shugendō no kenkyū*, Tokyo: Kōsei Shuppansha.

———. (1992) *Kumano shugen*, Tokyo: Yoshikawa Kōbunkan.

———. (2000) *Haguro Shugen: sono rekishi to mineiri*, Tokyo: Iwata Shoin.

———. (2002) *Shūkyō minzokugaku nyūmon*, Tokyo: Maruzen.

Mori, M. (2005) *Shikoku henro no kindaika: modan henro kara iyashi no tabi made*, Osaka: Sōgensha.

Numata, K. (1988) *Gendai nihon no shinshūkyō*, Osaka: Sōgensha.

Oda, M. (1996) 'Shōdoshima ni okeru utsushi reijō no seiritsu', in T. Shinno (ed.) *Nihon no junrei: junrei no kōzō to chihō junrei* Vol. 3, Tokyo: Yūzankaku.

Osada K., Sakata, M. and Seki, M. (2003) *Gendai no Shikoku henro: Michi no shakaigaku no shiten kara*, Tokyo: Gakubunsha.

Satō, H. (1989) 'Gendai no junrei: Saikoku junrei ni tsuite', in T. Maeda (ed.) *Kazoku shakaigaku nōto*, Kyoto: Kansai Daigaku.

———. (1990a) 'Osamefuda ni miru Shikoku henro', in Nakao Shunpaku Sensei Koki Kinenkai (ed.) *Bukkyō to shakai: Nakao Shunpaku sensei koki kinen*, Kyoto: Nagata Bunshōdō.

———. (1990b) 'Shikoku henro no shakaigakuteki kōsatsu', *Mikkyōgaku*, 26: 29–47.

———. (2004) *Henro to junrei no shakaigaku*, Kyoto: Jimbo Shoin.

Seishin Joshi Dai Kirisutokyō Kyōka Kenkyūjo (ed.) (1987) *Junrei to bunmei*, Tokyo: Shunjūsha.

Shinjō, T. (1960) *Shaji to kōtsū*, Tokyo: Shibundō.

———. (1964) *Shaji sankei no shakai keizaishiteki kenkyū*, Tokyo: Hanawa Shobō.

———. (1971) *Shomin no tabi no rekishi*, Tokyo: Nihon Hōsō Shuppan.

———. (1982) *Shinkō: Shaji sankei no shakai keizaishiteki kenkyū*, Tokyo: Hanawa Shobō (revised and expanded version of Shinjō 1964).

Shinno, T. (1980) *Tabi no naka no shūkyō*, Tokyo: NHK Books.

———. (1991a) *Nihon yugyō shūkyōron*, Tokyo: Yoshikawa Kōbunkan.

———. (1991b) *Sei naru tabi*, Tokyo: Tōkyōdō.

———. (ed.) (1996) *Nihon no junrei*, Tokyo: Yūzankaku, 3 volumes: Vol. 1: *Honzon junrei*. Vol. 2: *Seiseki junrei*. Vol. 3: *Junrei no kōzō to chihō junrei*.

Takeda, A. (1972) *Junrei no minzoku*, Tokyo: Iwasaki Bijitsusha.
———. (1987) *Nihonjin no shireikan: Shikoku minzokushi*, Tokyo: Sanichi Shobō.
Tanaka, H. (1983) *Junreichi no sekai*, Tokyo: Kokon Shoin.
Yamanaka, H. (ed.) (2012) *Shūkyō to tsūrizumu: Sei narumono no henyō to tokuzoku*, Tokyo: Sekaishisōsha.
Yamaori, T. (ed.) (1986) *Yugyō to hyōhaku* (Taikei Bukkyō to Nihonjin Vol. 6), Tokyo: Shunjūsha.

Western-Language Sources and Writings by Western Scholars in Japanese

Ambros, B. (2005) 'Geography and environment', in P. Swanson and C. Chilson (eds.) *The Nanzan Guide to Japanese Religions*, Honolulu: University of Hawaii Press.
Barbaro, P. (2013) *La mise en discours des pèlerinages au Japon depuis l'époque d'Edo: Pour une théorie de l'interversion réciproque entre expérience et récit.* Unpublished PhD dissertation, École Pratique des Hautes Études, Paris.
Christy, A. (2012) *A Discipline on Foot: Inventing Japanese Native Ethnography 1910–1945*, Lanham, MD, New York, and Plymouth, UK: Rowman & Littlefield.
Dubisch, J. (1995) *In a Different Place: Pilgrimage, Gender, and Practice at a Greek Island Shrine*, Princeton, NJ: Princeton University Press.
Ellwood, R. (1982) *Tenrikyo, a Pilgrimage Faith: The Structure and Meanings of a Modern Japanese Religion*, Tenri, Japan: Oyasato Research Institute.
Josephson, J. (2012) *The Invention of Religion in Japan*, Chicago: University of Chicago Press.
Kouamé, N. (1998) *Le Pèlerinage de Shikoku Pendant l'Epoque Edo: Pèlerins et Sociétés Locales.* Unpublished PhD dissertation, Institut National Des Langues et Civilisations Orientales, Paris.
———. (2001) *Pèlerinage et Société dans le Japon des Tokugawa: Le Pèlerinage de Shikoku entre 1598 et 1868*, Paris: École Française d'Extrême-Orient.
Maeda, T. (1971) *Junrei no shakaigaku*, Kyoto: Mineruba Shobō.
Moerman, D. (2005) *Localizing Paradise: Kumano Pilgrimage and the Religious Landscape of Premodern Japan*, Cambridge, MA: Harvard University Asia Center.
Reader, I. (1988) 'Miniaturization and proliferation: a study of small-scale pilgrimages in Japan', *Studies in Central and East Asian Religions*, 1 (1): 50–66.
———. (2005a) *Making Pilgrimages: Meaning and Practice in Shikoku*, Honolulu: University of Hawaii Press.
———. (2005b) 'Folk religion', in P. Swanson and C. Chilson (eds.), *The Nanzan Guide to Japanese Religions*, Honolulu: University of Hawaii Press.
———. (2009) 'Hikaku junrei kenkyū no kanten kara mita shikokuhenro: sono shisa suru mono to kongō no yukue', in Ehime Daigaku Shikoku Henro to Sekai no Junrei Kenkyūkai (ed.) *Shikoku Henro to Sekai no Junrei*, Matsuyama, Japan: Ehime Daigaku.
———. (2011) 'The Shikoku Pilgrimage online', in E. Baffelli, I. Reader and B. Staemmler (eds.), *Japanese Religions on the Internet: Innovation, Representation and Authority*, New York, NY, and Abingdon, UK: Routledge.
———. (2014) *Pilgrimage in the Marketplace*, New York, NY, and Abingdon, UK: Routledge.
———. and Swanson, P. (1997) 'Editors' introduction: pilgrimage in the Japanese religious tradition', *Japanese Journal of Religious Studies*, 24 (3–4): 225–270.

46   Ian Reader

Shultz, J. (2011a) 'Media transformation, evangelical continuity: enticement for a Japanese pilgrimage from woodblocks to homepages', in T. Yutaka and L. Tkach-Kawasaki (eds.) *Japan and the Internet: Perspectives and Practices,* Tsukuba, Japan: Center for International, Comparative, and Advanced Japanese Studies, University of Tsukuba.

———. (2011b) 'Pilgrim leadership rendered in HTML: bloggers and the Shikoku *Henro*', in E. Baffelli, I. Reader and B. Staemmler (eds.) *Japanese Religions and the Internet: Innovation, Representation, and Authority,* New York: Routledge.

3 Touching the Holy
Orthodox Christian Pilgrimage Within Russia

Stella Rock

INTRODUCTION

Although the nature and extent of the 'religious revival' in post-Soviet Russia continues to be debated, the dramatic cultural shift Russians have experienced since the late 1980s is embodied in a visibly and tangibly re-sacralised landscape. Desecrated shrines have been returned to the Russian Orthodox Church, sacred springs unblocked, ruins reconstructed, new monasteries built and old procession routes revived. Icons and relics have been released from museums—the former as valued works of art, often controversially—to temporarily participate in religious life or permanently reside in shrine environments. In scrutinising this landscape, which offers a rich field for comparative studies of contemporary European pilgrimage, one encounters kaleidoscopic variations of place, person/object, distance and movement.[1]

There is no academic survey of Russian Orthodox shrines comparable with Nolan and Nolan's 1989 overview of Catholic pilgrimage to help us navigate the shifting boundaries of the sacred, and Russian pilgrimage *per se* remains understudied by academics, with significant contributions to international debate made by only a handful of researchers.[2] This, however, belies a wealth of Russian-language material which contributes to mapping the inner and outer geographies of Russian religiosity and tests the idea of Orthodox pilgrimage as an activity distinct from other types of religious practice. Furthermore, what falls under the rubric 'pilgrimage' within the diverse and fluid sphere of Russian Orthodox tradition challenges both Western Christian models of pilgrimage, which tend to stress the state of transition and the importance of the journey, and Eastern Christian models, which emphasise veneration rather than movement.

Russian language has more than one word for the practice of visiting holy places and for those who engage in this activity. The terms *palomnik* [паломник, pilgrim—literally 'palmer'] and *palomnichestvo* [паломничество, pilgrimage] are most often used within the broad community of the contemporary Russian Orthodox Church. Pre-revolutionary publications in the late imperial period more commonly refer to *bogomolets* [богомолец, lit. 'one who prays to God'] and *bogomol'e* [богомолье], with *palomnik*

48   *Stella Rock*

glossed by the nineteenth-century lexicographer and folkorist Dal' as 'one who has venerated the grave of the Lord'. The first issue of *Pravoslavnyi palomnik*, a journal founded in 2001 by the Moscow Patriarchate to help 'revive the tradition of Orthodox pilgrimage', is keen to remind its readers that even within the Christian tradition there is no universal concept of pilgrimage because Western Christians—rejecting the principle of icon veneration—focus on travel and the mental recollection of holy events. At the beginning of the twentieth century, the editor argues, the term *poklonnik* [поклонник—worshipper, lit. 'one who bows down'] was often used to describe Russian pilgrims (Mark 2001). This translation of the Greek *proskynetes* [προσκυνητής] centres on veneration rather than the journey implied in a palm leaf souvenir from Jerusalem and the act of prostrating oneself before, kissing and touching a physical manifestation of the holy.

This difference in emphasis has also been stressed by academics studying contemporary Greek pilgrimage (e.g., Dubisch 1995: 46, Gothóni 1987) and Byzantine practice. Weyl Carr eloquently argues that in Byzantine pilgrimage 'the critical movement was over the threshold of access to the one venerated. The space claimed was one less of distance than of presence' (2002: 76). Orthodox pilgrimage, then, may be interpreted as an effort to be in the presence of—or to achieve maximum proximity to—the holy.

There is, however, another increasingly visible practice which challenges the suggestion that movement and distance are unimportant aspects of Russian pilgrimage. In 2007 the late Patriarch Aleksii II remarked on the 'extraordinary spread of multiple-day processions of the cross by thousands of people to holy places across all of Great Rus', declaring them a traditional form of Russian pilgrimage (2007). Processions of the cross (*krestnye khody*) are public and communal devotional acts, authorised by and involving clergy (in theory at least), which may last hours, days, or even months. Participants walk to a holy place carrying crosses, icons and banners on historically and/or religiously significant dates, or in times of crisis they may circumnavigate a threatened area in a protective or apotropaic procession. Although they are traditionally held on foot, there have been 'processions' in planes, on buses, on boats, on motorbikes and even in a submarine. The Soviet authorities made repeated efforts to curtail or eradicate processions which travelled beyond the walls of the church until the late 1980s, and in the last decade the extended procession-as-pilgrimage has seen an exponential rise in popularity. For many people, such mass processions provide a more accessible religious environment than a parish (where their behaviour may be closely scrutinised and corrected), but despite this apparent flexibility, processions of the cross challenge the notion of pilgrimage as an unstructured, extra-liturgical activity. Long processions will be punctuated by clerically led ritual and prayer and have been promoted and perceived as peripatetic prayer services, monasteries, or parishes (Naletova 2010, Rock 2012, 2014). In addition to forming a body of pilgrims moving (generally) towards a sacred goal, processions may also be interpreted as a form of 'inverted pilgrimage', in which icons (and sometimes relics) themselves travel to different regions.

STUDYING 'FOLK' RELIGION: ETHNOGRAPHIC LEGACIES

While this chapter does not attempt to do justice to the wealth of historical sources on pre-revolutionary pilgrimage in Russia, the work of pre-revolutionary folklorists and ethnographers has been so influential that the trajectories of subsequent study of religious practice cannot be fully understood without reference to it. Like their Western European counterparts, nineteenth-century folklorists were entranced by 'the people' but showed little interest in individuals, treating the object of their scrutiny as an amorphous reservoir of national cultural heritage. Peasant culture, viewed by the higher echelons of Russian society as conservative to the point of stasis and therefore untainted by modernity, was either the bearer of true Orthodoxy or of pagan survivals through which the pre-Christian religion of the Slavs might be deduced (Chulos 1995). However they conceived of the folk, the dedication of ethnographers like the aristocrat V. N. Tenishev—who in the closing years of the nineteenth century funded research on peasant life in twenty-three regions of European Russia—secured a vast resource on peasant culture which continues to be productively mined today.

Late imperial stereotypes of the devout or—conversely—anticlerical, materialistic and superstitious peasant have also proved enduring influences on academic studies of Russian religious culture. Within the Soviet Union, research on religious topics was circumscribed, shaped and sometimes compromised by ideological and institutional restrictions, perpetuating an emphasis on the archaic nature of folk culture as preserving pagan beliefs and practices under a thin veneer of Christianity—the so-called *dvoeverie* or 'double belief' (Levin 1993, Panchenko 1998: 42–61, Rock 2007). Moreover, the contentious heritage of Soviet atheist scholarship gave emotional and ideological weight to research findings on Russian Orthodoxy in particular, dividing some scholars into implicitly 'pro' and 'anti' Church camps (e.g., Chernetsov 1994). During the late 1980s and early 1990s, M. M. Gromyko led the development of a school of research on 'Orthodoxy in Russian folk culture' at the Russian Academy of Sciences Institute of Ethnology and Anthropology, publishing six edited volumes on this topic (Tishkov 2013: 21). The Institute later collaborated in the founding of a new journal, *Traditsii i sovremennost'* [Traditions and Contemporaneity], in which 'believing Orthodox academics can publish the results of their research without hiding their worldview'. Gromyko's introductory article outlines the legacy of 'false and tendentious' concepts and methodologies which post-Soviet humanities—and ethnography in particular—has grappled with and stresses the importance of overcoming the artificial contrast between 'folk and church religious life' (2002a: 3–5).

50 Stella Rock

At the same time, a drive to overcome such 'binary oppositions' as 'popular' and 'elite' or 'folk' and 'official' was evident in Anglophone academia (Dixon 1999, Engelstein 2003). Shevzov's examination of late imperial understandings of *'tserkovnost"* (ecclesiality or 'churchness')—in which she found an echo of Turner's *communitas*—promoted inclusive understandings of 'church' as a living body embracing the people as well as the clergy. Problematising the suggestion that there was one sort of Orthodox religiosity beyond the church, in everyday life, and another sort within it, she highlighted the diversity of clerical responses to practices deemed 'pagan' by some, while acknowledging that Orthodoxy still has 'recognisable boundaries' (2003: 68, 76). How to avoid thinking in terms of a two-tier model, and do justice to the diversity and complexity of religious culture in Russia—including the tensions and contradictions within the broad community of the Orthodox—is an ongoing debate (Shtyrkov 2006).

Gromyko's efforts have promoted and published research on pilgrimage and the veneration of holy objects or people as indicative of the vitality of Orthodoxy in Russian folk culture (see, for example, Gromyko 2002b, Kirichenko 2010 and various works by Poplavskaia and Tsekhanskaia). Forming something of a discreet school, a notable aspect of this scholarship is a conviction that Orthodox Christianity is an essential and vital aspect of Russian national identity, coupled with an understanding of the Russian people (*narod*) as a distinct, primordial ethnos. This, in itself, testifies to a difficult legacy of 'state ethnography', in which Soviet ethnographers had identified and defined acceptable Soviet 'peoples', fixing 'traditions' and emphasising ethnic difference whilst encouraging a shared Soviet identity (Baiburin, Kelly and Vakhtin 2012, Sokolovskiy 2012: 30). Early post-Soviet anthropology was also criticised for an idealised, ahistorical approach to 'folk knowledge', which was seen as homogenous and stable and considered genuine or 'traditional' by virtue of belonging to distinct ethnic group (Durand 1995). Moreover, the convergence of religious identity with ethnic identity has important implications for pilgrimage studies in a multi-ethnic, multi-confessional nation. As yet, these interactions during journeys to and time at shrines remain underexplored, although Luehrmann offers an inspiringly nuanced approach (2010).

Such essentialist understandings of 'the people' were problematic in the late imperial period—recent work on peasant women's pilgrimage suggests that village culture was subject to so many influences in this period that the concept of a distinct peasant worldview may have to be abandoned (Worobec 2012: 50). Today they are impossible to maintain, given the vast diversity, fluidity and dynamism of post-Soviet society. Treating 'Orthodox Russians' as one unified and undifferentiated category returns the researcher to the amorphous reservoir of unchanging tradition, which does not reflect the malleability and multiplicity of identities; the mobility of populations; the diverse information sources accessed by pilgrims and 'locals' alike; and the wide spectrum of Orthodox identity and allegiance, belief and practice, which fluctuates for individuals and families as for communities. Recent research on pilgrimage and local shrines is increasingly sensitive to these complexities.

As the editors of recent publications on post-socialist cultural anthropology point out, due to the virtual impossibility of conducting fieldwork in the Soviet Union, the Western anthropology of Soviet and former Soviet cultures began to develop only in the late 1980s (Rogers 2005, Baiburin, Kelly and Vakhtin 2012). When religious and ethnic identities became the subject of serious debate after *glasnost*, academics found themselves tackling the legacy of both domestic politics and the Cold War (Tishkov et al. 1992). Early efforts to share approaches internationally highlighted significant differences in 'preoccupations and discourses', but a similarly aimed conference in 2009 generated debate about the degree to which Russian scholars actually differ from their foreign counterparts and where Russian scholars engaged in postgraduate study and research at Western institutions fit into this putative home/abroad divide (Durand 1995: 327, Kormina 2009). Moreover, a number of collaborative projects continue to bring Russian academics together with their Western counterparts from various disciplines.[3] In this context, then, while pilgrimage research is necessarily a relatively new field in Russia and cross-fertilisation is still slow, Anglophone debates and theories concerning the anthropology of pilgrimage have made their mark on some recent research (discussed below).

It is difficult to divorce developments in the study of pilgrimage from the veritable explosion in studies of religiosity that followed the collapse of the Soviet Union. Research focussing on contemporary pilgrimage is also in dialogue with sociological assessments of religious revival and qualitative assessments of the nature of post-Soviet religious identity and allegiance. Although anthropologists and folklorists continue to examine local, rural cultures, challenging notions concerning 'pagan survivals' and highlighting the diversity to be found at village shrines, a broader interest in 'lived' Orthodoxy, which includes urban religious practices, is increasingly in evidence (Agadjanian and Russele 2006, 2011, Kormina, Panchenko and Shtyrkov 2006). Moreover, the flexible or fuzzy boundaries between groups (including different religious confessions) are acknowledged, as is the mutual influence between what is still generally referred to as 'folk' (*narodnoe*) or 'everyday' Orthodoxy and 'official', 'dogmatic', or 'canonical' Orthodoxy (e.g., Sibireva 2006).

CONTINUITIES AND DISCONTINUITY: DEALING WITH THE SOVIET PERIOD

Recent research has highlighted the importance of viewing these practices in historical context and examining Soviet-era religiosity as well as policy in order to appreciate the impact of state secularisation. This impact has

52   Stella Rock

practical as well as theoretical implications, as the Church makes efforts to reclaim her cultural property, to canonise those clerics and lay believers killed during the Soviet period, to 'church' the nominally Orthodox and to establish pastoral control over pilgrimage and holy places in contemporary Russia. Academics and archivists are often working in tandem with ecclesiastical institutions to research the history of pilgrimage places and objects of veneration, particularly on a local level, although federal level collaboration is also in evidence. The RAN Institute of Anthropology and Ethnography, for example, has co-organised annual conferences on such topics as 'the revival of Orthodox monasteries and the future of Russia', publishing five volumes of proceedings under the rubric 'Seraphim of Sarov's Legacy and the Fate of Russia' between 2004 and 2009 (Tishkov 2013: 22).

The Soviet past also generates one of the most important themes in contemporary pilgrimage research: what was the impact of Soviet secularisation on religious practice? Is today's pilgrimage so radically different that it cannot be compared with its historical precedents? In sharp contrast to the approach advocated by historians such as Chistiakov (2005) and Poplavskaia (2000), who trace pilgrimage in the Ryazan region from the beginning of the twentieth century to the end, one of the most prolific and pioneering researchers of contemporary pilgrimage in Russia argues that turning to analogous phenomena in Soviet or pre-revolutionary Russia is pointless. What we are witnessing, Kormina suggests, is not continuity but discontinuity, although everyone involved must believe that things are continuing just as before because this legitimises religious practices as authentic. Because those involved in this restoration aim to convince their audience this Orthodoxy is exactly the Orthodoxy that was before, academics should aim to expose this mimicry and not mistake a replica for real antiquity (2012).

The assumption that in examining post-Soviet religiosity 'we are dealing with a process of continuity—or interrupted continuity—between contemporary religious forms and their presocialist referents' has been problematised by others (Pelkmans 2009: 5). However, there are complex continuities between pre-revolutionary, Soviet and post-Soviet forms and practices, which challenge us methodologically and direct our attention to the 'legacy of the past' (Agadjanian and Rousselet 2010). As well as apparent 'elective affinities', researchers must grapple with the impact of the mass republication of pre-revolutionary Orthodox sources, including pilgrim memoirs and other shrine-related literature, and the ubiquity of the Internet through which, as Vinogradov points out, pilgrims share and republish academic research as well as their own impressions (2012).

The degree to which the Soviet period represents a radical break or interregnum is also debated. Our current picture of Soviet religiosity is more variegated than it was twenty years ago, and it is clear that the degree and extent of repression varied geographically as it did chronologically. While more work needs to be done, some researchers have considered the fluctuating practice of processions and pilgrimage during the Soviet era, highlighting the emergence of lay leaders, the decreasing participation of clergy and the increasing importance of natural features (such as springs) in the absence of functioning places of worship (Chistiakov 2006, Huhn 2012, Rock 2012).

Questions of dis/continuity and transformation will no doubt continue to preoccupy researchers, and Orsi's approach to the 'braided' nature of twentieth-century American Catholicism (which recognises transnational and intergenerational influences) could well be useful here (2005: 9). There have been calls for more micro-studies to examine the social and historical dynamics of religious practice, and such micro-histories will not just contribute to a richer picture of Orthodox pilgrimage but to working out the methodological challenges presented by the multilayered traditions (familial, local, ecclesiastical) and influences contemporary pilgrims are exposed to (Freeze 2001: 278, Panchenko 2012a: 11). We may, however, anticipate broader *longue durée* studies with equal enthusiasm.[4]

HISTORICAL MEMORY, DESECRATION AND THE TRAUMAS OF THE PAST

The desecration of holy places that took place during the Soviet period, particularly during the campaign against 'so-called holy places' launched in 1958 with the aim of eliminating unregulated pilgrimage, has a long echo. In addition to how the apparent fractures of the Soviet period impact upon pilgrim practices, the ways in which they are addressed in both individual and institutional narratives (such as diocesan or shrine publications) is also significant. Is the Soviet era 'skipped over' in embarrassment or meditated upon? How does adherence to Orthodoxy and/or atheism feature in the narratives pilgrims tell about their spiritual lives and family histories? Regardless of whether continuity is 'real' or imagined, its importance in the personal narratives of believers has been identified as a key point of difference between Russian Orthodoxy and the Protestant forms of Christianity which stress and celebrate discontinuities (Beneskovo-Sabkova et al. 2010, Hann and Goltz 2010: 7).

Close attention to narratives and rhetorical tropes is a particular strength of both Russian folklore studies and anthropology, and various approaches have been taken to the discourses that circulated as a result of Soviet acts of desecration and destruction. In addition to unpacking the internal structures of such narratives, researchers have interpreted tales of Soviet desecration as important in establishing and maintaining the holiness of a locally venerated object or place and fitted them into the sequence of oral narratives relating the life cycle of a sacred place: charter myths, relating miraculous origins; miracle tales, recounting events which testify to the sacred status of the place; narratives of destruction and of restoration (Fadeeva 2004). The

54   Stella Rock

relative importance of such tales to those living near a shrine—in contrast to those travelling some distance to venerate—has also been highlighted: oral narratives of desecration are maintained by locals rather than pilgrims and preserve memories of the Soviet closure and destruction of holy places even from the 1930s in stories recounting the punishments visited upon those who committed sacrilegious acts (Kormina 2006, Nikitina 2002, Panchenko 2012a: 262–263).

Ritual practices at desecrated sites—such as circumnavigation and leaving candles and other items—also maintained a local memory of sacrality (Moroz 2002), and some pilgrims perceive their actions as re-sacralising or cleansing desecrated ground. The way pilgrims experience and behave in desecrated space is a rich field for comparative research, as is the reclaiming of such space. Kozelsky's work, in particular, should generate further investigation of the interplay among grassroots activism, ecclesiastical policy and local and national politics in the revival of pilgrimage places, and indeed of the role of pilgrimage in appropriating contested territory and 're-Christianizing' the landscape (2010).

The relationship between pilgrimage and historical memory, and the degree to which history is significant to pilgrims (as opposed to those who live locally), is an important research question. Do pilgrims seek to avoid the traumas of Soviet history in Russia's holy places or to engage with them? Pilgrimage has been interpreted by some as a way for contemporary Russians to 'rediscover the historical past' of their country, which—particularly at sites related to the murder of the Romanovs—may prompt meditation on traumatic events and a desire to study the related history. Amongst the Soviet-era 'new martyrs', only the murdered Tsar and his family have attracted truly mass veneration, but as yet pilgrimage to sites associated with Soviet killings has been little scrutinised (Christensen 2012, Naletova 2007, Rousselet 2007, 2011). Conversely, an examination of pilgrimage as a leisure activity drawing on Soviet domestic heritage tourism, in which pilgrims on organised bus trips seek authenticity in Russian rusticity and find in holy places 'continuity between the ancient inhabitants and those of today', raises the question of whether such imagined continuity is enabling post-Soviet believers to avoid the challenges of the recent past and construct an '"anti-historical" historical consciousness' (Kormina 2010, Rogers 2010: 358).

PILGRIMAGE AND 'MISSION'

The fluctuating dynamics of pilgrimage to local shrines in the post-Soviet period, as the Church gained educational and pastoral resources (theologically educated clergy and laity as well as property, publications and media access), have been addressed by several researchers. A recurring theme is the relationship among local users of shrines, increasing numbers of nonlocal

Touching the Holy   55

pilgrims and ecclesiastical representatives who have—in many cases—only attempted to exert influence over shrine activities in the last one or two decades. In the absence of a priest, processions and collective prayers might be led by a lay person with some liturgical knowledge, although the collapse of rural culture observable from the 1970s meant that in some areas a new generation of spiritual leaders did not emerge (Panchenko 2012a: 268).

Where local conditions did not completely rupture tradition, those lay individuals who continued to lead religious practice lost authority in the post-Soviet period. Moreover, some pilgrimage practices, which developed during the Soviet period and were maintained by locals in the absence of clerical participation or functioning local churches, are being deemed 'pagan' and corrected by neophyte believers and clergy brought in to regulate worship (Filicheva 2006a, Kormina 2006, Panchenko 2012a, Vinogradov 2012). Taking a long view reveals that local shrines have been in dynamic tension with the ecclesiastical centre in earlier periods—notably during eighteenth-century reforms—and Panchenko has suggested that once a local shrine is recognised and embraced by the Church, peasant attitudes towards it change (2012b: 49).

Married to the close focus on discourses and narratives amongst Russian academics, Eade and Sallnow's conception of sacred space as 'able to absorb and reflect a multiplicity of religious discourses' has generated some fruitful analysis of shrines as contested environments (2000: 15, Kormina 2004). Recent work argues that not only do sacred places develop as a result of conflicts and competition but that contemporary folklore around shrines is both 'the subject, and the result of, social competition: the "struggle for authenticity"' (Panchenko 2012b: 58–9). Acknowledging the diversity to be found at both urban and rural shrines, Russian researchers have considered the ways in which different discourses are managed by clergy and the extent to which narratives maintained by locals, pilgrims and shrine guardians impact upon each other or remain discreet and stable. Exploring the discourses which affirm and explain the holiness of a rural place of pilgrimage, Kormina has noted that where ecclesiastical control over a shrine is weak, other meanings will supplant those given by local clergy (2004; see also Panchenko 2012a: 264–265). In an urban shrine which attracts pilgrims from all over Russia, a key factor in the ability of the clergy to influence behaviour at the shrine has been identified as the degree to which pilgrims are engaged with the liturgical life of the Church—it is this 'churchedness' which makes pilgrims receptive to clerical guidance (Filicheva 2006b).

The Church, for its part, is very well aware that a shrine or procession may be the point at which the 'nominally Orthodox' or unbaptised first encounter Orthodoxy. Given the opportunities pilgrimage offers for engaging with those who might otherwise be hard to reach, the ecclesiastical hierarchy is keen to ensure that such encounters are managed sensitively.

Part of the Moscow Patriarchate's strategy for developing the infrastructure to bring pilgrimage more firmly under the control of diocesan clergy is based on this desire to proselytise efficiently (Kirill 2005). Moreover, this infrastructure is firmly orientated at replacing private initiatives—including those of commercial tourist agencies—to ensure that a would-be pilgrim receives an appropriately Orthodox experience, supervised by clergy or properly 'churched' laity.

For the curious and the 'unchurched', pilgrimage may provide a more palatable taste of Orthodoxy than their local church. The obstacles which greet a neophyte (or potential neophyte) in parishes are identified similarly by researchers and clerics—services are long, difficult to follow and accompanied by a raft of behavioural rules, the infringement of which often attracts reprimands from parishioners. Group pilgrimages (which may be organised by charismatic individuals rather than parishes or diocesan providers) offer a gentler introduction to Orthodoxy: such bus excursions are generally intended to have a missionary-educational component, bringing pilgrims into a spiritual atmosphere in which they may imbibe Orthodoxy without enduring the tribulations of parish life but also playing educational DVDs, initiating group prayer and informing participants about the history of the holy place (Kormina 2012, Naletova 2007).

As various studies suggest, this proselytising strategy is not confined to group tours organised by ecclesiastical pilgrimage services but encompasses what might be deemed 'distance veneration' and 'inverted pilgrimage'. 'Distance veneration' encapsulates the practice of correspondence with a shrine, most thoroughly scrutinised in connection with the Petersburg saint Ksenia, whose cult has been interpreted as an advertising campaign aimed at believers who reject parish life and choose to turn directly to the saints. The Church's 'marketing strategy', as revealed by ecclesiastical publications of correspondence from devotees of the saint, is to present itself as a church for ordinary people and to stress the role of clerics as mediators with the saint (Kormina and Shtyrkov [2008] 2012, 2011).

The phenomenon of inverted pilgrimage encompasses Orthodox fairs, where a variety of holy objects are brought from parish churches and monasteries to one centre for a period of days, as well as travelling icons and relics such as the girdle of the Mother of God, which attracted millions of would-be venerators when it was brought to Russia from Athos in 2011. These function as both advertisement for the pilgrimage place and as a substitute for pilgrimage. At an Orthodox fair, therefore, would-be pilgrims who cannot reach a shrine for health or financial reasons may order prayers to be said *in situ*, and travelling holy objects enable believers to enjoy proximity to a devotional object they would otherwise be unable to venerate in person. Fairs, in particular, also provide opportunities to engage with visiting priests and monks and learn about distant or rural monasteries and parishes, but travelling relics may also bring the centre to the periphery, acting as agents or representatives of the Moscow Patriarchate (Naletova 2006, Kormina 2012).

In a doctoral dissertation based on fieldwork conducted in Russia in 2002–2004 and survey data from 2003, Naletova argues that pilgrimage is an important activity through which Russians can indicate their allegiance with Russian Orthodoxy and form part of a broader Orthodox community of believers (2007). The tendency to scrutinise pilgrimage as an alternative to parish life is reversed in a detailed study of parish life, which suggests that some priests may be attempting to build their parishes around miracle-working objects (Sergazina 2011). The priest promotes his parish as a place where healing occurs in order to encourage pilgrimage to his church, which is located in a sparsely populated village. By organising a weekly prayer service in front of a 'weeping' miracle-working icon, he attracts pilgrims and the summer visitors from nearby dachas. The icon itself is kept behind the altar and is only brought out for these special services, which are proving popular particularly with childless couples.

VENERATION AND MOVEMENT

While urban religiosity is attracting the attention of a new generation of anthropologists, there is continuing focus on rural shrines. Indeed, in contrast to the relative paucity of academic publications on contemporary pilgrimage to the Russian equivalents of Glastonbury or Jasna Góra, there is a flourishing body of work by folklorists, ethnographers and anthropologists which concentrates on marginal, small and/or 'unofficial' shrines (sviatyni). This partly reflects the historical strength of folk studies and kraevedenie (local history studies) in the Russian academic tradition, plus a long fascination with locally venerated objects, which at first sight appear to be extra-ecclesiastical—stones, caves, springs, trees—and, therefore, unambiguously 'folk'. The Russian word sviatynia [святыня] may refer to a holy place or venerated object and covers everything from relics in large monastic pilgrimage centres to icons in rural chapels and isolated natural features associated with a divine figure. Extensive work has been done particularly in the northwest of Russia by Petersburg academics, but local researchers have also been active in studying narratives and practices Russia-wide (see, for example, the special issues of Zhivaia starina [Living Antiquity] 2003: 3 and 2004: 2).

Two works in particular have shaped efforts by Russian scholars to analyse the meanings, structures and functions of local holy places, highlighting the complex relationship between ordinary religiosity and extraordinary efforts to access the sacred: between communal, calendrical devotions and private, personal appeals for divine assistance (Panchenko 1998, Shchepanskaia 1995). In a vast article exploring the relationship of

58   Stella Rock

people with shrines in the far north of Russia, Shchepanskaia argues that local holy places are turned to in times of misfortune, forming crisis networks which connect pilgrims, wanderers (poor, professional itinerants) and shrine guardians, and circulate information about cures and sufferings. Drawing on fieldwork with the Leningrad Institute of Ethnography and Anthropology (now Kunstkamera) conducted in the 1980s, supplemented by material from the Tenishev Bureau, Shchepanskaia analyses the 'cultural code' of this system—which she perceives as very conservative, changing little over centuries—as it existed in the late nineteenth and early twentieth centuries. The shrines comprise both built (chapels, monastery) and natural elements, and within the hierarchy of shrines, distance as well as type is significant. Rich in detail and highlighting the significance of votive objects, distance and gender in the organisation and functioning of the network, Shchepanskaia explores these shrines as locations where pilgrims might resort to a holy person (living or dead) in times of sickness and difficulty.

Panchenko's monograph on rural shrines in the northeast of Russia— also combining data from fieldwork conducted between 1986 and 1995 with archival evidence—similarly recognises the therapeutic nature of venerated stones, springs, trees and stone and wooden crosses. However, he concludes that such locally venerated objects answer a more fundamental peasant need for regulated and direct contact with the holy, and they help shape the local landscape into sacred space. This understanding of their broader function has been taken up by others. Stressing the fluidity and contextual character of folk Orthodoxy, Panchenko's study acknowledges the diversity of rural religious practice and rejects the concept of 'pagan survivals' (1998).

While recourse to small local shrines has continued to attract attention, post-Soviet pilgrimage to nationally or regionally significant monastic institutions has been less well researched. Russia's major monasteries have been the focus of mass pilgrimage particularly since the emancipation of the serfs in 1861, and recent historical research on this phenomenon adds further fuel to debates about the relationship between religion and modernity (see Chulos 1999, Robson 2007, Worobec 2009, Greene 2012). Monasteries are repositories not just of the sacraments and holy objects which allow pilgrims to access the divine but also of living intermediaries who may have substantial reputations for their diverse spiritual gifts. The networks around these *startsy*, and the institution of eldership both within and beyond monastic communities, have come under increasing scrutiny (Kormina 2011, 2013a, Mitrokhin 2006). In addition to visiting a monastery to receive guidance and consolation from the inhabitants, pilgrims may be asked to undertake an 'obedience' or volunteer to work for an extended period of weeks or months. These worker pilgrims (*trudniki*) may be testing a religious vocation, making a contribution to the monastery in return for extended or repeat visits, or fulfilling a vow (Kormina 2010,

Touching the Holy 59

Vedernikova 2002). For some committed believers who make regular pilgrimages, these holy places are perceived as oases of light in a dark, satanic world (Tarabukina 1998).

Contemporary pilgrims, like their pre-revolutionary predecessors, may approach a shrine in a variety of ways—through an organised bus trip, travelling independently by private or public transport, walking independently or in small groups, or participating in a procession of the cross. While modern, mechanised methods of travel are generally acceptable means of making a pilgrimage, the significance of the physical hardship involved in reaching a shrine has been observed by those scrutinising both contemporary and historic pilgrimage. One late imperial historian has suggested that this stress on physical sacrifice is 'the particularly Russian contribution to Orthodox Christian pilgrimage', bringing it closer to Western *peregrination* than Greek *proskinima* (Chulos 2003: 67). Walking is, of course, the most obvious way of 'labouring' *en route* to a shrine, but enduring long journeys on uncomfortable transport also counts. In her study of northern shrines, Shchepanskaia argues that the more serious the misfortune, the further pilgrims needed to travel in their appeal for divine assistance. The difficulty of getting to Solovki—one of the most geographically marginal pilgrimage sites in Russia—has been identified as one of the factors that makes it an attractive pilgrimage destination (Shchepanskaia 1995, Naletova 2007, Vedernikova 2002).

There is a strong tradition of studying ritual movement and related folklore, including the predominantly pre-revolutionary phenomenon of 'wanderers' (странники, *stranniki*)—itinerants who lived in continual movement from holy place to holy place (Shchepanskaia 2003). Walking, in particular, has been explored as an important ritual movement associated with Russian pilgrimage sites, engaged in by individuals appealing privately for divine assistance or collectively in a festive procession. Ritual walking (marked as such by behaviours such as keeping silent, praying or carrying icons) may mark the transition from secular to sacred, and often this movement within or on the bounds of the sacred territory will involve some form of circumnavigation of a natural or built feature. It may also involve following the footsteps of some holy figure associated with the landscape (Moroz 2002, Shevarenkova 1998, 2003). Here is another area where comparative research might prove fruitful, given the observed tendency amongst some Western pilgrims to perceive walking, and even processing, as a traditional way of moving towards or within a holy place (Coleman 2004: 65). Similarly, comparative work on long-distance processions could fruitfully test confessional paradigms of pilgrimage as veneration over movement. Research into processions, as both protest and performance of Orthodox identity in multi-confessional areas, is also to be hoped for.

In Kormina's recent work the importance of movement—as highlighted by Coleman and Eade (2004)—has prompted an approach which, rather than scrutinising modes of travel and ritual movement as cultural

60 *Stella Rock*

practices, considers movement as an ideology. Coining the term 'nomadic Orthodoxy' to describe the contemporary modes of religiosity Kormina views as fundamentally different to traditional forms of parish-based Orthodoxy, she identifies two basic models of the relationship between devotee and the holy. In the first devotees travel to a place in the landscape (monasteries, churches, or local shrines), while in the second, the holy itself migrates (travelling icons, relics, and more rarely, a living person). She then outlines four basic religious regimes, the first of which—parish ('structure')—encompasses the exotic minority in today's Russia, practitioners tied to one local church, a geographically fixed structure strictly controlled by a priest. The second is the pilgrim regime—'anti-structure'—where individuals seek religious experience beyond ecclesiastical control. The third group of networkers are nonconformists who exist on the social margins of Orthodoxy, seeking salvation mostly from charismatic elders and/or connected by long-term projects, such as the canonisation of a new saint or promotion of a particular icon. While the liminal social status of pilgrims is temporary, liminality becomes an organising principle for networks, which are egalitarian ventures allowing participants anonymity or another life detached from ordinary personality. Finally, flash mobs are groups which form—very temporarily—around the 'objectified charisma' of travelling holy objects. These new ways of being Orthodox display nomadic tendencies identified as specific to postmodern, post-secular Russia. Both networks and communities of pilgrims 'exploit the possibilities of liminal status', making it not a temporary, transitional state, as Turner suggests, but a comfortable social position. Pilgrimages are for those who live an alternative Orthodox life and for those who want to be Orthodox in their free time—away from family and work (2012).

PILGRIMS: INDIVIDUALS AND *COMMUNITAS*

Research which focusses on the pilgrims themselves has—unsurprisingly—engaged with the Turnerian model of *communitas*, in which pilgrims aspire to move away from everyday structures, lose their ordinary identities and enjoy a temporary feeling of community with others in a flexible, nonhierarchical, voluntary fashion. Kormina's *avtobusniki* or 'bus pilgrims' create a community at the moment of departure, but this ceases to exist when they return home. They call each other by first name only (thereby dispensing with the conventional Russian practice of addressing those who are not close friends by name and patronymic) and try to disguise social status; and the structural conditions they endure (on an uncomfortable bus) convey a degree of equality. Thus a temporary association (сообщество) is formed for the duration of the pilgrimage. However, no real community (община)

Touching the Holy   61

is created because pilgrims work hard to remain detached from each other and beyond the bureaucratic structure of the institutional church. Drawing on Mauss, Kormina sees the ideology of *communitas* as involving the avoidance of the reciprocity which creates lasting connections between people. Pilgrims, therefore, do not want to collaborate; they don't want to give up a more comfortable seat on the bus to a mother with disabled child or wash up together after eating. On weekend trips, at least, they remain 'strangers to one other, responsible for their own individual salvation and craving individual religious experience' (2012: 217).

Diametrically opposed to this vision of pilgrimage as a flight from social bonds and ecclesiastical unity is the presentation of pilgrimage as forming 'kenotic communities', where processions and the veneration of travelling holy objects provide 'one of the principal means through which people [seek] reintegration into society and new ways to communicate and congregate' in a fractured, uncertain, post-Soviet Russia. In this conception, pilgrims empty themselves in Christ-like fashion, avoiding the 'I' of Catholic pilgrims and embracing the 'we' that encapsulates the communal nature of Orthodox worship, and opening themselves towards others. Naletova's pilgrims, for example, welcome communal work and communal living but avoid emotional ecstasies which might be deemed Durkheimian 'effervescence' and have a deeper response than simply a 'Durkheimian-Turnerian feeling of togetherness'. They reflect on personal relationships and social issues, and their 'inner concentration [makes] the journey a collective reaffirmation of meaning-structures that [are] traditional and churchly' (Naletova 2010: 262, 257).

As the above contrast suggests, individualism is a recurring theme in recent publications on pilgrimage. Furthermore, it has been suggested that collective religious practice has become an *urban* phenomenon, carried out within the framework of town parishes and pilgrimage culture, rather than an aspect of religious culture in the countryside (Panchenko 2012a: 268, Kormina 2006). Do contemporary pilgrims prefer solitude to collectivism, or do they voluntarily limit their egos to better serve their fellows? Is there a fundamental difference between the way contemporary Catholic pilgrims behave in a group or relate personally to a saint and the way Orthodox pilgrims do? Is *sobornost'*—the conciliarity trope of Orthodox Christian studies which is commonly used to distinguish the Orthodox from other Christian confessions—a reality for Russian pilgrims? Are contemporary pilgrims more individualistic than their predecessors, and, if so, is this as a result of specific Soviet secularisation processes or a more general reflection of 'postmodern' tendencies visible elsewhere? Given the diversity of pilgrims and forms of pilgrimage, and the various traditions of Orthodox spirituality, which—like the Church as an institution—is far from monolithic, answers to these questions are likely to be anything but clear-cut.

Figure 3.1 Pilgrims who have walked for three days in a procession of the cross to the Kirov region shrine of Velikoretskoe are blessed with holy water, June 2009. (Photo: Sandra Reddin)

IN PLACE OF A CONCLUSION: SPACE, MATERIAL AND THE HOLY

Anthropologists are increasingly calling for an approach which is sensitive to the specifics of Eastern Orthodox Christianity. They are asking how these specifics challenge the models and methodologies of those working with other denominations and faiths and how an understanding of the Russian and Ukrainian experience can contribute to debates concerning secularisation and modes of religiosity elsewhere (Lubańska and Ładykowska 2013, Hann and Goltz 2010, Rogers and Verdery 2013, Wanner 2012: 7). Research on Russian Orthodox pilgrimage highlights various combinations and prioritisations of space and movement, people and objects, but a fundamental aspect of any pilgrimage is physical contact with the holy. This may be accessed via natural elements, such as water and stone, which function like contact relics by virtue of their connection with a holy figure and/or through living individuals, icons, relics, or graves. The act of walking has powerful religious significance in some contexts, but Orthodox Christian pilgrimage is, above all, about proximity to material conduits of the divine. As such, it is a rich field to plough in terms of material culture and somatic religiosity.

Robert Orsi has identified our academic apprehension of concepts such as 'the holy', which pilgrims understand 'as immediately and undeniably real', and which they use freely in articulating their experience both on the road to and at the shrine, and he suggests that the time is ripe for a reevaluation (2012). I would like to end by highlighting a related Russian concept which brings together a number of the themes raised above, *viz*. the relationship between history and Orthodox identity; the relationship between material culture and contact with the divine; and issues of tradition, desecration and continuity. In her exploration of the search for 'authenticity' and the correlation of age and value amongst contemporary pilgrims, Kormina has discussed the notion of *namolennost'*, a term which encapsulates the especial quality an object or place accrues as a result of the volume of prayers which have been said in the presence of that venerated place or item over time. The more prayers, the more grace or 'holy energy' it accumulates (2010, 2013b).

While we must be sensitive to the specifics of Russian Orthodoxy, we should also be alive to affinities and commonalities. A belief that prayers and pilgrims' visits contribute to sanctifying space is evident amongst Catholic and Protestant pilgrims, as well as Orthodox. Wynn has observed that one nineteenth-century Anglican pilgrim in the Church of the Holy Sepulchre felt on 'holy ground' not because of the sacred history of the site (as the place of Jesus's burial and resurrection) but because it has been the locus of fervent prayer for so long (2009: 140). A dynamic relationship between pilgrim action and divine grace is articulated by one Ukrainian Greek Catholic, who describes Medjugorje as a '*premolenoe mesto* (a "through-prayed" place)'. This pilgrim views pilgrimage sites as 'a common endeavour of God and humans—while God blesses the place, humans must sustain their sacredness through prayers' (Halemba 2011: 462). Comparative research on the way in which pilgrims articulate their religious experiences, which draws on the strengths of Russian intellectual traditions of folklore studies and philology and remains sensitive to historical, cultural and theological context, may generate some exciting new approaches to 'the holy'.

NOTES

1. My thanks to Alexander Agadjanian, Marion Bowman, Douglas Rogers, and Christine Worobec for comments on the conference paper that formed an early first draft, and to Katya Tolstaya for encouragement to think 'kaleidoscopically' (www.in-a-sec.com/method).

64 *Stella Rock*

2. The focus of this chapter is research on Orthodox Christian pilgrimage to Russian shrines, and this narrow lens necessarily excludes the sacred places and journeys connected with Russia's Islamic, Buddhist, pagan, and other communities, as well as pilgrimage across Russia's borders. Recent publications with a broader focus include Kathy Rousselet (ed.) *Pèlerinages en Eurasie et au-delà*, a special issue of *Slavica Occitania* 36 (2013); and a special issue of *Modern Greek Studies* 28/29 (2012/3).
3. Of particular note are the online journal *Anthropological Forum* (http://anthropologie.kunstkamera.ru/en/), a joint project of the Kunstkamera Museum, the European University of St Petersburg, and the European Humanities Research Centre, University of Oxford; the digital archive *The Russian Folk Religious Imagination* (http://rfri.rch.uky.edu/execSum.html); and *Gosudarstvo, religiia, tserkov' v Rossii i za rubezhom*, a peer-reviewed quarterly devoted to the multidisciplinary study of religion, published in Russian with English summaries (www.religion.rane.ru/?q=en). An English version is planned.
4. Christine Worobec is engaged in an interdisciplinary study examining Orthodox pilgrimages to holy sites within Russia and Ukraine as well as abroad from 1700 to the present, entitled 'Moving Faith: Pilgrimages in Modern Russia and Ukraine'. Vera Shevzov is currently writing a book on the image of Mary in modern and contemporary Russia and editing another on Marian veneration with a similar chronological scope. An already published example of this productive approach is Douglas Rogers's *The Old Faith and the Russian Land: A Historical Ethnography of Ethics in the Urals* (Cornell University Press, 2009).

REFERENCES

Agadjanian, A. and Rousselet, K. (eds.) (2006) *Religioznye praktiki v sovremennoi Rossii,* Moscow: Novoe izdatel'stvo. (Some of the contents are available in French in *Revue d'études comparatives Est-Ouest* 36 (4).)

———. and Rousselet, Kathy (2010) 'Individual and collective identities in Russian Orthodoxy', in C. Hann and H. Goltz (eds.) *Eastern Christians in Anthropological Perspectives,* Berkeley, Los Angeles, and London: University of California Press.

———. (eds.) (2011) *Prikhod i obshchina v sovremennom pravoslavii,* Moscow: Ves mir.

Aleksii, Patriarch (2007) 'Sviateishii Patriarkh Aleksii napravil privetstvie uchastnikam IV obshchetserkovnoi konferentsii "pravoslavnoe palomnichestvo: traditsii i sovremennost"', 28 November 2007, available online at www.pravoslavie.ru/news/25050.htm (last accessed 25 April 2014).

Baiburin, A., Kelly, C. and Vakhtin, N. (2012) 'Introduction: Soviet and post-Soviet anthropology', in A. Baiburin, C. Kelly and N. Vakhtin (eds.) *Russian Cultural Anthropology After the Collapse of Communism,* London and New York: Routledge.

Benovska-Sabkova, M. et al. (2010) '"Spreading grace" in post-Soviet Russia', *Anthropology Today,* 26 (1): 16–21.

Chernetsov, A. V. (1994) 'Dvoeverie: mirazh ili real'nost'?', *Zhivaia starina,* 4: 16–19.

Chistiakov, P. G. (2005) *Pochitanie mestnykh sviatyn' v Rossiiskom pravoslavii XIX–XXI vv (na primere pochitaniia chudotvornykh ikon v Moskovskoi eparkhii).* Candidate of historical sciences dissertation, defended in Moscow.

———. (2006) 'Pochitanie mestnykh sviatyn' v sovetskoe vremia: palomnichestvo k Kurskoi Korennoi Pustyni v 1940–1950-e gody', *Religiovedenie,* 1: 38–49.

Christensen, K. V. H. (2012), 'Remembering the New Martyrs and Confessors of Russia', in C. Raudvere, K. Stala and T. Stauning Willert (eds.), *Rethinking the Space for Religion: New Actors in Central and Southeast Europe on Religion, Authenticity and Belonging*, Lund: Nordic Academic Press/Svenska historiska media AB.

Chulos, C. (1995) 'Myths of the pious or pagan peasant in post-emancipation Central Russia (Voronezh Province)', *Russian History/Histoire Russe*, 22 (2): 181–216.

——. (1999) 'Religious and secular aspects of pilgrimage in modern Russia', *Byzantium and the North/Act Byzantina Fennica*, 9 (1997–8): 21–58.

——. (2003) *Converging Worlds: Religion and Community in Peasant Russia, 1861–1917*, Dekalb: Northern Illinois University Press.

Coleman, S. (2004) 'From England's Nazareth to Sweden's Jerusalem: movement, (virtual) landscapes and pilgrimage', in S. Coleman and J. Eade (eds.), *Reframing Pilgrimage: Cultures in Motion*, London and New York: Routledge.

Dixon, S. (1999) 'How holy was Holy Russia? Rediscovering Russian religion', in G. Hosking and R. Service (eds.), *Reinterpreting Russia*, London: Arnold.

Dubisch, J. (1995) *In a Different Place: Pilgrimage, Gender, and Politics at a Greek Island Shrine*, Princeton: Princeton University Press.

Durand, J.-Y. (1995) '"Traditional culture" and "folk knowledge": whither the dialogue between Western and post-Soviet anthropology?' *Current Anthropology*, 36 (2): 326–330.

Eade, J. and Sallnow, M. J. (2000) *Contesting the Sacred: The Anthropology of Christian Pilgrimage*, Urbana, IL, and Chicago: University of Illinois Press.

Engelstein, L. (2003) 'Old and new, high and low: Straw horsemen of Russian Orthodoxy', in Valerie A. Kivelson and R. H. Greene (eds.) *Orthodox Russia: Belief and Practice Under the Tsars*, University Park, PA: Pennsylvania State University Press.

Fadeeva, L. V. (2004) 'Rasskazy o mestnochtimykh sviatyniakh: k probleme tsikla', in V. M. Gatsak and N. V. Drannikova (eds.) *Kompleksnoe sobiranie, sistematika, eksperimental'naia tekstologiia, vyp. 2: Materialy VI mezhdunarodnoi shkoly molodogo fol'klorista (22–24 noiabria 2003)*.

Filicheva, O. (2006a) '"Narodnoe pravoslavie" v gorode i derevne: sviashchennik i ozhidanii pastvy (religioznye prazdniki v 2001–2004 godakh)', in Agadzhanian and Russele, op. cit.

——. (2006b) 'Zapiski dlia Ksenii Blazhennoi: pozitsiia tserkovnosluzhitelei i narodnyi obychai', in Zh. V. Kormina, A. A. Panchenko and S. A. Shtyrkov (eds.) *Sny bogoroditsy: Issledovaniia po antropologii i religii*.

Freeze, G. L. (2001) 'Recent scholarship on Russian Orthodoxy: a critique', *Kritika: Explorations in Russian and Eurasian History*, 2 (2): 269–278.

Gothóni, R. (1987) 'The revival on the holy mountain reconsidered', in *Byzantium and the North Acta Byzantina Fennica*, III: 7–18.

Greene, R. H. (2012) 'Bodies in motion. Steam-powered pilgrimages in late imperial Russia', *Russian History*, 39: 247–268.

Gromyko, M. M. (2002a) 'O edinstve pravoslaviia v Tserkvi i ve narodnoi zhizni russkikh', *Traditsii i sovremennost'*, 1 (1): 3–31.

——. (2002b) 'Pochitanie Presviatoi Bogoroditsy, sviatykh i sviatyn'. Palomnichestvo', in *Russkie: narodnaia kul'tura (istoriia i sovremennost')*. *Tom 5: Dukhovnaia kul'tura. Narodnye znaniia*, Moscow: Rossiiskaia akademiia nauk, In-t etnologii i antropologii.

Halemba, A. (2011) 'National, transnational or cosmopolitan heroine? The Virgin Mary's apparitions in contemporary Europe', *Ethnic and Racial Studies*, 34 (3): 454–470.

Hann, C. and Goltz, H. (2010) 'Introduction', in C. Hann and H. Goltz (eds.) *Eastern Christians in Anthropological Perspective*, Berkeley, Los Angeles, and London: University of California Press.

66 *Stella Rock*

Huhn, U. (2012) 'S ikonami i pesnopeniiami, ili episkop, sbezhavshii ot svoikh prikhozhan. Massovye palomnichestva v Rossii epokhi Stalina i Khrushcheva', *Gosudarstvo, Religiia, Tserkov' v Rossii i za Rubezhom*, 3–4 (30): 232–256.

Kirichenko, O. V. (ed.) (2010) *Sviatyni i sviatost' v zhizni russkogo naroda: etnograficheskoe issledovanie*, Moscow: Nauka.

Kirill, Mitropolit Smolenskii i Kalingradskii (2005) 'Problemy i puti razvitiia sovremennogo pravoslavnogo palomnichestva', in *Pravoslavnoe palomnichestvo: traditsii i sovremennost': sbornik materialov konferentsii*, Moscow: Palomnicheskii tsentr Moskovskogo Patriarkhata.

Kormina, Zh./J. (2004) 'Pilgrims, priest and local religion in contemporary Russia: contested religious discourses', *Folklore*, 28, available online at www.folklore.ee/folklore/vol28/pilgrims.pdf (last accessed 24 August 2011).

———. (2006) 'Religioznost' russkoi provintsii: K voprosu o funktsii sel'skikh sviatyn', in Zh. V. Kormina, A. A. Panchenko and S. A. Shtyrkov (eds.), op. cit.

———. (2009) 'Russkoe pole: vzgliad iz-za rubezha', *Antropologicheskii forum*, 11, available online at http://anthropologie.kunstkamera.ru/files/pdf/011online/11_online_08_kormina.pdf (last accessed 30 August 2013).

———. (2010) 'Avtobusniki: Russian Orthodox pilgrims' longing for authenticity', in Hann and Goltz, op. cit.

———. (2011) 'Rezhimy pravoslavnoi sotsialnosti v sovremennoi Rossii: prikhozhane, palomniki, seteviki', in Agadzhanian and Russele, op. cit.

———. (2012). 'Nomadicheskoe pravoslavie: o novykh formakh religioznoi zhizni v sovremennoi Rossii', *Ab imperio*, 2: 195–227.

———. (2013a) 'Russian saint under construction: portraits and icons of Starets Nikolay', *Archives de sciences sociales des religions*, 58 (162): 95–119.

———. (2013b) 'La langue des pèlerins orthodoxes: « l'énergie sacrale d'un lieu chargé de prière»', in K. Rousselet (ed.) *Pèlerinages en Eurasie et au-delà*, a special issue of *Slavica Occitania*, 36.

———. and Shtyrkov, S. A. [2008] (2012), 'Believers' letters as advertising: St Xenia of Petersburg's 'National Reception Centre', in Baiburin, Kelly and Vakhtin, op. cit. (A translation by E. Griffiths of 'Pis'ma veryiushchikh kak reklama: "Vsenarodnaia priemnaia" sv. Ksenii Peterburgskoi' *Antropologicheskii forum*, 2008 (9): 154–184.)

———. and Shtyrkov, S. (2011) 'St Xenia as a patron of female social suffering: an essay on anthropological hagiology', in J. Zigon (ed.) *Multiple Moralities and Religions in Post-Soviet Russia*, Oxford and New York: Berghahn Books.

———., Panchenko, A. A. and Shtyrkov, S. A. (eds.) (2006) *Sny Bogoroditsty. Issledovaniia po antropologii religii*, St Petersburg: Izd. Evropeiskogo universiteta v S-P.

Kozelsky, M. (2010) *Christianizing Crimea: Shaping Sacred Space in the Russian Empire and Beyond*, DeKalb: Northern Illinois University Press.

Lubańska, M. and Ładykowska, A. (2013) 'Prawosławie—"chrześcijaństwo peryferyjne"? O teologicznych uwikłaniach teorii antropologicznej i stronniczości perspektyw poznawczych antropologii chrześcijaństwa', *Lud*, 97: 195–220.

Levin, E. (1993) 'Dvoeverie and popular religion', in S. K. Batalden (ed.), *Seeking God: The Recovery of Religious Identity in Orthodox Russia, Ukraine, and Georgia*, DeKalb, IL: Northern Illinois University Press.

Luehrmann, S. (2010) 'A dual struggle of images on Russia's Middle Volga: icon veneration in the face of Protestant and pagan critique', in Hann and Goltz, op. cit.

Mark, Archimandrite (Golovkov) (2001) 'O smysle pravoslavnogo palomnichestva', *Pravoslavnyi palomnik*, 1(1): 14–16.

Mitrokhin, N. (2006) 'Archimandrit Naum i 'naumovtsy' kak kvintessentsiia sovremennogo starchestva', in Agadzhanian and Russele, op. cit.

Moroz, A. B. (2002) 'Sviatyni Russkogo Severa i traditsionnaia kul'tura', in N. I. Reshetnikov (ed.) *Sviatye i sviatyni severorusskikh zemel'*, Kargopol': Kargopol'skii istoriko-arkhitekturnyi i khudozhestvennyi muzei.

Naletova, I. (2006), 'Sovremennye pravoslavnye iarmarki kak vyrazhenie pravoslvanoi very vne khrama', in Agadzhanian and Russele, op. cit.
———. (2007) *Orthodoxy beyond the walls of the church: a sociological inquiry into Orthodox religious experience in contemporary Russian society.* PhD dissertation, University of Boston.
———. (2010) 'Pilgrimages as kenotic communities beyond the walls of the church', in Hann and Goltz, op. cit.
Nikitina, S. E. (2002) 'Solovetskii monastyr' i narodnaia vera' [Solovetsky monastery and folk belief], in Reshetnikov, op. cit.
Orsi, R. A. (2005) *Between Heaven and Earth: The Religious Worlds People Make and the Scholars Who Study Them,* Princeton and Oxford: Princeton University Press.
———. (2012) 'The problem of the holy', in *The Cambridge Companion to Religious Studies,* Cambridge: Cambridge University Press.
Panchenko, A. A. (1998) *Issledovanie v oblasti narodnogo pravoslavia: Derevenskie sviatyni Severo-Zapada Rossii,* Sankt-Peterburg: Aleteiia.
———. (2012a) *Ivan i Iakov—neobychnye sviatye iz bolotistoi mestnosti: 'krest'ianskaia agiologiia' i religioznye praktiki v Rossii Novogo vremeni,* Moskva: Novoe literaturnoe obozrenie.
———. (2012b) 'How to make a shrine with your own hands: local holy places and vernacular religion in Russia', in M. Bowman and Ü. Valk (eds.) *Vernacular Religion in Everyday Life: Expressions of Belief,* Sheffield [u.a.]: Equinox Pub.
Poplavskaia, Kh. V. (2000) *Narodnaia traditsiia pravoslavnogo palomnichestva v Rossii v XIX–XX vekakh: po materialam Riazanskogo kraia.* Candidate of historical sciences dissertation, defended in Moscow.
Pelkmans, M. (2009) 'Introduction: post-Soviet space and the unexpected turns of religious life', in M. Pelkmans (ed.) *Conversion After Socialism: Disruptions, Modernisms and Technologies of Faith in the Former Soviet Union,* New York and Oxford: Berghahn Books.
Robson, R. R. (2007), 'Transforming Solovki: pilgrim narratives, modernization, and late imperial monastic life', in M. D. Steinberg and H. J. Coleman (eds.) *Sacred Stories: Religion and Spirituality in Modern Russia,* Bloomington, IN: Indiana University Press.
Rock, S. (2007) *Popular Religion in Russia: 'Double-Belief' and the Making of an Academic Myth,* Routledge: Abingdon and New York.
———. (2012) '"They burned the pine, but the place remains all the same": pilgrimage in the changing landscape of Soviet Russia', in C. Wanner (ed.), *State Secularism and Lived Religion in Soviet Russia and Ukraine,* Oxford: Oxford University Press.
———. (2014) 'Rebuilding the chain: tradition, continuity and processions of the cross in post-Soviet Russia', in K. Tolstaya (ed.), *Orthodox Paradoxes: Heterogeneities and Complexities in Contemporary Russian Orthodoxy,* Leiden and Boston: Brill.
Rogers, D. (2005) 'Introductory essay: the anthropology of religion after socialism', *Religion, State and Society,* 33 (1): 5–18.
———. (2010) 'Epilogue: ex oriente lux, once again', in Hann and Goltz, op. cit.
———. and Verdery, C. (2013) 'Postsocialist societies: Eastern Europe and the Former Soviet Union', in J. G. Carrier and D. B. Gewertz (eds.) *The Handbook of Sociocultural Anthropology,* London and New York: Bloomsbury Academic.
Rousselet, K. (2007) 'Butovo: la création d'un lieu de pèlerinages sur une terre de massacres', *Politix,* 1 (77): 5–78.
———. (2011) 'Constructing moralities around the tsarist family', in J. Zigon (ed.) *Multiple Moralities and Religions in Post-Soviet Russia,* Oxford and New York: Berghahn Books.

68 Stella Rock

Sergazina, K. (2011) ' "Palomnichestvo" ili "votserkovlenie": o raznykh tipakh pravoslavnykh prikhodov na primere trekh tserkvei severo-vostochnogo Podmoskv'ia', in Agadzhanian and Russele, op. cit.

Shchepanskaia, T. V. (1995) 'Krizisnaia set' (Traditsii dukhovnogo osvoeniia prostranstva)', in T. A. Bernshtam (ed.) *Russkii sever. K probleme lokal'nykh grupp*, Sankt-Peterburg: MAE RAN.

———. (2003) *Kul'tura dorogi v russkoi miforitual'noi traditsii XIX–XX vv.*, Moscow: Indrik.

Shevarenkova, IU. M. (1998) 'Diveevskie legendy', *Zhivaia Starina*, 4: 25–27.

———. (2003) 'Sviatye istochniki i ritual khozhdeniia k nim v Nizhegorodskom krae', in Iu. M. Shevarenkova (ed.) *Mestnye sviatyni v nizhegorodskoi ustnoi narodnoi traditsii: rodniki, chasovni pro nikh*, Nizhnii Novgorod: Rastr-NN.

Shevzov, V. (2003) 'Letting the people into church: reflections on Orthodoxy and community in late Imperial Russia', in V. A. Kivelson and R. H. Greene (eds.) *Orthodox Russia: Belief and Practice Under the Tsars*, University Park, PA: Pennsylvania State University Press.

Shtyrkov, S. (2006) 'Predislovie. Posle "narodnoi religioznosti"', in Kormina, Panchenko and Shtyrkov, op. cit.

Sibireva, O. (2006) 'Sovremennyi sviashchennik i 'narodnoe pravoslavie', in Agadzhanian and Russele, op. cit.

Sokolovskiy, S. (2012) 'Writing the history of Russian anthropology', in Baiburin, Kelly and Vakhtin (eds.), op. cit.

Tarabukina, A. V. (1998) 'Sviatye mesta v kartine mira sovremennykh "tserkovnykh liudei"', *Zhivaia Starina*, 4: 28–30.

Tishkov, V. A. (2013) *Institut Etnologii i Antropologii im. N. N. Miklukho-Maklaia Rossiiskoi Akademii Nauk: 80 let*, Moscow: Indrik.

———. et al. (1992) 'The crisis in Soviet ethnography [and comments]', *Current Anthropology*, 33 (4): 371–394.

Vedernikova, N. M. (2002) 'Solovetskie palomniki', in Reshetnikov, op. cit.

Vinogradov, V. V. (2012) 'Sovremennye tendentsii pochitaniia sviatykh mest (na material severo-zapada Rossii)', *Traditsionnaia kul'tura*, 3: 67–75.

Wanner, C. (2012) 'Introduction', in C. Wanner (ed.) *State Secularism and Lived Religion in Soviet Russia and Ukraine*, New York: Oxford University Press.

Weyl, Carr A. (2002) 'Icons and the object of pilgrimage in Middle Byzantine Constantinople', *Dumbarton Oaks Papers*, 56: 75–92.

Worobec, C. D. (2009) 'The unintended consequences of a surge in Orthodox pilgrimages in late Imperial Russia', *Russian History*, 36: 62–76.

———. (2012) 'Russian peasant women's culture: three voices', in W. Rosslyn and A. Tosi (eds.) *Women in Nineteenth Century Russia: Lives and Culture*, Cambridge: Open Book.

Wynn, M. (2009) *Faith and Place: An Essay in Embodied Religious Epistemology*, Oxford: Oxford University Press.

4 Old and New Paths of Polish Pilgrimages

Anna Niedźwiedź

Pilgrimage in Poland has been deeply influenced by its partition at the end of the eighteenth century and incorporation within the Austrian, Prussian and Russian empires as well as by border changes and political transformations during the twentieth century. This chapter focusses on Roman Catholic pilgrimage, on its changes and developments within last two centuries and on its stance within contemporary Poland, where the Marian shrine of Częstochowa holds a prime position. Recently, other shrines have emerged as important national pilgrimage centres in the continuing dynamic between Polish nationalism and Roman Catholicism. The development of new pilgrimages expresses this dynamism but also signals changes in contemporary religious practices of Polish people.

NINETEENTH-CENTURY LITERARY REPORTAGE: WŁADYSŁAW REYMONT

In May 1894 Władysław Reymont, who years later would become one of the best-known Polish novelists and a Nobel Prize laureate in literature, but then a twenty-seven-year-old aspiring writer, departed from Warsaw with a group of local pilgrims, mainly from Praga, one of the poorer Warsaw districts, on a ten-day journey on foot to the Marian shrine at Jasna Góra in Częstochowa.[1] Dressed simply and modestly, revealing neither his occupation nor the real reasons behind his decision to join the pilgrimage, he became one of the 'brothers' walking in a typical 'company' (Polish: *kompania*). Soon after completion of the pilgrimage, a popular Warsaw weekly, *Tygodnik Ilustrowany* (Illustrated Weekly), published a series of reports by Reymont entitled 'Pilgrimage to Jasna Góra: Impressions and Pictures', which in 1895 was issued in book form (Reymont 1895/1988).

Historians of Polish literature cite Reymont's book as one of the first examples of Polish literary reportage (see Starnawski 1987: 215). Apart from appreciating Reymont for his contribution to the development of a new literary genre, his first book, about seventy pages long, was one of the first (if not *the* first) detailed Polish accounts, which documented ethnographic

70 *Anna Niedźwiedź*

experiences drawing on participant observation of religious ritual. Reymont was a Catholic and thus wholly familiar with Catholic prayers, songs, art and symbols. A few years before this pilgrimage he had even considered joining the Pauline monastery at Jasna Góra (Wyka 1979: 34). By the time of his journey, however, he had become somewhat sceptical, at least about some religious practices (including pilgrimages), as revealed in the initial pages of his report (see Jakacka-Mikulska 2001: 164).

His chief area of interest was the reasons and motives, which led his companions to undertake the costs and difficulties of a time-consuming and tiring pilgrimage. Interestingly, his diary includes many elements typical of ethnographic field research notes because they mixed ethnographic descriptions with personal annotations revealing his changing attitude, as an 'observer', towards his subjects and companions (see Kawa 2004). While walking with his 'sisters' and 'brothers', he documented his feelings, emotions and physical sensations as he got closer to understanding his companions and becoming 'one with this crowd kneeling nearby and flowing together in the same stream with them' (Reymont 1988: 26). Three days before entering Częstochowa, Reymont experienced classical Turnerian *communitas*:

> I let myself be carried away with this stream and I am flowing—where? . . . I do not ask, for I am feeling good. I feel as if I were becoming more and more fused with them. I am entering a sort of warm, mystical affinity with these souls, I am starting to feel the same, to feel the simplest things [. . .].
>
> I am not even a will, I am only a set of muscles which are impelled into motion and automated, with constant intense emotionality. I am only one beat of this heart which has more than four thousand heads. Nobody has a mask here, or even a name. (Reymont 1988: 67–68)

Reymont, an ideal observer, depicts in detail the *imponderabilia* of daily walking: sleeping on hay in overcrowded barns, washing in local ponds together with other pilgrims, buying milk and bread from peasants, visiting small country churches filled with 'primitive' sculptures, etc. He provides detailed descriptions, giving the reader comprehensive information about landscapes, weather conditions (so important during a journey on foot lasting several days), towns and villages he passed through, interiors of cottages, furniture, farm animals, crops growing in the fields, people's faces, clothes, food, smells, sounds, various dialects and accents, words of sermons, songs and prayers, fragments of conversations among pilgrims overheard while walking and descriptions of numerous incidents and interactions in which he was involved as one of the pilgrims.

Certainly, his perseverance, combined with his deep sensitivity, empathy and ability to overcome his assorted prejudices, social stereotypes and physical limitations, made him perfect material for an ethnographer—at least from the perspective of today's self-conscious and self-critical anthropology, which accepts not only participant observation but also 'observant participation' as key field research strategies. Of course, neither Reymont nor his contemporaries were able to consider his experiences in those terms. Reymont's domain, towards which he was steering at the end of the nineteenth century, was not scholarly research but literature. Yet it is thanks to his literary rather than scholarly interests that we can enjoy his deep and sensitive insight into the late-nineteenth-century pilgrimage to Jasna Góra. The scholarly language of his times probably would not have allowed him to reveal his personal feelings and his ability to empathise with his fellow pilgrims.[2]

NINETEENTH-CENTURY STUDIES: OSKAR KOLBERG AND FOLKLORE

Given that Reymont's reportage is a unique source concerning historical Polish pilgrimages and the experiences accompanying them, it is worth taking a closer look at numerous other sources dating back to the times before and during the emergence of self-conscious social sciences in Poland and their maturing and theoretically framed interests in pilgrimage and religion.

Surprisingly, especially in light of the predominantly peasant character of the most popular pilgrimages throughout the nineteenth century (Olszewski 1996: 190), the direct contribution by the first ethnographers and folklorists to the study of Christian pilgrimage seems relatively modest. When they did look at pilgrimage, they concentrated on collecting information about shrines, documenting their histories, recording legends of their origins and describing the religious practices and beliefs concerning the most sacred objects within a given shrine, such as images, statues and relics.

Hence, shrines appeared in the monumental regional monographs of Oskar Kolberg as important generators of religious practices and orally distributed texts and folk songs. A founding father of Polish folklore studies, ethnomusicology and ethnography and an indefatigable researcher of folk culture, Kolberg (1814–1890) spent his life travelling through various regions which had belonged to the Polish-Lithuanian Commonwealth before the Partitions,[3] documenting diverse aspects of the cultures of the inhabitants and publishing an impressive cycle, consisting of several dozen tomes entitled *Lud* [*The Folk*] (Kolberg 1857–1890).[4] His immense work has been recognised as 'a unique collection of sources on a European and a world scale' (Millerowa and Skrukwa 1982: 25). A new edition of *The Collected Works of Oskar Kolberg* (launched in 1961 and still in progress), which, apart from reedited original works, includes material preserved in manuscripts, is intended to include as many as eighty-six volumes filled with detailed ethnographic descriptions of peasants and their villages, fields,

72   Anna Niedźwiedź

tools, physical appearance, costumes, cottages, rituals, music, songs and dances, riddles, tales and so on (Kolberg 1961–).

Kolberg's astonishing work is organised according to geographical and ethnographic regions. Within individual monographs, among other assorted information, we can find, sometimes scattered, sometimes more consistent and outstanding, descriptions of numerous local shrines. However, a researcher of pilgrimages might often be disappointed with Kolberg because his notes tend to be very general and laconic, even when describing important and thriving shrines and pilgrimage routes. For instance, Kalwaria Pacławska, one of the typical Passion and Marian shrines, which in Kolberg's day (as today) was popular among both Roman Catholic and Greek Catholic pilgrims (Olszewski 1996: 183), received only a short note describing it as 'a Roman Catholic parish church and Stations of the Cross to which nearby folk and folk from distant lands make numerous pilgrimages' (Kolberg 1964b: 8).

Probably the most extensive information is given for the Częstochowa shrine. Kolberg not only provided readers with a brief history and description of the town and the Jasna Góra Pauline monastery but also recalled historical facts and legendary themes related to the image of Our Lady of Częstochowa. Based on the scientific knowledge about the image then available, he briefly explained its origins and iconography (pointing to probable Byzantine influences). He also collected 'folk legends' about the miraculous origins of the image, including the most popular legend about St Luke, who was said to have painted the image on a table belonging to the Holy Family with miraculous help from an angel, who added the finishing touches to St Mary's face (for various versions of this legend, its origins and development, see Niedźwiedź 2010: 11–16.)

In his descriptions of the 'companies', which walked to and from Częstochowa, Kolberg attached the words and melodies of thirty religious songs, which were sung by pilgrims. He also described a typical 'company' as comprising several dozen people, usually from one parish, with a lay elder as a guide responsible for both the organisational and spiritual dimensions of the pilgrimage. This guide had to know the route; arrange accommodation; and be able to read, preach and lead prayers and songs. According to Kolberg, 'companies' were only occasionally led by clergymen. He also described a typical itinerary followed by pilgrims during their stay in Częstochowa. This included falling to the ground while approaching Jasna Góra and getting a first glimpse of the Monastery's soaring tower (repeating the same ritual on the way home at their last glimpse of the Monastery), walking on their knees three times around the altar where the image was displayed, listening to sermons and taking part in religious ceremonies, as well as visiting St Barbara's church in the town to wash their eyes and drink water famous for its miraculous healing properties (Kolberg 1964a).[5]

Figure 4.1 'A company arriving to Częstochowa'. From the collection of The National Library of Poland, available through http://polona.pl, originally published in a Warsaw weekly, Kłosy, 1872, Vol. XIV, no. 363, p. 400.

OTHER NINETEENTH-CENTURY TEXTS: ACADEMIC AND RELIGIOUS DISCOURSES

While the ethnographic material on pilgrimages and religious practices provided by Kolberg might—especially in the case of many smaller shrines—be disappointingly modest and lacking detailed descriptions, other nineteenth-century sources fill the gap reasonably well. They were produced mainly by archaeologists and historians, who recorded the shrines' histories, searched for archival documents, offered scholarly comments on old devotional books, analysed the iconography and style of images and transcribed legends and miraculous stories, which had been circulating orally (Łepkowski 1850, Grabowski 2009). These publications were often supplemented with the author's personal impressions and descriptions of their own visits to shrines, which they themselves identified as 'pilgrimages' (see Baliński 1846).

A separate group of interesting sources consists of writings produced by the Catholic Church and its clergy. To a certain extent, nineteenth-century devotional writings continued the mediaeval and Baroque traditions of devotional literature inspired by shrines. The seventeenth and eighteenth

74 Anna Niedźwiedź

centuries witnessed the appearance of numerous Marian shrines in the Polish-Lithuanian Commonwealth, as well as the growth of old ones (a similar development in Hungary is discussed by Barna in Chapter 5). The post-Tridentine Catholic revival within Poland-Lithuania and the growing number of pilgrims spurred the development of devotional literature. Larger shrines, founded through richer donations, promoted themselves by printing their own devotional cards, prayers, songs, panegyrics, lists of miracles and so on. Jasna Góra established its own printing house in 1693 and soon became an important centre of Catholic devotional literature (Witkowska 1987). The shrine at Kalwaria Zebrzydowska printed its own guidebooks from the end of the seventeenth century, providing elders of 'companies' with prayers, the words of 'Kalwarian songs' and knowledge enabling them to lead pilgrims along so-called pathways—complicated chains of the Passion and Marian chapels which sprang up around Kalwaria's monastery, covering the surrounding hills and valley.

During the nineteenth century, the growing level of literacy among peasants, who visited shrines in large numbers, sparked a new boom for devotional literature, which glorified the shrines, provided basic information about them and promoted various forms of devotion related to particular sanctuaries. At the beginning of the twentieth century, Kraków's Jesuits published a four-volume collection listing hundreds of 'miraculous Marian images' and their 'histories' related to individual shrines (see Fridrich 2008). This ambitious publication, covering a vast and very diverse geographical area (including not only most of today's Poland but also parts of present-day Ukraine, Belarus and Lithuania), supplied readers with detailed historical facts about images and shrines as well as information about devotional practices, cults and miraculous events.

NINETEENTH-CENTURY NATIONAL DISCOURSES

During the lengthy period of the Partitions (1795–1918), shrines and pilgrimages appeared in Polish discourse on yet another level. They began to be related to the concept of national identity. The period of extinction of the Polish state coincided with the development of the modern concept of nationhood and the awakening of various national identities, especially among newly emancipated peasants inhabiting the region of the former Polish-Lithuanian Commonwealth. The development of various national identities was often amplified, especially in the eastern regions, by denominational differences (mostly between Roman Catholic and Orthodox and between Greek Catholic and Orthodox). In these circumstances Roman Catholic shrines (and, to a certain extent, some Greek Catholic shrines as well) started to promote and generate a Polish national identity. In this process Jasna Góra gained a leading role as a 'national sanctuary': a place where a 'real Queen' (as opposed to partitioning usurpers) 'resided' and could unite Poles arriving at this shrine from the three partitioned regions (see Niedźwiedź 2010: 126–127; Olszewski 1996: 185). Despite the strict censorship of printed materials implemented by Russian government, these patriotic feelings were expressed through songs, prayers and sermons, as well as visual signs, such as the flags used by the 'companies' arriving at Jasna Góra.

In the Prussian area at the end of the nineteenth century, the small village of Gietrzwałd gained the nickname 'Warmian Częstochowa' (Jackowski 1999: 73). In 1877 two young Polish girls reported apparitions of Mary, who spoke to them in Polish. Given the attempt by the Prussian authorities to suppress the Polish language, Gietrzwałd's popularity as a sacred site for Poles living in Warmia skyrocketed. When the authorities tried to hinder the organisation of pilgrimages to Jasna Góra by forbidding Poles to cross the Russian border, locals turned to Gietrzwałd as a 'substitute for Częstochowa' (Olszewski 1996: 185).[6]

During this Partition period pilgrimage also saw the appearance of 'national pilgrims'—those who focussed on 'discovering the beauty of the motherland, learning about its past and collecting national memorabilia' (Ziejka 1996: 99). Of course, 'national pilgrimages' were often intertwined with religion and eagerly adopted religious places, symbols, or religious phraseology. After all, Jasna Góra promoted a Marian-centred vision of Polish history and referred to Our Lady of Częstochowa as 'the Polish Queen'. Furthermore, Polish Romantic writers frequently equated 'Nation' with 'Religion'. In *The Books of the Polish People and of Polish Pilgrimage* (1832), published in Paris by the most famous Polish Romantic poet, Adam Mickiewicz, partitioned Poland was compared to the Messiah, Jesus Christ, who had been killed only to be resurrected and save others. In other words, the mission of a martyred (partitioned) but resurrected Poland was to save other European nations. Although not everyone shared Mickiewicz's ideas in detail, his visions, and especially the religious language and symbols he used, reflected the sanctification and mythologisation of the 'nation', which attracted a broader audience, especially among Polish intelligentsia and artists, during the first half of the nineteenth century.

Hence, searching for a national past, discovering the beauty of national traditions (often said to be hidden in folk customs and folklore), and studying national history were often seen as para-religious activities. During the nineteenth century 'national pilgrims' travelled to Jasna Góra, therefore, not only to pray before the holy image of Mary and the baby Jesus but also to admire jewels donated by old Polish kings and study historical events related to the monastery. After visiting the monastery some travelled on to Puławy to visit the first Polish 'national museum' ('Temple of Memory') founded by the aristocratic Polish Czartoryski family (Ziejka 1996: 99).[7] Also, those who contemplated the beauty of remote landscapes and listened to folk songs of the 'Polish people' eagerly called themselves 'pilgrims'.

76 *Anna Niedźwiedź*

Almost all of them glorified the city of Kraków, the 'ancient Polish capital', which soon gained fame as a 'must-see' place on the itinerary of Polish 'national pilgrims'. Wincenty Pol, poet, geographer, ethnographer and writer, came to Kraków in 1834 and left in his *Memoirs* a very moving and emotional description:

> Kraków! Kraków! How much is hidden in this one word! For a Pole this one word reveals so much! Upon entering Kraków anyone who does not feel himself a Pole must be transformed into one. (after Grodziska 2003: 72)

Kraków began to be perceived as a preserved and condensed symbolic manifestation of Polish history and national ideology. Churches, towers, cathedral, monuments—even pavements, smells, sounds and landscapes— were seen not only as mementoes but also as relics and witnesses of the national past and as an 'open history book', which could be 'read'. Wawel Cathedral, with its relics of saints and tombs of kings, enjoyed a special status. Thanks to two periods of relatively looser control by the partitioning powers over the city (1815–1846, 1867–1914),[8] a new national 'Pantheon' was created in Kraków. Next to the graves of old kings and queens, newer graves appeared with the 'relics' of patriotic heroes (Tadeusz Kościuszko), soldiers fighting for Polish independence (Prince Józef Poniatowski), and famous artists and poets (for example, in 1890 Adam Mickiewicz's remains were brought from abroad and buried in the cathedral). The city began to be called by such symbolic nicknames as 'national temple', 'heart of Poland', 'bastion of Polishness', 'Slavic Rome' and 'treasury of relics and mementoes' (Grodziska 2003: 67–80).

In his analysis of these national pilgrimages, Franciszek Ziejka points out a very important shift in the social strata of the pilgrims (Ziejka 1994). Whereas in the first part of the nineteenth century the idea of 'national pilgrimage' was invented, promoted and popularised mostly among the intelligentsia and people socially related to higher society, the last decades of the century witnessed the popularisation of patriotic pilgrimages to Kraków among peasants. Organised peasants' pilgrimages arrived not only during important religious festivals but also for public funerals of national heroes and for patriotic jubilee celebrations, such as the two hundredth anniversary of the Battle of Vienna (1683) commemorating the victory of the Polish king Jan III Sobieski over the Ottomans (Ziejka 1994: 23). (This historical jubilee was directly associated with a religious event: the coronation of the image of Our Lady from the Carmelite church in Kraków with papal crowns.) The city also became a typical stopover for peasants' pilgrimages travelling to Częstochowa from the southern Polish regions. All of these visits combined religious experiences with patriotic education and manifestations of national feeling.

TWENTIETH-CENTURY TEXTS:
PILGRIMAGE AND PEASANT RELIGIOSITY

The dawn of the twentieth century and the creation of the Polish Republic in 1918 brought about the rebuilding of Polish universities and scholarly institutions alongside the development of the social sciences. Numerous sociologists and anthropologists became interested in issues related to religious studies, including analyses of Polish Catholicism as well as other denominations and religions present within the borders of newly independent Poland. The religiosity of peasants became a focal issue for folklorists, religious and cultural historians, ethnographers and some sociologists.

A number of concepts and theories conceived in the 1920s and 1930s were considered so fundamental that they have influenced Polish anthropological and sociological discourses on religion ever since. Here I will point out the most vivid and the most widely discussed ideas. Starting with a few original texts, I will discuss later works and studies which were inspired and influenced by them. Although many only mention pilgrimage in passing, I recognise their value and their potential contribution to pilgrimage studies.

THOMAS AND ZNANIECKI ON POLISH
PEASANT RELIGIOSITY

One of the first works, which attempted to systematise the diverse folklore-related materials on religion collected in the previous century by Oskar Kolberg and his contemporaries was a chapter titled 'Religious and Magical Attitudes' published by William I. Thomas and Florian Znaniecki in the first volume of their classic study, *The Polish Peasant in Europe and America* (1918: 205–288). The American sociologist and his younger Polish colleague[9] were interested in 'religious and magical attitudes' as important factors influencing the organisation of social groups and the social process. They systematised the beliefs of the 'Polish peasant', dividing them into four groups, which they called 'systems', described as progressive stages leading toward 'individual mysticism'. Certainly, today's reader easily picks up echoes of evolutionist concepts present in their analysis. Additionally, the theoretical distinctions between religion and magic they proposed ring dubiously in contemporary ears and their analysis seems to be strongly influenced by a Protestant-shaped ethic-centred concept of religion (Zowczak 2000: 28). However, their work contains numerous thorough observations concerning 'traditional folk culture' deduced from careful studies of nineteenth-century ethnographic sources. To understand the organisation of peasant beliefs and explain their worldview, which was based on partnership with nature, animals, elements, atmospheric phenomena and so on, Thomas and Znaniecki introduced the concept of the 'principle of

78   *Anna Niedźwiedź*

solidarity'. They also seemed to understand that various and often supposedly contradictory beliefs, originating from different traditions, might coexist in the worldviews of people who might hold them without any feeling of inconsistency.

Pilgrimages are mentioned only twice but in a context, which was pursued in subsequent discussions about 'peasant mysticism' by Polish ethnologists. For Thomas and Znaniecki, pilgrimages were first and foremost collective events, greatly valued by peasants, who often would 'economise for many years in order to be able to make such a pilgrimage' (Ibid.: 280). The authors agree that during pilgrimages 'there are cases in which a mystical attitude develops' and 'the individual is aroused from his normal state' (Ibid.: 287). In their conclusion, however, they describe these occurrences as 'occasional outbreaks of mysticism' and deny that peasants can have fully 'proper mystical' experiences (Ibid.). They contend that peasants are inclined towards 'collective' forms of religion, which distance them from 'individual mysticism'.

CZARNOWSKI AND PEASANT RELIGIOUS CULTURE

The distinction, which Thomas and Znaniecki made between 'proper mystical' experiences and peasant religiosity reflected current images of historical Christian mystics, usually associated with well-educated monks and nuns who express their 'inner life' in elaborate writings rather than by participating in emotional public and communal religious rituals like Polish villagers. The distinction also appeared in a highly influential article titled 'The Religious Culture of Polish Villagers' written by Stefan Czarnowski (1879–1937), a cultural historian and a sociologist, educated in Leipzig and Berlin as well as in Paris, where he was a student of Marcel Mauss. His article is probably the most important twentieth-century text on 'popular Catholicism' in Poland. Even today students enrolled on anthropology of religion courses at Polish universities carefully study it. The several dozen pages are so dense with pertinent and inspiring remarks and accurate examples that my own copy of his article is full of underlining, highlights in various colours and exclamation marks!

Czarnowski's first book concerned the cult of St Patrick as a national hero in Ireland and was originally published in Paris in French (Czarnowski 1919). His academic career in Poland was mostly connected with the University of Warsaw. His famous article appeared posthumously in another book, which the author had managed to finish before his sudden death in December 1937 (Czarnowski 1938).[10] Despite the important contribution made by the article, his comments about the 'religious inner life' and 'private religiosity' of peasants are highly questionable. Like Thomas and Znaniecki, he is reluctant to associate mystical experiences with the 'communal' religion of villagers. He admits that mystical experiences do occur and that 'individual mystics and sporadic mystical movements [appear]' also among peasants. Nevertheless, the general tone of his text suggests that 'Polish people as a mass [. . .] have little inclination toward mysticism' (Ibid.: 184). Even when he refers to the 'popular' Beguines, Czarnowski distinguishes them from Polish peasant spirituality, which is not only far 'from non-pareil examples like St Teresa of Avila but also from the mysticism of the Flemish Beguines, which was crude but concentrated on inner spiritual life' (Ibid.: 170).

These parts of Czarnowski's article have often been discussed and heavily criticised. Recently, Michał Łuczewski has suggested that Czarnowski described villagers and their 'religious culture' in terms 'resembling colonial discourse rather than impartial analysis' (Łuczewski 2007: 9). While I certainly disagree with Czarnowski's generalisations about the nonexistent 'inner life' of villagers, I also reject Łuczewski's overgeneralised statement and his one-sided and biased reading of Czarnowski's article. Apart from his dubious sentences about mysticism, Czarnowski sees religion not as an attribute of the 'lower, non-rational strata of society' but rather as a complex, multifaced and changing 'culture' (hence the term 'religious culture' appearing in the title of his article), integrally related to people's experiences and lifestyles.

The pilgrimages discussed by Czarnowski are one of many elements involved in the 'religious culture' of Polish peasants. Years before the debate about *communitas*, which emerged in Anglophone literature in the 1980s and 1990s, Czarnowski's apparent intuitions about the ambiguity and variety of experiences related to pilgrimages had led him to write:

> In spiritual elevation during services and processions, then in unreserved participation in joy, in dance and drunkenness, in walking from stall to stall, the individual somehow becomes immersed in the community. (Czarnowski 1938: 158)

This description of community solidarity is followed a few paragraphs later by a description of festive pardons (annual parish feasts) and pilgrimages, which emphasise how groups of peasants split into various subgroups according to age, gender and village affiliation. A closer look at these 'companies' of pilgrims also reveals that they are well ordered and hierarchical. The various subgroups within a 'company' walk together and identify themselves with their own symbols: the images they carry, processional floats, flags and emblems. Hence, during religious feasts and pilgrimages, individuals manifest and strengthen their various communal bonds while feelings of solidarity intermingle with hierarchical order.

Czarnowski recognises the identity-building aspect of pilgrimage and its complexity when he writes: 'Pilgrimages create organic bonds between a villager and a regional group, as well as between a villager and the whole nation' (Ibid.: 161). Not surprisingly, he mentions Częstochowa as a 'national shrine', which bonds Polish people from various regions, but he

80 *Anna Niedźwiedź*

also points to numerous regional shrines, discussing, among others, a multi-ethnic shrine in Wejherowo in Pomerania. In his day, Wejherowo attracted Pomeranian Slavic people called Kashubians as well as local Catholic Germans, and he shows how both groups used the place as their identity-building shrine to support two different ethnic identities present within one regional and religious group. Czarnowski points that both ethnic groups organised their pilgrimages separately and on different days.

CZARNOWSKI'S SIGNIFICANCE: STUDIES
ON IMAGES, SENSES AND SACRED PLACES

Probably the most interesting of Czarnowski's comments, and those most widely discussed by contemporary anthropologists of religion in Poland, concern 'miraculous images', which have been central holy objects and the focus of most Polish pilgrimages:

> Images of holy figures are, for our people, something more than mere pictures. They are symbols in the most literal meaning of the word, i.e. objects taking part in the nature of the imagined figure and summarising it. (Ibid.: 171)

Most Polish shrines are dedicated to Mary, the mother of Jesus, and devotions centre on depictions of Mary alone or with an infant Christ. Art historians have pointed out that these images reveal Byzantine, Ruthenian, and Russian influences and Czarnowski, along with many other researchers, also noticed the link between the popularity of panel paintings and their importance in the religious cults of Polish Catholics as well as the historical influence of Orthodox culture and the Orthodox cult of icons (see Rock's remarks in Chapter 3 about the centrality of icons in Russian Orthodox pilgrimages).

Czarnowski's remarks on the cult of images and their role in the religious life of Polish peasants are significant mostly because he was probably the first Polish scholar to point out the importance of the senses, bodily participation and physical stimuli in religious experience. He introduced the term 'religious sensualism' to explain the relationship between peasants and holy images.[11] Images are perceived and approached by peasants as real holy figures and thus possess the physical features of a living person:

> Images live their own lives. They are sensitive and reveal their emotions as living creatures. They sweat drops of blood. They cry when they feel that a catastrophe is approaching. (Ibid.: 172)

The relationship between people and holy images is an important topic, which is being studied extensively within contemporary Polish anthropology.

In 2000 Joanna Tokarska-Bakir, for example, published a massive volume dedicated to the analysis of experiences, beliefs, behaviours and rituals related to 'miraculous images' in Polish Catholicism. Inspired by Czarnowski, and adopting Hans-Georg Gadamer's concept of 'non-differentiation' (Gadamer 2004: 134), she introduced the category of 'sensual non-differentiation', which she describes as 'adhesion of image and referent' which 'establishes and enables' religious experience involving images (Tokarska-Bakir 2000: 230). When, in 2005, I was preparing the publication of my book on Our Lady of Częstochowa, I had no doubt that it should be titled *The Image and the Figure*. Numerous interviewees during ethnographic field research had experienced 'sensual non-differentiation'. They were able to talk to Mary, listen to her, sense her feelings and build a deep religious and personal relationship with her through images, i.e., material pictures they saw in shrines or kept in their homes, often as souvenirs brought from pilgrimages (see Niedźwiedź 2005).

Apart from describing 'religious sensualism', Czarnowski raises other issues related to images, which are very important with respect to studies of pilgrimage. He is interested in the origins (and legends of origins) of sacred

Figure 4.2 Women from Klimontów near Kraków in their traditional attires, holding a local Marian image when welcoming the peregrinating image of 'Our Lady of Częstochowa', 2008. (Photo: Anna Niedźwiedź)

82　*Anna Niedźwiedź*

places built around images. He highlights the crucial role played by 'miraculous images' in the construction of sacred places, whereby images are usually said to have appeared miraculously: discovered in a forest, on a tree, floating in a well, shining with a heavenly glow, or revealing healing abilities when kept in a poor peasant's cottage. Czarnowski calls these miraculous happenings 'apparitions of images' (Czarnowski 1938: 172). Images are the most important of the holy objects, which attract pilgrims searching for bodily and spiritual healing. He also realises that within 'religious mentality' the distinction between a copy and an original is not always obvious. For religious people, copies of images can reveal the same (or even greater) powers as the originals. This principle also works in respect to shrines. Czarnowski cites numerous Polish *Kalwarias* (Calvaries) as sacred places, perceived and experienced by pilgrims as holy because they are 'authentic copies'[12] of Calvary, Jerusalem and other places in the Holy Land.

Years later these remarks about the perception of images and sacred places as 'miraculous' and 'holy' were developed in ethnographic case studies by Jacek Olędzki. He introduced the term 'miraculous consciousness' (Olędzki 1989) to describe the pilgrims' 'expectation and readiness to experience miraculous happenings' (Niedźwiedź 2010: 159) through sacred objects, places and rituals. In more recent studies on contemporary pilgrimages related to not-officially-recognised apparitions, Hubert Czachowski reveals the crucial role of 'miraculous religiosity' in creating new sacred places in today's Poland (Czachowski 2003). Thus, on the one hand, sacred places and objects generate 'miraculous consciousness', while on the other, 'miraculous consciousness' enables the creation of new places and objects, which come to be treated as holy.

NEW POLISH ETHNOLOGY DURING THE 1980s

In discussing how issues related to pilgrimages have appeared in Polish scholarly debate, it is important to recognise not only the achievements but also the obstacles and mental loops, which have afflicted Polish ethnological discourse on religion during the last decades. In the 1970s, after several decades of the materialist, limited and politicised version of Polish Marxism, which had dominated research after the Second World War, newly reviving Polish ethnology reopened itself to the study of religion. Once again, the initial focus was on *religijność ludowa*: 'folk religiosity', sometimes also translated as 'folk religion' or 'popular religion'.[13]

This stage was crowned with two publications on 'popular religion' in traditional Polish folk culture. Recalling Czarnowski's earlier work, Ryszard Tomicki and Ludwik Stomma each enumerated typical features of 'folk religiosity', listing ritualism, the communal dimension of religious life, the coexistence of religious feasts and symbols with the agricultural calendar and natural yearly cycle, Marian-centred piety, the role of shrines and images

Old and New Paths of Polish Pilgrimages 83

and sensual religiosity (Tomicki 1981, Stomma 1986). However, Stomma distanced himself from Czarnowski's sceptical approach towards 'folk mysticism', arguing that while ethnology focusses on 'external' manifestations of religion, it cannot deny the existence of deep 'inner religious experiences' in the lives of the people it studies. Hence, ethnology should be sensitive to various 'external' manifestations of people's 'inner' lives. Tomicki, on the other hand, drew on Mircea Eliade's phenomenological approach towards religion and concentrated on developing a deep symbolic analysis of the relationship between people and nature.[14] Both writers described and analysed the chronologically remote reality of nineteenth-century peasants.

Stomma, as one of the leaders of the new trend in Polish ethnology during the 1980s, was aware that before Polish ethnology could seriously study culture from a new perspective and turn from studies limited only to 'folk culture' or the 'peasant class' (as it was often described in Communist phraseology) towards studies of the 'internal mechanisms of any cultures' (Stomma 1981: 71), new concepts and new theories would be necessary. While the return to old sources and to interwar concepts was an attempt to restore a broken chain in Polish research, he also proposed the concept of 'folk-type culture' (*kultura typu ludowego*). The idea behind this term was that the cultural and social mechanisms, which were identified and discovered through the thorough analysis of traditional folk culture, could be applied in the study of other cultures. He claimed that this application was especially relevant to the study of contemporary societies because they also revealed many 'folk-type' characteristics.

This proposal was certainly helpful for research on contemporary Polish Catholicism and its practices, including pilgrimages. In my own study of the religious and cultural meanings attached to the image of Our Lady of Częstochowa, for example, I drew on the concept of 'religion of a folk-type' when analysing the relationship between contemporary Polish Catholics and this image (Niedźwiedź 2005: 232; Niedźwiedź 2010: 140). It was especially helpful when I was analysing behaviours, shared beliefs and myths related to a 'peregrination of the copy of the image of Our Lady of Częstochowa'. This ritual, which was initiated by the Polish Catholic Church in 1957, might be actually seen as an 'inverted pilgrimage' while the holy image has travelled to 'visit' its devotees in their parishes and homes (on similar practices within Russian Orthodoxy, see Rock's Chapter 3, where she introduces the term 'inverted pilgrimage'). Using the concept of 'folk-type religiosity' I focussed on long-lasting structures related to traditional cult of images, veneration of Mary and national Polish mythology, showing how they were revived within the framework of a newly invented ritual of 'peregrination'.

Yet more recently, I have realised that the concept of 'folk-type religiosity' is problematic. Although its introduction was an important and necessary step in Polish ethnology during a period of moving from traditional studies of historic 'folk' towards studies of contemporary cultures, on further inspection its continued application appears to be extremely limited.

Figure 4.3 Members of a voluntary firemen unit in Klimontów village near Kraków, bringing a copy of the image of 'Our Lady of Częstochowa' to their parish church during a 'peregrination of the image', 2008. (Photo: Anna Niedźwiedź)

First of all, even though 'folk-type religiosity' was coined in opposition to the term 'folk religion', it still fails to resolve basic problems related to the concept of 'folk'. 'Folk-type' evokes the concept of 'non-elite' and 'lower' and thus bears a hidden stigma, or at least suggests a paternalistic approach towards what is called 'folk religion'. Secondly, it may be impossible to apply the concept to cultural, geographical, historical and religious contexts, which are very different from those in east-central Europe. 'Folk-type religiosity' has failed, therefore, to acquire a more universal theoretical application.

Even so, it can be used in the study of Polish Catholicism to emphasise certain enduring cultural structures and historical background. Thus, in studies of pilgrimages and pilgrimage-related topics, such as the cult of images, the identity-building dimension of shrines, the national aspect of specific pilgrimages and the durability of narrative patterns related to sacred places and objects, 'folk-type religiosity' might successfully reveal some ossified mental and behavioural structures rooted in cultural patterns of the historic Polish countryside. Having said that, the term does not seem to provide a strong theoretical basis for uncovering the complexity of pilgrimages and pilgrims' attitudes.

TOWARDS NEW ROUTES: BIOGRAPHICAL ASSOCIATIONS

My maternal grandmother spent her life in a small village around fifty kilometres southeast of Częstochowa. All her life she was a devoted Catholic, deeply committed to the cult of Mary. Her home was located on one of the historic pilgrimage routes leading to Częstochowa; as a young girl she would join 'companies' of pilgrims who were passing through her village and walk for two days to reach the Jasna Góra monastery and pray before the image of Mary. However, soon after World War II, long-distance walking pilgrimages to Częstochowa became less popular because parishes organised pilgrimages by train and coach. But still some pilgrimages walked for many days to reach the Częstochowa shrine. The largest and the most famous was the foot pilgrimage from Warsaw. Every year since 1711, the Warsaw pilgrimage has followed the route described so vividly at the end of the nineteenth century by Władysław Reymont in his 'Impressions and Pictures'.

At the end of the 1970s and the beginning of the 1980s, these walking pilgrimages were revived on a grand scale, sparked by the election of Karol Wojtyła, archbishop of Kraków, as Pope John Paul II. His first papal visit to Poland in 1979, which drew millions of Poles from all over Poland to attend open-air masses, inspired a major revival of the pilgrimage movement (Jackowski and Soljan 2000). This revival also coincided with political developments in Poland, especially the appearance of the 'Solidarity' movement in 1980 and the Catholic Church's support of political resistance.

86   *Anna Niedźwiedź*

The emergence of Kraków's foot pilgrimage, for example, was directly associated with the Polish pope. A few days after his attempted assassination in May 1981, students in Kraków organised the so-called White March, numbering half a million people, all wearing white as a symbol of solidarity with the wounded Pope. During an open-air mass celebrated at the end of the march in Kraków's Market Square, it was declared that as an *ex-voto* offering for saving the pope's life, the people of Kraków would organise a walking pilgrimage to Częstochowa. Thus, in August 1981 the first pilgrimage from the Kraków diocese arrived at Jasna Góra after a five-day walk.

Throughout the decade many other dioceses began to organise their own walking pilgrimages, some lasting even longer than two weeks. Of course, during the 1980s, apart from their purely religious dimension, pilgrimages often included features of political and social protests against the government. National-religious bonds were revealed in the intentions and prayers offered during those pilgrimages, e.g., 'for the motherland' or for 'those who are interned'. 'Solidarity' movement banners, often carried by pilgrims all the way from distant places, were lifted high as they entered the Jasna Góra monastery. Following the political changes in 1989 and subsequent democratisation of Poland, the popularity of foot pilgrimages waned slightly; however, they still attract as many as 150,000 pilgrims every year (Jackowski and Soljan 2000, Bilska-Wodecka and Soljan 2011: 348).

Marysia Galbraith, an American anthropologist who joined a foot pilgrimage from the city of Rzeszów in 1992, observed:

> Participation in the pilgrimage also extends beyond those who actually walk. People who live along the route greet pilgrims with water, fruit compote, tomatoes, apples, or on hot days they spray pilgrims with water from hoses. Some parishes offer soup; on the first day parishioners gave pilgrims piles of homemade cakes as well. Parishioners open their homes to pilgrims, allow them to sleep in barns or even in their houses, and many provide food, warm tea, and water for washing. Many ask about experiences on the pilgrimage; others ask pilgrims to say a prayer for them when they reach the shrine at Częstochowa. These numerous voluntary contributions to the pilgrimage are central to creating an atmosphere of spontaneous involvement, outside of formal institutions and structures. (Galbraith 2000: 63–64)

I find this observation, as well as numerous other remarks and detailed descriptions of walking pilgrimages made by Galbraith, very accurate and successful in conveying the atmosphere of a typical Polish pilgrimage. In the early 1990s I myself, as a high school student, twice joined such a pilgrimage to Częstochowa and thus could have been one of Galbraith's subjects (her study was particularly focussed on teenaged pilgrims and their experiences during pilgrimages, which, as she observed, did not necessarily conform to the clergy's 'official' rhetoric).

To add something to the picture presented by Galbraith, I would like to recall here my grandmother's participation in pilgrimages and her experiences when, due to advanced age, she could not walk to Częstochowa herself. In the 1980s a few major foot pilgrimages returned to the historic route, passing by my grandmother's kitchen window. One of the groups had a scheduled overnight stay in her village. Every year, on one night in August, twenty or more pilgrims slept in her home or on her property, on improvised beds, mattresses and blankets laid out around the house and barn. My brothers, cousins and I used to spend long portions of our holidays at our grandmother's and remember the fun and excitement associated with the arrival of pilgrimages in the 1980s. Of course, for this one night, the place was terribly overcrowded, and we children had to squeeze into one bedroom. But I can readily recall the feeling of spontaneity and communal participation mentioned by Galbraith.

My grandmother welcomed pilgrims until her death. Rather than putting up twenty people as in the 1980s, beginning in the late 1990s she provided comfortable accommodation for a few 'sisters'.[15] Two of them, despite the age difference (they were much younger than Grandma), became her close friends. They returned each year with the same group, always bringing news about their families, sharing an evening prayer with my grandmother and singing a morning novena to the Virgin Mary before leaving at dawn with freshly prepared sandwiches in their backpacks and prayer intentions (my grandmother would ask them to pray for her in Częstochowa) in their heads. During the year they sent Christmas and name-day cards to one another. Since my grandmother's passing in 2007, the same pilgrims have been welcomed by my grandmother's neighbours. And every year, when stopping in my grandma's village on their way to Częstochowa, they visit a local cemetery to light candles on their 'sister's' grave.

I recall this family story to illustrate that pilgrimages in contemporary Poland are a part of the lives of many people. Even those who do not participate in pilgrimages themselves, or who have little or no connection with Catholicism, usually know somebody who has participated in some sort of pilgrimage at least once, especially given the diversity of Catholic pilgrimage in contemporary Poland. The most common pilgrimages now include bus tours lasting from one to several days to various shrines. There are also pilgrimages on bicycles, on horseback, in canoes and so on. Almost every age, social and professional group has its official pilgrimage to one of the most popular shrines. Every year new types of pilgrimages appear. In 2009 a Kraków priest organised the 'Extreme Way of the Cross'. This event is an overnight walk, physically very demanding, dedicated to prayer and meditation on the Passion of Christ. The route leads from the city of Kraków to the Passion shrine in Kalwaria Zebrzydowska (a distance of approximately forty kilometres). Since 2009, the 'Extreme Way of the Cross' has been organised every year during Lent. The idea has become so popular that it has spread to several other locations in Poland as

88   Anna Niedźwiedź

well as to England, where it attracts young recent immigrants from Poland (see www.edk.org.pl/).

TOWARDS NEW ROUTES: ANTHROPOLOGICAL APPROACHES

Given the huge variety of Polish Catholic pilgrimages and their vitality and innovative character, which coexist with numerous traditional and ossified forms of religious ritual, Polish ethnology must answer important questions about its ability and readiness to study this complex, diverse and ever-changing phenomenon. The option of defining pilgrimages as either 'folk' or 'folk-type' seems unlikely to provide a frame for fruitful discussion of contemporary and future Polish pilgrimages. Several of the newest anthropological case studies undertaken by Polish ethnologists of the younger generation suggest a way out of the historically framed obstacle course, which characterises today's anthropology of religion in Poland. The thorough analysis of contemporary passion plays, proposed by Kamila Baraniecka-Olszewska, shows that certain inspiring terms can be coined within the Polish tradition. She reformulates the term 'religious culture', originally proposed by Czarnowski, and draws on the concept of performativity, adopting the general approach of anthropology of experience (Baraniecka-Olszewska 2013). Inga Kuźma also turns to the anthropology of experience and finds further inspiration in feminological theories (Kuźma 2008). She focusses on the 'inner worlds' of her female interviewees, who are engaged in pilgrimage to Kalwaria Zebrzydowska through their participation in the 'funeral and triumph of the Virgin Mary' procession conducted there every August.

This turn towards the anthropology of experience indicates that the Polish ethnology of religion has begun to fill the gap in studies related to religious experience and individualistic approaches towards Catholicism. Yet the study of identity and the communal dimension of religion, whose long history I have outlined above, has acquired a second wind in recent years. Interesting studies of the newest Polish shrines, such as Licheń and Łagiewniki, demonstrate the structural relationship among religion, place and power, while also showing the cracks in the hegemonic position of the post-1989 Catholic Church in Poland and the new transnational relationships in which Polish Catholics are trying to situate themselves (Sekerdej, Pasieka and Warat 2007, Sekerdej and Pasieka 2010, Niedźwiedź 2014).

Disputes between Catholics and non-Catholics regarding shared landscape, community and social life, and the sharing of sacred places and public space, are also topics which are appearing in significant new publications by Polish researchers (see Kubica 2002, Pasieka 2013). There is also an emerging discourse concerning the pursuit of anthropology of religion in

Old and New Paths of Polish Pilgrimages   89

a country which is dominated by one religious institution (Sekerdej and Pasieka 2013). It is also important to point to non-Polish researchers, such as Judith Samson, Cathelijne de Busser, or Chris Hann, who conduct field research in Poland and bring new perspectives to pilgrimage-related topics (see Samson 2012, Hann 2000, de Busser and Niedźwiedź 2009).[16]

The perspective of 'lived religion' is probably the most promising new approach to be applied to studies on pilgrimages in Poland and elsewhere. As pointed out by Willy Jansen, in her introduction to one of the latest publications on contemporary European pilgrimages, a focus on 'lived religion' means a focus on 'what people actually believe and do, and on how this constitutes various identities' (Jansen 2012: 6). 'Lived religion' thus combines the tradition of community building and identity studies (already well developed in Poland) with emerging studies on religious experience.

CONCLUDING THOUGHTS

Although other Christian denominations and religions conduct pilgrimages in Poland, I have focussed here on Roman Catholic pilgrimage because of its long-established, hegemonic position. Moreover, due to lack of space, I have omitted a discussion of the many pilgrims who also travel abroad. As we have seen, given the deep influence of folklore studies on Polish anthropological research, Roman Catholic pilgrimage was often observed and analysed within the framework of the 'folk' or, at best, as a 'folk-type' religion. Although this approach led towards a blind alley, it still enabled deep, contextualised, detailed and ethnographically sensitive analyses of Polish Catholic beliefs and practices. Probably the most valuable achievements of this approach was its emphasis on the significance of images, the sensual and material dimensions of religious rituals and the variety of communal bonds generated by pilgrimages.

Roman Catholic pilgrimage has also played a long-established role in political and social processes. The emancipation of peasants and the emergence of national identity during the nineteenth century, as well as the social influence of the Catholic Church during the Communist period, illustrate the continual interplay between the ossifying and innovative character of pilgrimages and between their religious and nonreligious (e.g., political) dimensions.

Since the collapse of the Communist regime, Polish anthropologists have drawn on developments in Western pilgrimage studies to develop new insights and perspectives towards research and ethnographic material in Poland. As the hegemony of Roman Catholic Church has begun to be questioned, researchers are looking beyond the traditional focus on Roman Catholic pilgrimage within Poland to transnational processes and the relationship between Catholics and non-Catholics. Researchers from outside the country, especially in central and Western Europe, are also contributing

Figure 4.4 A 'Pilgrimage in the Footsteps of Karol Wojtyła the Worker', Kraków, 2013. On their way to a newly built shrine dedicated to John Paul II, pilgrims visit an old quarry where Wojtyła used to work during the Nazi occupation of Poland. (Photo: Anna Niedźwiedź)

to this diversifying field of pilgrimage research, and this chapter is written in the hope that it will encourage a deeper understanding of Polish research among non-Polish scholars. The mutual exchange of knowledge is especially important when we think about contemporary trends, such as the increasingly mobile and rapidly changing attitudes towards 'religion' and 'pilgrimage', in particular.

NOTES

1. The main Warsaw pilgrimage (1711 to date) has always been made in the summer months (see Ziejka 1996: 105). Reymont describes smaller May pilgrimage.
2. Reymont's reportage was noticed by at least some Polish social scholars. Already in 1895 Ludwik Krzywicki (1859–1941), who worked across sociology, anthropology and economics, published a lengthy comment on Reymont's book, noticing its value for social sciences and naming it 'a significant contribution to studies of psychology of communal life' (Krzywicki 1923: 148).
3. Between 1772 and 1795 Russia, Prussia and Austria partitioned the Polish-Lithuanian Commonwealth among them. Poland as a state was reborn in 1918 as the Second Polish Republic.
4. Sometimes the title of Kolberg's book *Lud* is translated as *The People* (see Thomas and Znaniecki 1918).

Old and New Paths of Polish Pilgrimages   91

5. The spring near St Barbara's church is related to the image of Our Lady of Częstochowa. According to legend, the spring appeared miraculously when the image fell and hit the ground there (see Niedźwiedź 2010: 58–59).
6. However, Olszewski points out that the ethnic and religious composition of Gietrzwałd pilgrims at the turn of the twentieth century was diverse. He mentions pilgrims from Germany, the Netherlands and Lithuania, as well as Polish-oriented Protestant pilgrims from the Masuria region (Olszewski 1996: 185).
7. In 1830, before the Polish national uprising, the collection was moved first to Paris and then to Kraków.
8. Between 1815 and 1846 the Republic of Kraków existed as a free city. In 1867 part of the Austrian Partition (Galicia, with the cities of Kraków and Lvov) was granted partial autonomy within Austria-Hungary.
9. Florian Znaniecki (1882–1958) was a philosopher and a sociologist and deeply influenced the development of Polish sociology, especially at the University of Poznań.
10. Actually, 'The Religious Culture of Polish Villagers' was originally published in 1937 as an article. However, most scholarly works refer to the 1938 edition, published as a book chapter.
11. He also wrote about 'naïve sensualism', leading to criticisms about his paternalistic attitude towards peasants and their religious behaviour.
12. The term 'authentic copy' does not appear in Czarnowski's work. It is discussed in detail, however, in later works related to images (see Tokarska-Bakir 2002).
13. There are many problems with the proper translations of the Polish terms *lud* (folk, people), *kultura ludowa* (folk culture) and *religijność ludowa* (folk religiosity/religion). To avoid direct connotations with *lud* ('folk' understood as peasants in traditional feudal and postfeudal societies) some Polish ethnologists prefer the terms *kultura/religia popularna* (popular culture/religion). Additionally, the term *lud* was propagandised during the period of the Polish Peoples' Republic when it was used to describe 'peoples', understood as the working masses.
14. During the 1980s and 1990s many Polish ethnologists were fascinated with Eliade's theories, whose works were extensively translated into Polish. In Tomicki's approach it is also possible to trace echoes of Thomas and Znaniecki's 'principle of solidarity'.
15. As in Reymont's times, today's walking pilgrims call each other 'sisters' and 'brothers'. Interestingly, this is rarely true of pilgrimages travelling by bus or other means of transportation. Somehow, foot pilgrimages are seen as 'more real' than coach pilgrimages, which are sometimes regarded as tourist excursions rather than religious experiences.
16. I should also mention the emergence of studies related to religious geography and the geography of pilgrimages initiated by Professor Antoni Jackowski at the Jagiellonian University. Since 1995 the journal *Peregrinus Cracoviensis*, dedicated to the geography of pilgrimages, has been published there.

REFERENCES

Baliński, M. (1846) *Pielgrzymka do Jasnej Góry w Częstochowie odbyta przez Pątnika XIX wieku*, Warszawa: G. Sennewald.
Baraniecka-Olszewska, K. (2013) *Ukrzyżowani. Współczesne Misteria męki Pańskiej w Polsce,* Toruń: Fundacja na rzecz Nauki Polskiej.

92 Anna Niedźwiedź

Bilska-Wodecka, E. and Sołjan, I. (2011) 'Przemiany krajobrazu religijnego Częstochowy w XX wieku', *Peregrinus Cracoviensis*, 22: 335–355.

De Busser, C. and Niedźwiedź, A. (2009) 'Mary in Poland: a Polish master symbol', in A.-K. Hermkens, W. Jansen and C. Notermans (eds.), *Moved by Mary: The Power of Pilgrimage in the Modern World*, Farnham, UK, and Burlington, VT: Ashgate.

Czachowski, H. (2003) *Cuda, wizjonerzy i pielgrzymi. Studium religijności mirakularnej końca XX wieku w Polsce*, Warszawa: Oficyna Naukowa.

Czarnowski, S. (1919) *Le culte des héros et ses conditions sociales. Saint Patrick, héros national de l'Irlande*; preface M. H. Hubert, Paris: Librairie Félix Alcan.

———. (1938) *Kultura*, Warszawa: 'Wiedza i Życie'.

Fridrich, A. (original 1903–1911, reprint 2008) *Historye cudownych obrazów Najświętszej Maryji Panny w Polsce*, Kraków: Wydawnictwo WAM.

Gadamer, H.-G. (2004) *Truth and Method* (2nd, revised edition, translation revised by J. Wiensheimer and D. Marshall), London and New York: Continuum.

Galbraith, M. (2000) 'On the road to Częstochowa: rhetoric and experience on a Polish pilgrimage', *Anthropological Quarterly*, 73: 61–73.

Grabowski, A. (2009) *Religijność w dawnym Krakowie* (A. Wawryszczuk, ed.), Kraków: Wydawnictwo Jagiellonia SA.

Grodziska, K. (2003) *'Gdzie miasto zaczarowane. . .'. Księga cytatów o Krakowie*, Kraków: Wydawnictwo Znak.

Hann, C. (2000) 'Problems with the (de)privatization of religion', *Anthropology Today*, 16: 14–20.

Jackowski, A. (ed.) (1999) *Miejsca święte Rzeczpospolitej. Leksykon*, Kraków: Wydawnictwo Znak.

———. and Sołjan, I. (2000) 'The millenium of Polish pilgrimage', in *Polski pielgrzym*, Częstochowa: Stowarzyszenie 'Nasza Częstochowa', Muzeum Częstochowskie.

Jakacka-Mikulska, K. (2001) 'Pielgrzymki w literaturze przełomu XIX i XX wieku. Emil Zola, Joris-Karl Huysmans i Władysław Reymont', *Peregrinus Cracoviensis*, 12: 153–169.

Jansen, W. (2012) 'Old routes, new journeys: reshaping gender, nation and religion in European pilgrimage', in W. Jansen and C. Notermans (eds.) *Gender, Nation and Religion in European Pilgrimage*, Farnham, UK, and Burlington, VT: Ashgate.

Kawa, M. (2004) 'Pątnik czy badacz? O Reymontowskim opisie pielgrzymki na Jasną Górę', in P. Kowalski and M. Sztandara (eds.) *O granicach i ich przekraczaniu*, Opole: Wydawnictwo Uniwersytetu Opolskiego.

Kolberg, O. (1857–1890) *Lud. Jego zwyczaje, sposób życia, mowa, podania, przysłowia, obrzędy, gusła, zabawy, pieśni, muzyka i tańce*, Kraków: Drukarnia Uniwersytetu Jagiellońskiego.

———. (1961–) *Dzieła Wszystkie Oskara Kolberga* [abbreviation: *DWOK*] (various places, various editors).

———. (1964a) DWOK 23 *Kaliskie cz. I. Lud. Jego zwyczaje, sposób życia, mowa, podania, przysłowia, obrzędy, gusła, zabawy, pieśni, muzyka i tańce*, Wrocław-Poznań: Polskie Wydawnictwo Muzyczne, Ludowa Spółdzielnia Wydawnicza.

———. (1964b) DWOK 35 *Przemyskie. Zarys etnograficzny*, Wrocław-Poznań: Polskie Wydawnictwo Muzyczne, Ludowa Spółdzielnia Wydawnicza.

Krzywicki, L. (1923) *Studja Socjologiczne*, Warszawa-Kraków-Lublin-Łódź-Poznań-Wilno-Zakopane: Gebethner i Wolff.

Kubica, G. (2002) 'Catholic crosses, and Jewish void: the polish landscape and its religious dimension', *Mediterranean Ethnological Summer School*, 4: 91–100.

Kuźma, I. (2008) *Współczesna religijność kobiet. Antropologia doświadczenia*, Wrocław: Polskie Towarzystwo Ludoznawcze.

Łępkowski, J. (1850) *Kalwaria Zebrzydowska i jej okolice pod względem dziejowym i archeologicznym*, Kraków: Wydawnictwo Dzieł Katolickich.

Old and New Paths of Polish Pilgrimages 93

Łuczewski, M. (2007) 'Popular religion as morality, interpretation and process', *Ethnologia Polona*, 28: 5–21.

Millerowa, E. and Skrukwa, A. (1982) 'Oskar Kolberg (1814–1890)', in H. Kapełuś and J. Krzyżanowski (eds.) *Dzieje folklorystyki polskiej 1864–1918*, Warszawa: Państwowe Wydawnictwo Naukowe.

Niedźwiedź, A. (2005) *Obraz i postać. Znaczenia wizerunku Matki Boskiej Częstochowskiej*, Kraków: Wydawnictwo Uniwersytetu Jagiellońskiego.

———. (2010) *The Image and the Figure: Our Lady of Częstochowa in Polish Culture and Popular Religion*, Kraków: Jagiellonian University Press.

———. (2014) 'Competing sacred places: making and remaking of national shrines in contemporary Poland', in J. Eade and M. Katić (eds.) *Pilgrimage, Politics and Place Making in Eastern Europe: Crossing the Borders*, Farnham, UK, and Burlington, VT: Ashgate.

Olędzki, J. (1989) 'Świadomość mirakularna', *Polska Sztuka Ludowa. Konteksty*, 3: 147–157.

Olszewski, D. (1996) *Polska Kultura religijna na przełomie XIX i XX wieku*, Warszawa: Instytut Wydawniczy PAX and Instytut Tomistyczny OO. Dominikanów.

Pasieka, A. (2013) 'Being normal in Poland', *Tr@nsti online*, Vienna: Institute for Human Sciences, available at www.iwm.at/read-listen-watch/transit-online/being-normal-in-poland/ (last accessed 20 December 2013).

Reymont, W. (1988) *Pielgrzymka do Jasnej Góry*, Warszawa: Instytut Prasy i Wydawnictw "Novum"; originally published as W. Reymont (1895) *Pielgrzymka do Jasnej Góry: wrażenia i obrazy*, Warszawa: Gebethner i Wolf.

Samson, J. (2012) 'EU criticism in two transnational Marian anti-abortion movements', in W. Jansen and C. Notermans (eds.), *Gender, Nation and Religion in European Pilgrimage*, Farnham, UK, and Burlington, VT: Ashgate.

Sekerdej, K., Pasieka, A. and Warat, M. (2007) 'Popular religion and postsocialist nostalgia: Licheń as a polysemic pilgrimage centre in Poland', *Polish Sociological Review*, 4: 431–444.

———. and Pasieka, A. (2010) '"Bogu co boskie, cesarzowi, co cesarskie. A co ludziom?" Negocjowanie przestrzeni w Licheniu', in A. Bukowski, M. Lubaś and J. Nowak (eds.) *Społeczne tworzenie miejsc. Globalizacja, etniczność, władza*, Kraków: Wydawnictwo Uniwersytetu Jagiellońskiego.

———. and Pasieka, A. (2013) 'Researching the dominant religion: anthropology at home and methodological Catholicism', *Method and Theory in the Study of Religion*, 25: 53–77.

Starnawski, J. (1987) 'Władysław Stanisław Reymont jako reporter pielgrzymki do Jasnej Góry', *Studia Claromontana*, 7: 215–229.

Stomma, L. (1981) Etnografia - etnologia - antropologia kultury - ludoznawstwo. 'Czym są? Dokąd zmierzają? (odpowiedzi na ankietę)', *Polska Sztuka Ludowa*, 35: 71–72.

———. (1986) *Antropologia kultury wsi polskiej XIX w.*, Warszawa: Instytut Wydawniczy Pax.

Thomas, W. I. and Znaniecki, F. (1918) *The Polish Peasant in Europe and in America: Monograph of an Immigrant Group. Volume I Primary-Group Organization*, Boston: Richard G. Badger, The Gorham Press.

Tokarska-Bakir, J. (2000) *Obraz osobliwy. Hermeneutyczna lektura źródeł etnograficznych*, Kraków: UNIVERSITAS.

———. (2002) 'Why is the holy image 'true'? The ontological concept of truth as a principle of self-authentication of folk devotional effigies in the eighteenth and nineteenth century', *Numen*, 49: 255–281.

Tomicki, R. (1981) 'Religijność ludowa', in M. Biernacka, M. Frankowska and W. Paprocka (eds.) *Etnografia Polski. Przemiany kultury ludowej*, t. 2, Wrocław: Ossolineum, Instytut Kultury Materialnej PAN.

94   *Anna Niedźwiedź*

Witkowska, A. (1987) 'Książka dewocyjna w duszpasterskiej posłudze jasnogórskiego sanktuarium w XVII–XVIII wieku', *Studia Claromontana,* 7: 50–60.

Wyka, K. (1979) *Reymont czyli ucieczka do życia,* Warszawa: Państwowy Instytut Wydawniczy.

Ziejka, F. (1994) 'Krakowscy pątnicy', in R. Godula (ed.) *Klejnoty i sekrety Krakowa. Teksty z antropologii miasta,* Kraków: Wydawnictwo Wawelskie.

——. (1996) 'Pisarze czasów narodowej niewoli na jasnogórskim szlaku pielgrzymkowym', *Peregrinus Cracoviensis,* 3: 97–117.

Zowczak, M. (2000) *Biblia ludowa. Interpretacje wątków biblijnych w kulturze ludowej,* Wrocław: Fundacja na rzecz Nauki Polskiej.

5 Pilgrimages in Hungary
Ethnological and Anthropological Approaches

Gábor Barna

BACKGROUND

The structures, development and specific practices of pilgrimages are a good reflection of the nature of religiosity in a particular age; they also are influenced by the cultural, denominational, social, economic and political conditions of their time. Consequently research on pilgrimages draws on various disciplines. In general, social and political relations determine what researchers are interested in and how they study it. According to the census of 2011, around 40% of the country's population describe themselves as Roman Catholics, while Protestants (Calvinists, Lutherans, Unitarians) represent approximately 14%, and the remaining 46% are divided between the dynamically growing small Christian and non-Christian (Buddhist, Jewish, etc.) churches and nonbelievers (27% of Hungarians did not declare membership of any denomination). The different Roma groups mostly subscribe to Roman Catholicism, but Pentecostal congregations have recently proved a powerful magnet because of their use of music.

As in other parts of Europe the first scholarly descriptions of Hungarian pilgrimage appeared during the second half of the nineteenth century. Scholars mainly adopted a historical perspective, exploring the history of the Catholic Church, its religious orders and artistic production, all of which are still important areas for Hungarian pilgrimage research. The most important study on pilgrimage and Marian devotion is still Ágost Flórián Balogh's magisterial book (1872), a kind of *summa Mariana*. Written in Latin (Hungary's official language at the time), it dealt not only with Hungary but also Croatia and Poland. Because it was written in Latin, it was addressed to the priesthood across the Central European region and to the limited audience of people versed in the language. Balogh concentrated on providing a historical and descriptive portrait of the various Marian cults, which is still useful today because it examines numerous sources that are no longer readily accessible. His work also marked the departure from a devotional or literary tradition, which had served the demands of religious practice from earlier centuries, and the beginning of scholarly research.

96   *Gábor Barna*

Marian devotion in Hungary had been encouraged during the Catholic Counter-Reformation in the seventeenth and eighteenth centuries. An increasing emphasis was placed on the idea that, through the dedication of the country made by the first Hungarian king, Saint Stephen, Hungary was Mary's country. This was also given iconographic expression in the form of the Woman clothed with the Sun (Apocalyptic Woman). This image was transformed into the portrayal of *Patrona Hungariae*, when the so-called Holy Crown used for the coronation of Hungarian kings was placed on Mary's head. During the Counter-Reformation the notion of the *Regnum Marianum* (*Mary's Kingdom*) assisting Catholic restoration and renewal took shape, intertwined with the veneration of Hungarian saints. From then on Hungarian pilgrimages were imbued with a strongly Marian character.

From the seventeenth century up to the mid-nineteenth century a major publication series—the *Atlas Marianus*—commented on this Marian devotional tradition from various disciplinary perspectives. The final book in the series was produced by Elek Jordánszky (1836). It was both devotional and scholarly in its aims and represents a transition between providing sources about pilgrimage and studying it in a scholarly fashion (see Tüskés 1993: 82). Ágost Balogh decided to summarise both these and similar publications and critically evaluate them. He defined the concept of shrines (*loca gratiarum*) and followed the same criteria in describing the different places. He outlined each place's history, presented the main features of the cult and its devotional objects, described the feast days, estimated the number of pilgrims, reported the most significant community pilgrimages to the place and also listed his sources (Balogh 1872: 441–693).

During the second half of the nineteenth century more and more information about the history of different shrines and relics and the various manifestations of pilgrimage appeared in a diverse literature produced by the Church and by those studying the history of the Church, its parishes, religious orders and religious art in various regions across the country. Yet those who were developing ethnology and the study of folklore chose to ignore this literature and concentrate on the reconstruction of archaic religion and Hungarian mythology. Some considered that the task of ethnology was to examine only the autochthonous elements rather than those generated by external influences, i.e., Christianity (see Szendrey 1940: 90).

ETHNOLOGICAL RESEARCH ON PILGRIMAGE

After this sporadic publication of data, a systematic ethnological and folkloristic study of pilgrimages began to emerge. The emphasis increasingly shifted away from the earlier historical descriptions of shrines and their votive images towards an analysis of the series of social and cultural activities that constitute the pilgrimage. This approach was pioneered by Sándor

Bálint. He provided the first description of the pilgrimage made by the people of Szeged to Máriaradna (Bálint 1936), which drew mainly on German research, especially the work of Georg Schreiber. (The German influence remains important in Hungarian research on religious ethnology because Hungary is linked by its cult connections mainly to Austrian and Bavarian, as well as Italian regions; see Barna 2001d and Eberhart's chapter in this volume). In this pilgrimage and the customs of the most popular shrines, Bálint saw the expression of the community's demand for 'representation' and the vows of the Baroque age (Bálint 1938: 25–27). The Baroque age brought spectacle and theatricality to its praise of God. People often made a vow to undertake a pilgrimage to a sacred place with the aim of averting natural disasters and epidemics. Bálint was the first to publish the prayers that were said by the walking pilgrims when they departed, along the route, on arrival at the shrine and during their return home (1938: 29–43).

In this first major ethnological study Bálint outlined the prime features of the pilgrimage and revealed its psychological dimensions, its communal nature and regional characteristics. He placed special emphasis on material culture (the pilgrim's staff, souvenirs, small devotional pictures, decorated honey cakes, candles) and the influence of pilgrimages on local economic and cultural traditions—for example, how the so-called sacred wells strengthened the local pottery industry. This approach was very forward looking because it was only taken up by others in the second half of twentieth century (see Hahn 1969, Barna 1986), and Anglophone researchers are only now addressing it seriously in the context of pilgrimage and material religion, more generally (see Reader's chapter earlier).

Bálint was also the first to refer to the special rites, which characterised pilgrimage's devotional practices, in particular. The latter included sleeping in the church, specific prayers, pilgrim baptism where those making a pilgrimage to a shrine for the first time are baptised with water from the sacred well and a bond forged between the novice and the godparent (see Barna 1995).

Recognising the importance of the role of pilgrim leaders, Bálint also published and analysed in 1942 the autobiography of István Orosz of Jászladány, known as a 'holy man', most of which is devoted to a description of the Orosz's pilgrimages in Hungary and abroad. Sándor Bálint saw in the figure of the 'holy man' the successor of the licentiates (Juhász 1921) who, because of the shortage of Catholic priests following the Turkish occupation (1526–1686) and the Reformation, had been allowed to perform pastoral work, except saying mass and hearing confession. From his visits to the different shrines Bálint produced descriptions of their spirituality that are still valid today (Bálint 1944). In these publications he alerted researchers to such novel sources as small devotional pictures and booklets of songs and prayers, which were illustrated with naive engravings.

During the mid-1940s Károly Gaál wrote his doctoral dissertation on the Franciscan place of pilgrimage at Andocs. He analysed the miracle records

98 *Gábor Barna*

kept by the shrine, projected its catchment area on a map, presented the pilgrimage songs and described the patronal festival, placing great emphasis on the shrine's cheap popular literature (Gaál 2009). He later reinterpreted his research in the context of Marian devotion through Loreto chapels across central Europe. He saw in these chapels a mystical line of defence that protected the western part of the Kingdom of Hungary from the danger of the Ottoman Turks (Gaál 1983).

Influenced by Sándor Bálint, a growing number of studies were published on the religious rites and customs performed during pilgrimage, votive objects left at shrines and the role of pilgrimage in folk medicine (Vajkai 1942). Many shrines in Hungary are associated with sacred wells or springs, and people attribute healing power to the water and use it to wash sick parts of their bodies (see Barna 2010a). As a result the study of folk medicine and medical history also began to contribute to pilgrimage research.

The search for ethnographic data was carried out not only among the Hungarian population but also by the country's Catholic ethnic minorities. Germans, generally known as *svábok* (Swabians) in Hungarian, constituted the most important of these minorities. They brought many distinctive types of votive images and cults to Hungary, and their religious culture and religiosity was studied by Bonomi (1936, 1969, 1970, 1971). However, Hungarian pilgrimage was not only influenced by cult connections established through these German settlers—Austrian, Italian and Polish ties have been at least as important right up to the present day. Their influence was channelled through both official church institutions and the different religious orders (Barna 2001). Since the 1970s on September 8, the birthday of Mary, the Roma have held a Roma fair at Csatka (north of Lake Balaton). Together with the religious events this offers families an opportunity for representation, for meals held in luxurious circumstances and to make marriage matches for their daughters.

During the 1940s researchers also made use of photography to document religious life (Manga 1946). The processions were spectacular sights at the shrines. The processional crosses and banners of the different groups, as well as the portable statues and the girls and young men carrying them, could be seen in the crowd of thousands or tens of thousands. The so-called Marian girls and young men were and still are a distinctive group in local communities. They stand out even today with their special costumes, and their task is to add to the procession's pomp (Dám 1944).

PILGRIMAGE IN FICTION AND FILM

The shrine festivals that attracted thousands of people, the mingling of the sacred and the profane and the moving forms of devotional practice also had a great influence on Hungarian writers and poets. Before the Second World War these performances were the subject of many works of fiction. Factually precise novels and poems that described the atmosphere of the shrines, their festivals and their rites on the basis of personal experience were very popular. To cite just a few emblematic works there were the poems by Gyula Juhász (1883–1937) and the novels written by Ferenc Móra (1879–1934), Zsigmond Móricz (1879–1942) and László Németh (1901–1975).

During the 1940s pilgrimage was also a central theme in two art films. In 1941 István Szőts, the director of *Emberek a havason* [Men on the Mountain], made his film about mountain woodcutters in the Székelyföld region. The wife of the film's main protagonist falls ill, and in the hope of a recovery they make a pilgrimage to the Marian shrine of Csíksomlyó, where the film recorded the original pilgrimage festival. István Szőts was also the director of *Ének a búzamezőkről* [Song of the Wheatfields] (1947), adapted from a novel by Ferenc Móra, in which scenes of the pilgrimage festival at Pálosszentkút, a shrine on the Great Plain, play an important part in the life of a soldier, who has returned home from the First World War.

Besides these two feature films, a number of documentary films were made both before 1990 and after the collapse of the Communist regime. In 1986–1989 Mihály Hoppál and János Tari made a film in colour titled *Búcsújárás Magyarországon* [Pilgrimage in Hungary], while Ágnes Orbán directed *Búcsújárás* [Pilgrimage] in 2001. A series of ethnological films were also produced by József Mester, e.g., *Búcsújárás* [Pilgrimage] (1993) and *A csíksomlyói búcsú* [The Pilgrimage Feast in Csíksomlyó] (1994).

These films also portrayed pilgrimages being made to countries outside of Hungary after 1990. István Szakály's film, *Zarándokút* [Pilgrimage], for example, covered the Hungarian pilgrimage to Aachen in 1993. He shows the pilgrims visiting shrines, which contain Hungarian relics along the Vienna-Regensburg-Mainz-Andernach-Cologne-Aachen route, as well as the pilgrimage festival in Aachen. The increasingly popular walking pilgrimages, partly influenced by the international reputation of the Santiago pilgrimage and growing religious tourism, led József Birinyi to produce his 2010 films *Mária-kegyhelyek* [Marian Shrines] and *Élménylánc: vallási turizmus a dél-alföldi régióban* [Chain of Experience: Religious Tourism in the South of the Great Plain]. He also followed the less well-known Portuguese branch of the Santiago pilgrimage in *Út a csillagok alatt* [Route Under the Stars] (2011). Duna Television pursued similar goals when it made a documentary film with a cultural historical approach on a number of popular shrines in the Carpathian Basin, directed by Tamás Barlay. Most of these films drew on the expertise of Gábor Barna and other researchers as consultants.

Hungary's Jewish minority has also attracted filmmakers. Over a period of years János Tari has documented how Jews, originally from Makó, continue to maintain ties with their native town (*Távoli templom* [Distant Temple] 2002). Each year during the Festival of Weeks (*shavuot*) they come to the tomb of the Rabbi of Makó, Mózes Vorhad (1862–1944), to remember their rabbi. Vorhad had operated an influential Talmudic school,

100 *Gábor Barna*

and on his deathbed he promised to intercede in heaven for his community, most of whom survived the Holocaust.

HISTORICAL, CULTURAL HISTORICAL AND HISTORICAL ETHNOLOGICAL RESEARCH

Historians continued to show a great interest in pilgrimage during the first half of the twentieth century. Their interest was stimulated by the Hungarian national jubilees of the 1930s, and they paid increasing attention to the Middle Ages and Early Modern Age through the study of the emergence and functioning of shrines as well as pilgrimages to places outside the country. In his still unsurpassed monograph, Lajos Pásztor (1940) discussed the religiosity of the Jagiellonian period (between the early fifteenth and sixteenth centuries) and explored pilgrimage in terms of motivations, destinations and forms.

After the conversion of the Hungarians between the ninth and eleventh centuries and the establishment of Church institutions, the country was joined to an already existing international pilgrimage network, where the main destinations were the Holy Land, Rome and Santiago de Compostela. This network expanded during the thirteenth and fourteenth centuries to include the shrines of Saint Patrick's Purgatory in Ireland (Posonyi 1942), Mariazell, Aachen, Cologne, Loreto and Częstochowa, as well as pilgrimages to Rome during the holy years. Lajos Pásztor revealed the substitutional and penitentiary forms of pilgrimage,[1] as well as the accommodation provided for Hungarian pilgrims and their customs (Pásztor 1940: 94–133).

Between the fourteenth and eighteenth centuries the pilgrimage to Aachen was especially important for Hungarians (see Thoemmes 1937). The generous patronage of the Hungarian Angevin king, Louis the Great (1326–1382), in support of the dynastic cult of saints, encouraged these strong links with Aachen. Louis had a Hungarian chapel erected beside the Aachen cathedral, which had been founded in 800 by Charlemagne, and donated relics of the Hungarian royal saints to both Aachen and Cologne, where a pilgrim house and poorhouse cared for Hungarians, who made the pilgrimage there every seventh year (Thoemmes 1937). Louis's patronage also extended to Mariazell and Częstochowa closer to home.

Shrines also emerged in Hungarian territories around the graves and relics of royal saints (Stephen, Ladislas, Emmerich) and other saints, such as Saint Gerard, Saint Margaret of Hungary and Saint John Capistran (Pásztor 1940: 133–135). The graves of Saint Stephen at Székesfehérvár and Saint Ladislas at Nagyvárad (now Oradea, Romania) emerged as sacred centres in the Kingdom of Hungary. With the increasing veneration, which surrounded Margaret of Hungary during the first half of the twentieth century when her canonisation process was under way, the legends concerning her were published and these contain numerous references to the practice of pilgrimages in her lifetime. Art historians also contributed to the study of her cult, with Jajczay (1944) producing an analysis of the seven hundred years of iconography surrounding her. In the fifteenth century Eucharistic shrines in Hungary were also very important, and the most renowned shrine was located at Báta beside the Danube where a bleeding host was the focus of the cult (Kónyi, Holub, Csalog and Dercsényi 1940, Pásztor 1940: 135–138).

The Communist takeover in 1948 set back research on the history of Hungarian pilgrimages for decades. It was not until the end of the twentieth century that Enikő Csukovits brought the scattered data on medieval pilgrimage together. She presented the sources for mediaeval pilgrimages, the destinations, the motivations for pilgrimages and their different types. On the basis of these sources she traced the structure of the pilgrimages from the departure through the journey and to the arrival back home, and she analysed the social composition of the pilgrims and the role pilgrimages played in religiosity (Csukovits 2003). It is only recently, too, that research has turned to other phenomena related to mediaeval pilgrimages, such as pilgrim badges (Benkő 2002).

In the first half of the twentieth century the disciplines of history, art history, cultural history and historical ethnology also turned their attention towards pilgrimage after the Middle Ages, especially the Baroque period. Lajos Pásztor again produced an outstanding study of the most important

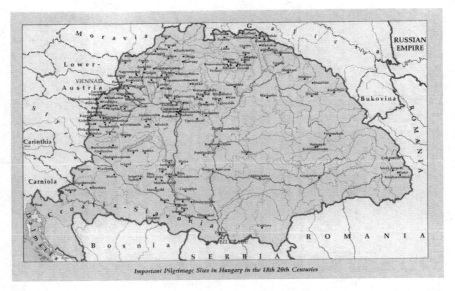

Figure 5.1 Map of important pilgrimage sites in Hungary in the eighteenth through twentieth centuries.

102 Gábor Barna

Baroque shrine in Hungary—Máriavölgy, which was close to Pozsony, the capital of the country at that time (now Bratislava, the capital of Slovakia) and called today Marianka. Drawing on contemporary sources he analyses the shrine's foundation legend, the history of the Pauline order, its rebuilding in the Baroque age, the pilgrimages to the shrine, its catchment area, the records of miraculous healings and the votive objects offered for answered prayers (Pásztor 1943).

The dynamic religiosity of the Baroque age favoured the emergence of local and regional shrines. Pilgrimages abroad declined and only those to Rome, Mariazell, Aachen, and, for a while, to the Holy Land and Częstochowa retained their importance. Throughout the Early Modern Age the holy years were the most important magnet for pilgrimages to Rome. Monks, priests and well-travelled aristocrats also journeyed on official business. Numerous pilgrim passports have survived in our archives (Barna 2001), while many pilgrim badges have also been preserved (Gohl 1912) as well as *vera icon* prints. These visits inspired the introduction of Holy Stairs to Hungary,[2] e.g., Malacka, Selmecbánya, Kassa (after 1920 these three settlements became part of Czechoslovakia and are now called Malacky, Banska Štiavnica and Košice), and various forms of Marian devotion were strengthened, such as Our Lady of Snows, Our Lady of Mount Carmel, Mother of Good Counsel and the Bleeding Virgin Mother shrines (Bálint and Barna 1994: 120–122, Barna 2001a).

The Benedictine abbey at Mariazell deeply influenced not only Hungarian religious devotion between the seventeenth and eighteenth centuries but also cults elsewhere across Europe. Historians have examined the festivals held at the abbey from the perspectives of art, architecture, music and literature, and ethnologists have also contributed to this research (Barna 1996, Farbaky and Serfőző 2004). The Franciscans were the most important leaders of these festivals and included Hungarians, who had travelled to the Holy Land (see Kiss 1958). The Pauline order also contributed to this development of Marian devotion. Although the order's presence in the country had been destroyed by the Reformation and the Turkish occupation, it returned during the mid-seventeenth century and brought copies of the Black Madonna of Częstochowa's miraculous image and spread its cult (Barna 2004, Szilárdfy 2003).

With the end of the Turkish occupation in 1686 and the reorganisation of the Catholic Church, many shrines with roots going back to the Middle Ages were revived, and a large number of new ones emerged. Under the leadership of the Jesuits the Roman Catholic Church won over many Orthodox believers in the eastern part of the country, especially in northern Transylvania. This development led to the establishment of the Greek Catholic Church, which retained the Eastern rite but acknowledged papal authority. As the beginning of the eighteenth century approached, Catholic evangelisation and the spread of union between Latin and Greek Catholic communities was strengthened by the flourishing of many miraculous apparitions and the emergence of shrines where cult images were seen to weep, bleed, or perspire, or were wounded and bleeding (Bálint and Barna 1994: 108–114, Barna 2001e). Máriapócs in today's eastern Hungary became the most famous of these shrines, although its original weeping votive image is now displayed in Vienna's St Stephen's Cathedral. Máriapócs is still the biggest place of pilgrimage in the Greek Catholic world (Manga 1996) and has important offshoots abroad (Méhes 1963).

To understand these seventeenth- and eighteenth-century developments, scholars drew on the concept of sacred landscape (*Sakrallandschaft*), devised by the German scholar Georg Schreiber (1937). Jánosi (1939) applied the concept to the churches, chapels, Ways of the Cross, etc., erected under the influence of the shrines within a local and micro-region catchment area, while Mária Lantosné followed suit in her study of holy wells in the Pécs diocese (Lantosné 1995). Recent research has interpreted the concept more broadly, however, so that it can be deployed to analyse the interaction between religion and the spatial landscape, including pilgrimage (Bartha 1992).

The best overview in Hungary of pilgrimage during the Baroque period has been produced by Gábor Tüskés, drawing on the records of miracles taking place at the shrines (Tüskés 1993). In his analysis he explored the characteristics of the roads leading to the shrines, the practices pursued by shrine custodians and the pilgrims and the influence of pilgrimage on everyday life. He analysed thirty-six shrines, showing their legends of origin, the historical and social motivations for visiting the shrines, their ethnic and denominational links, the intensity of the pilgrimages and changes in their catchment areas. In numerous studies written jointly with Éva Knapp, he has summarised the complex material and written source material for pilgrimages, the sacred spatial structures and the Austrian-Hungarian interethnic connections in the area of pilgrimage (Tüskés and Knapp 2001, 2002, Barna 2009). They have also shown how the printed miracle books, devotional pictures and engravings of miracle stories were utilised as effective tools of religious propaganda (Tüskés and Knapp 2004). This research has been deepened by the contribution of art historians who have studied relics, cult objects and copies made of them, the portrayals in small prints and other cult objects (Szilárdfy, Tüskés and Knapp 1987, Szilárdfy 1995, 1997, 2008).

ETHNOLOGICAL, SOCIOLOGICAL AND ANTHROPOLOGICAL RESEARCH FROM THE SECOND HALF OF THE TWENTIETH CENTURY

After the pioneering research during the first half of the twentieth century on Hungarian places of pilgrimage by those trained in ethnology, folkloristics and history, a long hiatus followed during the decades of Communism.

104 *Gábor Barna*

From 1948 up to the 1980s researchers had no hope of publishing their findings. This hiatus is particularly regrettable because it was during this period that the traditional forms of pilgrimage were undergoing change, partly due to modernisation and the spread of technical civilisation and partly as a result of ideological influences. The few sporadic studies, which were undertaken were imbued with harsh criticism of pilgrimage activity from the perspective of historical materialism (Mihályfi 1962, Manga 1962, Nyárády 1966). Studies that appeared from the 1970s dealt only with particular aspects of material culture, such as small graphic prints, small devotional pictures, pilgrim songs, pilgrim's bags, wax votive objects, copies of votive objects and convent work. Yet they deepened our knowledge in specific areas and research because art historians also began to examine the cult and the people behind the cult rather than just analysing the artefact.

Outstanding among the few publications, which sought a comprehensive approach was the theoretical overview and periodisation published by the ethnologist Ferenc Schram in a theological journal (Schram 1968). At the same time new research was produced by Hungarians, who had emigrated to the West, while the Hungarian Institute of Religious Sociology, based in Vienna, also played an important role here. Its bilingual parallel series, *UKI Berichte über Ungarn/UKI Reports about Hungary*, included several volumes on pilgrimage. The most important of these was Jenő Bangó's book, *Pilgrimage in Hungary*, which undertook a sociological analysis of fifty pilgrimage shrines (Bangó 1978), while Maria-Kornelia Fasching also produced a historical ethnological examination of shrines in southern Pannonia (Fasching 1991). Furthermore, during the 1980s the study of the history of pilgrimage to Mariazell was deepened by articles published in *Katolikus Szemle*, a journal produced in Rome (Szamosi 1987).

Within Hungary, during the 1970s Sándor Bálint was preparing to write a national history of pilgrimage and its ethnology, and after his sudden death this task was completed by Gábor Barna during the 1980s. The monograph, *Búcsújáró magyarok* [Hungarians on Pilgrimage], constituted the first ethnological synthesis of pre-1949 Hungarian pilgrimage traditions (Bálint and Barna 1994). Ethnological research strove to pick up the threads that had been dropped in the 1940s, but real progress only came around the time of the change in the political system.

The first results of this transformation were seen in the 1990s. By this time research was beginning to reflect not only German influence but also the impact of Anglo-Saxon and French ethnology and cultural anthropology. Special courses in religious ethnology were launched at the University of Szeged, which had been the cradle of ethnological research during the 1930s and 1940s. A research programme was developed through conferences, research initiatives and publications, and this still operates through the Department of Ethnology and Cultural Anthropology. Applying new methods, researchers began to investigate modern forms and functions of pilgrimage. The inscription books in votive churches (and churches, in

Pilgrimages in Hungary 105

general) provided a new source for the study of written communication with the sacred (see Frauhammer 1999, 2012, Barna 2000, István 2003).

The researchers at Szeged also examined the custom of donating votive images, which still survives at Máriaradna (from 1920 it became part of Romania) through an inventory of around two thousand such images (Barna 2002). Furthermore, they have documented the religious and secular components of the Szeged-Alsóváros feast day (August 5, Our Lady of the Snows) (Pusztai 1999) and published bilingual monographs on the history and folklore of the shrines (Tóth 2002, Barna 2003). János Hetény's book on the Karancs-hegy feast day is not only methodologically a fine example of participant observation but is also our most detailed description so far of this pilgrimage feast day (Hetény 2000). Szeged researchers have also studied pilgrimage songs and published some of them, as well as the first catalogue of small prints, most of which are associated with pilgrimage shrines (Szabó and Zombori 2010). Last but not least, Barna produced the first overview of Hungarian pilgrimage in English (Barna 2001).

JEWISH PILGRIMAGE

In the Jewish tradition pilgrimages were made to the 'Holy Land'. Elderly Orthodox and Hasidic Jews had long moved to spend their last years in Jerusalem. Members of Hungarian Reform and Orthodox communities also joined organised trips by Western European middle-class Jews to spend part of the feasts, prescribed in scripture, in Jerusalem, but this involved only a tiny fraction of the population. More significant in terms of numbers were the pilgrimages by rural Orthodox and Hasidic Jews, who joined the festivals held by the followers of the Hasidic 'rebbes' in Galicia. During the early twentieth century these pilgrimages were very similar to Catholic pilgrimages in Hungary, with pilgrims arriving not only in carts but also by train and bus.

During the late nineteenth century those involved in the study of Jewish communities (*Wissenschaft des Judentums*) were also attracted to the pilgrimages made by pious Eastern European Jews to the shrines of Jewish holy men (Gleszer 2006). However, their research remained within the earlier conceptual frame of *Wissenschaft des Judentums* and focussed mainly on legends (Dobos 1990). This approach was deeply influenced by ghetto nostalgia and the secularisation perspective (Schön 1997, Glässer 2014a).

During the 2000s, however, Norbert Glässer provided an analysis of the history of 'Jewish pilgrimage', focussing initially on the rites and written communication with the sacred (Gleszer 2010). Through the study of the pilgrimage infrastructure and the tombs of holy men, he moved towards an exploration of the social context within which the veneration of *tsadiks* (spiritual master) took place (Gleszer 2008). Historical evidence revealed that people not only came to the shrines of rabbis and rebbes during

106 *Gábor Barna*

individual crises and community visits but also to perform the anniversary rites of rebbe dynasties and attend meetings of the Talmudic schools of Ashkenazi Hasidic rebbes. In the communal memory of Orthodox Jews, who emigrated from Hungary, these places of pilgrimage became important spaces of memory and points of attachment to the homeland they had left behind (Glässer 2013). Following the collapse of Communism, researchers were able to investigate how intense pilgrimage practices were intertwined with heritage tourism. The question of visits to tombs has led to questions about the communal strengthening of religious authority and the communal engagement with modernity and secularisation (Glässer 2014b).

As we have seen, ethnological research on Hungarian pilgrimage has been dominated by a historical perspective. The contribution by art historians has been particularly rich because an image, statue, relic, holy well, or spring is usually the centre of veneration at sacred places. Many historical analyses have been written about these places, the answers to prayers said there and miraculous recoveries. Research in Hungary today always examines the historical territory of the country, despite the dramatic border changes during the twentieth century.

NEW CONSIDERATIONS IN RESEARCH— RELIGIOUS TOURISM

Systematic research on pilgrimages, the veneration of saints and religious communities became very difficult in the period from the 1950s to the 1980s, when the authorities pursued an anticlerical and antireligious policy. However, the study of contemporary pilgrimage was stimulated by the collapse of the regime and the resurgence of pilgrimage in diverse forms. The network of pilgrimage places in the Carpathian Basin was completely restructured together with the organisation of pilgrimage. The tradition of pilgrimage by parish communities had already largely disappeared and the dominance of the shrine network had also changed. This process had been set in motion by the Treaty of Trianon (4 June 1920), where two-thirds of Hungary's territory was allocated to the neighbouring countries (Czechoslovakia, Romania, Yugoslavia and Austria). Millions of Hungarians found themselves in new nation-states where the borders cut across pilgrimage routes, and it became impossible to go on pilgrimage for decades. Hence, visiting such places as Máriaradna in Romania and Doroszló in Serbia is today also an expression of religious and Hungarian national identity because the Romanians and Serbs belong to the Orthodox Church, while Hungarians are Roman Catholics and Protestants.

New shrines, routes and catchment areas emerged with Csíksomlyó on the eastern edge of Transylvania, annexed by Romania, becoming the symbolic expression of religious and national survival. Csíksomlyó/Șumuleu had long been a regional shrine, but it has now become a transnational

Figure 5.2 New state borders after the Trianon Peace Treaty, 4 June 1920. Map of the Central Statistical Office of Hungary, Census 1920 VI.

shrine because it attracts those from Hungary as well as members of Romania's Hungarian minority. This has created a special situation: a Hungarian national shrine in the territory of another state. Tamás Mohay has critically reinterpreted the historical sources concerning the shrine, pointing out the possibilities and limitations of mythification (Mohay 2009). Others have drawn on Victor Turner's work to examine pilgrimage as ritual drama in the context of both Roman Catholics and the Romanian Orthodox communities (Vass 2009). Walking pilgrimages have reappeared involving small groups or individuals; some of these can also be interpreted as religious and cultural tourism. The pilgrimages by particular status groups, which had been forbidden earlier, began again and the youth pilgrimages on foot have become particularly attractive.

Nevertheless, the most striking change has been the appearance of tourism offices organising pilgrimages, and researchers began to explore this change, drawing on Anglophone publications by anthropologists and other social scientists (Bhardwaj and Rinschede 1988, Eade and Sallnow 1991, Post 1994). From the 1990s a number of researchers have analysed the relationship between pilgrimage and tourism and have drawn on the concept of religious tourism. Within this interpretative frame they have analysed pilgrimages organised by travel offices (Korpics 2000, Pusztai 1999, 2004) and extended their interest to secular pilgrimages, as well as national religion and neo-pagan (syncretic) religions (Povedák 2008, 2011, 2012).

108 *Gábor Barna*

After 1990 pilgrimage to Compostela also became popular and pilgrimages were organised in Hungary on the Compostela model. Individual and group pilgrimages were developed by various associations along various routes, e.g., the Saint James, Saint Martin and Saint Elizabeth routes; the *Via Margaritarum* or Route of Pearls; the route of Saint Mary; the Hungarian Pilgrimage Route; and the Saint Stephen Route. The promoters of these various routes seek to attract people by developing their own websites.

Significant changes have also taken place in other modes of travel. Since 2000 pilgrimage trips by special train were also revived to Csíksomlyó, Częstochowa and Mariazell, for example, recalling the heyday of pilgrimages by train between 1870 and 1940 to popular European destinations such as Rome and Lourdes. Trips by bus were organised more from the end of the 1960s. Researchers are just beginning to analyse these changes through the study of travel reports concerning pilgrimages abroad.

Pilgrimages were and still are occasions and places for meetings and interactions. Pilgrims meet other people, other languages, cultures, nature, themselves and, at the end of the journey, the venerated saint. The encounter with others can awaken pilgrims to differences in language, customs and other things, as well as encourage them to reflect on their own life worlds. Their identity is thereby strengthened. The shrines and the pilgrimage routes leading to them can be said to contain in condensed form the history and everyday life of the place and the region. Writers and poets have described the special atmosphere of different shrines. The pilgrimage can result in getting to know the other person, the environment, the past and present; it can bring persons, peoples, languages and cultures closer together. The pilgrim routes are sacred routes (*via sacra*) marked with small structures (crosses, statues, chapels). Visiting shrines can foster ties within the traditional (parish, settlement) community or the tourist office group, functioning religious societies established at the shrines and pilgrimage societies organising pilgrimages.

NOTES

1. In the Middle Ages and Early Modern Age many people were unable to fulfil their vows to make a pilgrimage. They hired someone to visit the shrine in their place. Secular courts often sentenced persons found guilty to make visits to distant sacred places—thereby removing them from the community for years and forcing them to do penance.
2. These were copies of the stairs in the Scala Sancta church in Rome, originally from Jerusalem, which were believed to have been used by Jesus when he was tried.

REFERENCES

Bálint, S. (1936) 'Szegediek búcsújárása Radnára' [People of Szeged on Pilgrimage to Radna] *Ethnographia*, XLVII: 317–318.

Pilgrimages in Hungary 109

————. (1938) *Népünk ünnepei* [Feasts of our People], Budapest.
————. (1944) *Boldogasszony vendégségében* [Guests of Our Lady], Budapest: Veritas.
————. and Barna, G. (1994) *Búcsújáró magyarok. A magyarországi búcsújárás története és néprajza* [Hungarians on Pilgrimage: History and Ethnology of Pilgrimage in Hungary], Budapest: Szent István Társulat.
Balogh, A. (1872) *Beatissima Maria Mater Dei, qua Regina et Patrona Hungariarum.* Historico-pragmatice-adumbravit Augustus Florianus Balogh de Nemcsicz, parochus Kocskóczensis. Agriae.
Bangó, F. (1978) *The Pilgrimage in Hungary.* UKI Reports about Hungary, Vienna.
Barna, G. (1986) 'A búcsúvásár' [The Pilgrim Market], in J. Szabadfalvy and G. Viga (eds.) *Árucsere és migráció* [Exchange of Goods and Migration], Miskolc.
————. (1995) 'Pilgrim baptism: an initiation rite in the Hungarian Catholic paraliturgy', *Etnološka Tribina*, 18: 91–102.
————. (1996) 'Mariazell und Ungarn', in H. Eberhart and H. Fell (eds.) *Schatz und Schicksal. Steierische Landesausstellung*, Graz.
————. (2000) 'Vendégkönyvek kegyhelyeken, kórházakban és szállodákban—A ritualizált viselkedésmódok új, írásos formái és forrásai' [Inscription Books in Shrines, Hospitals and Hotels—New Written Forms and Sources on Ritualised Forms of Behaviour], in K. Kuti and B. Rásky (eds.) *Azonosságok és különbségek. Mai néprajzi kutatások Ausztriában és Magyarországon* [Similarities and Differences. Current Ethnological Research in Austria and Hungary], Budapest.
————. (2001a) *Búcsújárók. Kölcsönhatások a magyar és más európai vallási kultúrákban.* [Pilgrimages: Interactions in Hungarian and Other European Religious Cultures], Budapest: Lucidus Kiadó.
————. (2001b) 'Hungarian pilgrims in Europe—places of pilgrimage in Hungary', in I. Zombori, Z. Cséfalvay and M. de Angelis (eds.) *A Thousand Years of Christianity in Hungary: Hungariae Christianae Millennium*, Budapest: Hungarian Catholic Episcopal Conference.
————. (2002) '"Mária megsegített" Fogadalmi tárgyak Máriaradnán/"Maria hat geholfen" Votivgegenstände in Maria-Radna I-II' ['Mary has helped'. Votive objects in Mariaradna I-II), *Devotio Hungarorum 9*, Szeged: Néprajzi Tanszék.
————. (2003) 'Egy szent raktár. Tárgyak, szimbólumok, kommunikáció'/'A Sacred Depot. Objects, Symbols, Communication', *Devotio Hungarorum*, 10, Szeged: Néprajzi Tanszék.
————. (2004) 'A Czestochowai Szűzanya tisztelete Közép-Európában' [Cult in Central Europe of the Virgin Mother of Czestochowa], in G. Barna (ed.) *". . . szolgálatra ítéltél . . ." Bálint Sándor Emlékkönyv.* [Sándor Bálint Festschrift], Szeged: Lazi Kiadó.
————. (2009) 'A barokk szakrális térszerkezet kialakulása. Zarándoklatok, kegyhelyek a 18. század első évtizedeiben' [The Formation of the Baroque Sacral Space Structure. Pilgrimages and Shrines in the First Decades of the 18th Century], in Z. Gőzsy, S. Varga and L. Vértesi (eds.) *Katolikus megújulás és a barokk Magyarországon.* [Catholic Revival and Baroque Hungary], Pécs.
————. (2010a) 'Szent kutak, szent források a búcsújáró helyeken' [Holy Wells and Holy Springs in Places of Pilgrimage], in E. Bartha, R. Keményfi and V. Lajos (eds.) *A víz kultúrája.* [The Culture of Water], Debrecen: Debreceni Egyetem Néprajzi Tanszék.
Bartha, E. (1992) *Vallásökológia* [Religious Ecology], Debrecen: Néprajzi Tanszék.
Benkő, E. (2002) *Erdély középkori harangjai és bronz keresztelő medencéi* [Mediaeval Bells and Bronze Baptismal Fonts in Transylvania], Budapest-Kolozsvár: Teleki László Alapítvány and Polisz Könyvkiadó.
Bhardwaj, S. and Rinschede, G. (eds.) (1988) *Pilgrimage in World Religions*, Berlin: Reimer.

110   Gábor Barna

Bonomi, E. (1936) *Budaőrs, ein vergessener Wallfahrtsort*, Budapest.

———. (1969) 'Die Mirakelbücher der Wallfahrtsorte Óbuda-Kiscell/Kleinzell bei Altofen und Makkor Mária/Maria Eichel bei Budakeszi in Ungarn', *Jahrbuch für Ostdeutsche Volkskunde*, 12: 271–300.

———. (1970) 'Ungarndeutsche Wallfahrten nach Mariazell/Österreich im 200. Jahrhundert', *Jahrbuch für Ostdeutsche Volkskunde*, 13: 136–190.

———. (1971) 'Deutsche aus dem Ober Bergland in Ungarn auf Wallfahrt', *Jahrbuch für Ostdeutsche Volkskunde*, 14: 239–277.

Csukovits, E. (2003) *Középkori magyar zarándokok* [Mediaeval Hungarian pilgrimages], *História Könyvtár Monográfiák* 3, Budapest: MTA Történettudományi Intézet.

Dám, I.O.F.M. (1944) *'A "Hordozó Mária" valláséleti szerepe Mátraalján. Tanulmány a lelkipásztori néprajz köréből'* [The Role of the 'Mary Pendant' in Religious Life in the Mátraalja Region: Studies in Priestly Ethnology], Gyöngyös.

Dobos, I. (1990) 'A csodarabbi alakja a néphagyományban' [The figure of the miracle-working rabbi in folk tradition], in I. Kríza (ed.), *A hagyomány kötelékében. Tanulmányok a magyarországi zsidó folklór köréből* [In the Bonds of Tradition: Studies on Jewish Folklore in Hungary], Budapest: Akadémiai.

Eade, J. and Sallnow, M. (eds.) (1991) *Contesting the Sacred: The Anthropology of Christian Pilgrimage*, London and New York: Routledge.

Farbaky, P. and S. Serfőző (eds.) (2004) *Ungarn in Mariazell—Mariazell in Ungarn. Geschichte und Erinnerung*, Budapest.

Fasching, M.-K. (1991) *Die Wallfahrtsorte Südwestpannoniens*, Vienna: UKI Berichte über Ungarn.

Frauhammer, K. (1999) 'Levelek Máriához. A máriakálnoki kegyhely vendégkönyve/ Briefe an Maria. Das Gästebuch des Gnadenortes Máriakálnok/Gahling', *Devotio Hungarorum*, 6, Szeged: Néprajzi Tanszék.

———. (2012) *Írásba foglalt vágyak és imák. Magyar kegyhelyek vendégkönyveinek összehasonlító elemzése* [Desires and Prayers Communicated in Writings. Comparative Analysis of Inscription Books on Places of Pilgrimage in Hungary], Szeged: Néprajzi és Kulturális Antropológiai Tanszék.

Gaál, K. (1983) 'Auxilium Christianorum. A lorettói szűz tisztelete Kelet-Közép-Európában' [Cult of the Virgin of Loreto in Eastern Central Europe], *Szolgálat*, 58 (2): 22–28.

———. (2009) *Az andocsi Mária gyermekei. Adatok az andocsi búcsújárás néprajzához.* [Children of Mary in Andocs. Ethnological Data on the Andocs Pilgrimage], Bibliotheca Religionis Popularis Szegediensis 24, Szeged—Dunavarsány.

Glässer, N. (2013) 'Úgy mint az óhazában: az újrateremtett közösség' [As in the Old Country: The recreated community], in V. Bányai, C. Fedinec and S. Komoróczy (eds.) *Zsidók Kárpátalján: Történelem és örökség a dualizmus korától napjainkig* [Jews in Sub-Carpathia: History and Heritage From the Age of the Dual Monarchy to the Present], *Hungaria Judaica*, 30: 347–352.

———. (2014a) 'A kállói Szent Pap. Egy neológ izraelita integrációs narratívum a Horthy-korszakban' [The Holy Priest of Kálló. A Reform Jewish integration narrative in the Horthy era], in G. Barna and I. Kerekes (eds.) *Vallás, egyén, társadalom* [Religion, Individual, Society], Szegedi Vallási Néprajzi Könyvtár 39. A vallási kultúrakutatás könyvei 7. SZTE-BTK Néprajzi és Kulturális Antropológiai Tanszék—MTA-SZTE Vallási Kultúrakutató Csoport, Szeged.

———. (2014b) *Találkozás a Szent Igazzal: A magyar nyelvű orthodox zsidó sajtó cádik-képe 1891–1944* [Encounter with the Holy Just Men: The image of the tsadik in the Hungarian-language Orthodox press, 1891–1944], Szegedi Vallási Néprajzi Könyvtár 40. MTA-SZTE Vallási Kultúrakutató Csoport a Vallási Kultúrakutatás Könyvei 8. Néprajzi és Kulturális Antropológiai Tanszék—Gabbiano Print Kft, Szeged, 2014.

Pilgrimages in Hungary 111

Gleszer, N. (2006) 'Pilgrimages in Jewish folk religion in Hungary—from the Chassidic courts to the virtual communities', *Acta Ethnographica Hungarica*, 51 (1–2): 91–104.

———. (2008) 'Sacred and modernity in a changing group culture: just men, saints and community strategies in the Jewish denominational press in Hungary in the late 19th and early 20th century', in U. Wolf-Knuts and K. Grant (eds.) *Rethinking the Sacred*. Proceedings of the Ninth SIEF Conference in Derry.

———. (2010) 'Üzenetek e világból A kvitli elhelyezésének ritualizálása a magyarországi cádik-síroknál' [Messages from this world: The ritualisation of the placing of quitli at the tombs of tsadiks in Hungary], in G. Barna and O. Gyöngyössy (eds.) *Ritus és ünnep—Rite and Feast*, Szegedi Vallási Néprajzi Könyvtár 25. Néprajzi és Kulturális Antropológiai Tanszék, Szeged.

Gohl, Ö. (1912) 'Magyar egyházi emlékérmék III. Helyi vonatkozású érmék'. [Hungarian Ecclesiastical Commemorative Medals III. Medals of Local Relevance], *Numizmatikai Közlöny*, XI: 90–110.

Hahn, M. (1969) *Siedlungs- und wirtschaftsgeographische Untersuchungen der Wallfahrtstätten*, Düsseldorf.

Hetény, J. (2000) *A győri vérrel könnyező Szűzanya kultusztörténete*. [History of the Cult of the Bleeding Virgin Mother of Győr], Szeged: Bibliotheca Religionis Popularis Szegediensis 5. Néprajzi Tanszék.

István, A. (2003) *Most segíts meg Mária . . ." A futásfalvi Sarlós Boldogasszonynapi búcsú szövegrepertóriuma* ['Help me now Mary . . .' Texts of the Feast of the Visitation in Futásfalva], Kriza Könyvek 20. Kriza János Néprajzi Társaság, Kolozsvár.

Jajczay, J. [1944] *Árpádházi Szent Margit hétszázéves arculata* [Seven Hundred Years of the Image of Saint Margaret of Hungary], Budapest: Szent István Társulat.

Jánosi, G. (1939) *Barokk búcsújáró helyeink táji vonásai* [Regional Features of our Baroque Pilgrimage Places], Pannonhalma.

Jordánszky, E. 1836. *Magyar Országban s ahoz tartozó részekben lévő Szűz Mária kegyelem képeinek rövid leírása* [Short Description of Miraculous Pictures of Virgin Mary in Hungary], Pozsony.

Juhász, K. (1921) *A licenciátusi intézmény Magyarországon* [The Institution of Licentiate in Hungary], Budapest.

Kiss, I. (1958) *Jeruzsálemi Utazás* [Journey to Jerusalem]. With introduction and notes by P. Lajos, Roma.

Kónyi, M., J. Holub, J. Csalog and D. Dercsényi (1940) *A bátai apátság és Krisztusvére ereklyéje* [The Báta Abbey and the Relic of Christ's Blood], Pécs.

Korpics, M. (2000) 'Zarándok és turista. Gondolatok a szent helyekről a turizmus kontextusában' [Pilgrims and Tourists. Thoughts on sacred places in the context of tourism], in Z. Fejős and Z. Szíjártó (eds.) *Turizmus és kommunikáció. Tanulmányok* [Tourism and Communication. Studies], Budapest and Pécs: Néprajzi Múzeum and PTE Kommunikációs Tanszék.

Lantosné, I. M. (1995) 'Szakrális táj és kultusz a pécsi egyházmegyében I. Csodaforrások és szentkutak', *A Janus pannonius Múzeum Évkönyve*, 39: 197–211.

Manga, J. (1946) *Magyar katolikus népélet képekben* [Hungarian Catholic Folk Life in Pictures], Budapest.

———. (1962) 'A hasznosi tömegpszichózis' [Mass Psychosis in Hasznos], *Ethnographia*, LXXIII: 353–388.

Méhes, I. (1963) *Die blutweinende Gottesmutter. Ein berühmtes Gnadenbild aus Ungarn und Unsere Liebe Frau in Siebeneich*, Siebeneich.

Mihályfi, E. (1962) *A mérges csók* [*The Poisoned Kiss*], Budapest: Móra Ferenc Könyvkiadó.

Mohay, T. (2009) *A csíksomlyói pünkösdi búcsújárás: Történet, eredet, hagyomány* [The Whitsun Pilgrimage to Csíksomlyó: History, origin, tradition], Budapest: Nyitott könyv and L'Harmattan.

112 Gábor Barna

Nyárády, G. (1966) *Búcsúsok. Hitetlen beszélgetések a hazai búcsújáró helyekről* [Pilgrims. Unbelieving conversations on places of pilgrimage in Hungary], Budapest.

Pásztor, L. (1940) *A magyarság vallási élete a Jagellók korában* [Religious Life of the Hungarians in the Jagiellonian Period], Budapest.

———. (1943) 'A máriavölgyi kegyhely a XVII–XVIII. században' [The Shrine Máriavölgy in the 17th-18th century], *Regnum 1942–1943: Egyháztörténeti Évkönyv,* 563–600.

Posonyi, E. (1942) 'A Tar Lőrinc-monda és a szent Patrik purgatóriumi víziók keletkezése' [The Lőrinc Tar Legend and the Origin of the Visions of Saint Patrick's Purgatory], *Magyarságtudomány I. évf.,* 1: 26–54 and 2: 195–224.

Post, P. (1994) 'The modern pilgrim: a study of contemporary pilgrims' accounts', *Ethnologia Europaea,* 24: 85–100.

Povedák, I. (2008) 'The apostle of love: secular pilgrimage in post-socialist Hungary', in P. J. Margry (ed.) *Shrines and Pilgrimage in the Modern World: New Itineraries Into the Sacred,* Amsterdam: Amsterdam University Press.

———. (2011) 'Shrines and pilgrimage in the modern world: new itineraries into the sacred', *Acta Ethnographica Hungarica,* 56 (1): 262–265.

———. 2012 'MOGY: a vessel of ritual in post-socialist Hungary', *Traditiones,* 41: 1: 147–158.

Pusztai, B. (ed.) (1999) *Szent és profán között: A szeged-alsóvárosi búcsú /Between the Sacred and the Profane: The Pilgrimage Feast of Szeged-Alsóváros,* Szeged: Bibliotheca Religionis Popularis Szegediensis 3. Néprajzi Tanszék.

———. (2004) *Religious Tourists. Constructing Authentic Experiences in Late Modern Hungarian Catholicism,* Jyväskylä: University of Jyväskylä.

Schram, F. (1968) 'Búcsújárás Magyarországon' [Pilgrimage in Hungary], *Teológia,* 2: 94–100.

Schön, Dezső. 1997. *Istenkeresők a Kárpátok alatt.* A haszidizmus regénye. [Seekers for God in the shadow of the Carpathians. The story of Hasidism.] Múlt és Jövő Lap- és Könyvkiadó, Budapest.

Schreiber, Georg. 1937. *Die Sakrallandschaft des Abendlandes mit Besonderer Berücksichtigungvon Pyranäen, Rhein und Donau.* Düsseldorf.

Szabó, M. and I. Zombori (eds.) (2010) *Vallásos ponyvanyomtatványok Bálint Sándor hagyatékában/Religöse Kolportagedrucke in Sándor Bálints Nachlass. Devotio Hungarorum 14,* Szeged.

Szamosi, J. (1987) 'Magyar zarándoklatok Máriacellbe' [Hungarian Pilgrimages to Máriazell], *Katolikus Szemle,* 4: 318–338.

Szendrey, Á. (1940) 'Adatok a magyar búcsújárás néprajzához' [Data on the Ethnology of Hungarian Pilgrimage], *Ethnographia,* L: 87–90.

Szilárdfy, Z. (1995) *A magánáhítat szentképei a szerző gyűjteményéből I. 17–18. Század/ Kleine Andachtsbilder aus der Sammlung des Verfasseres I. 17.–18. Jahrhundert.* [Sacred Images of Private Devotions from the Collection of the Author I. 17th–18th century], *Devotio fungarorum 2,* Szeged.

———. (1997) *A magánáhítat szentképei a szerző gyűjteményéből II. 19–20. század/ Kleine Andachtsbilder aus der Sammlung des Verfassers II. 19.–20. Jahrhundert* [Sacred Images of Private Devotions from the Collection of the Author II. 19th–20th century], *Devotio Hungarorum 4,* Szeged.

———. (2003) 'A pálos rend két kegyképe: A Częstochowai és Sasvári Boldogasszony' [Two Votive Images of the Pauline Order: Our Lady of Częstochowa and of Sasvár].

———. (2008) *A magánáhítat szentképei a szerző gyűjteményéből III. Alkalmazott szentképek (16–21. század). Kleine Andachtsbilder aus der Sammlung des Verfassers III. Angewandte Andachtsbilder (16.–21. Jahrhundert)* [Sacred Images

Pilgrimages in Hungary   113

of Private Devotions from the Collection of the Author III. Applied Devotional Pictures, 16th–21st century], *Devotio Hungarorum*, 12, Szeged—Budapest.

Szilárdfy, Z., Tüskés, G. and Knapp, E. (1987) *Barokk kori kisgrafikai ábrázolások magyarországi búcsújáróhelyekről* [Baroque Small Prints from Places of Pilgrimage in Hungary], Budapest: Egyetemi Könyvtár.

Thoemmes, E. (1937) *Die Wallfahrten der Ungarn an den Rhein*, Aachen.

Tóth, J. (2002) 'A barkai Skapuláré Társulat története/History of the Scapular Confraternity in Barka', *Devotio Hungarorum*, 8, Szeged: Néprajzi Tanszék.

Tüskés, G. (1993) *Búcsújárás a barokk kori Magyarországon a mirákulumirodalom tükrében.* [Pilgrimages in Baroque Hungary in the Mirror of the Miracle Literature], Budapest: Akadémiai Kiadó.

——. (2002) *Az egyházi irodalom műfajai.* [The Genres of Church Literature] Irodalomtörténeti füzetek 7, Budapest: Argumentum.

——. (2004) *Populáris grafika a 17–18. században.* [Popular Prints in the 17th–18th Centuries], Budapest: Balassi Kiadó.

——. and E. Knapp (2001) *Népi vallásosság Magyarországon a 17–18. században.* [Vernacular Religion in Hungary in the 17th–18th centuries], Budapest: Osiris.

Vajkai, A. (1942) 'Népi orvoslás dunántúli búcsújáróhelyeken' [Folk Medicine in Places of Pilgrimage in Transdanubia], *Magyarságtudomány*, 1: 116–139.

Vass, E. (2009) *A búcsú és a búcsújárás mint rituális dráma.* [The Pilgrim Feast and Pilgrimage as Ritual Drama], Budapest: Lexica Kiadó.

6 From Religious Folklore Studies to Research of Popular Religiosity
Pilgrimage Studies in German-Speaking Europe[1]

Helmut Eberhart

THE TRADITIONAL APPROACH

In the introduction to their 2012 edited volume *Pilgern gestern und heute* [Pilgrimages Yesterday and Today], Christian Kurrat and Patrick Heiser state that a steadily increasing number of people are going on pilgrimage in German-speaking countries. This development has led to a growing body of research over the last thirty years by folklorists, ethnologists, sociologists, historians and theologians in marked contrast to the period immediately after the Second World War when pilgrimage was largely pushed into the background because the focus was primarily on technological change and 'progress'.

When pilgrimage was investigated, it was usually approached from the perspective of folklore studies. Hence, at the beginning of the 1980s, the Graz church historian Karl Amon, in a private conversation, claimed that pilgrimage should be studied within folk studies rather than church history. Meanwhile, a number of disciplines had begun to study pilgrimage intensively not only in German-speaking countries but also in neighbouring areas (see Gábor Barna's contribution to this volume, the research in Switzerland by Paul Hugger [1999] and the study on similar developments at Ptujska Gora by Tuchschaden [2005]). Research became more and more interdisciplinary and studies were developed at an international comparative level. Pilgrimage also became the subject of public and media discourse.

The growing interest in pilgrimage paralleled changes in the fields of quantitative and qualitative research, more generally. Pilgrimage had been traditionally studied in terms of the history of pilgrimage, cult images, votive offerings, votive pictures and votive tablets. The data collected led to the cultural history of particular pilgrimage centres or a comparative analysis of corresponding objects (see Schmidt 1948b, Kriss, 1953/6, Kriss and Kriss-Heinrich 1955, Gugitz 1955/58, Kretzenbacher 1957a, 1957b, 1960, 1977, Grabner 1972, 2002, Kriss-Rettenbeck 1963, 1972, Beitl 1973, Harvolk 1979, Wiebel-Fanderl 1982). Ethnographic museums played a key role in making this research available to the public, mainly through the display of votive pictures, votive offerings and devotional images. Yet this focus

From Religious Folklore Studies to Research of Popular Religiosity 115

on everyday cultural items and questions about the origin of certain cultural phenomena, such as customs, rituals, pilgrimage centres and costumes, directed attention away from people's behaviour, meanings and beliefs.

Richard Andree's work deeply influenced this focus on cultural items because he was the first to elaborately describe and systematically collect votive materials and votive offerings from an evolutionary perspective towards folklore (Andree 1904). He lived in Germany where he was head of the Geographische Anstalt at the Velhagen and Klasing publishing house. Although he sometimes referred to people's relationship to the saints and pilgrimage shrines, he concentrated on votive offerings as reminders of human destiny and reduced their meaning to abstract sufferings and problems, which could be attributed to specific individuals. Most of these objects were taken out of context, therefore, and did not provide any information about the pilgrims' journeys and the importance of particular shrines.

The attention which early folklore studies paid to votive offerings led to the historical study of votive pictures and national costumes, as portrayed in these votive pictures, in particular (see Geramb 1932/35). In 1901 Frank had already pointed out the value of these votive pictures as sources and bemoaned their loss, blaming the Roman Catholic Church for their destruction. He declared that it was an 'irreplaceable loss for folklore studies, since through votive pictures [we] could learn about old national costumes, customs, local saints and patron saints' (cited from Andree 1904: 184).

At this point it should be pointed out that, quite early on, comprehensive research was undertaken on pilgrimage in German-speaking Europe, which looked beyond these aspects of material culture. However, researchers concentrated on pilgrimage to Jerusalem, which was very popular during the second half of the nineteenth century. The study by the German researcher on the Crusades Reinhold Röhricht (1875) is a fine example of this research despite his work has attracting scant interest within folklore studies.

FROM THE PLACE OF PILGRIMAGE TO THE PILGRIM: THE REVERSAL OF PERSPECTIVE

Hence, when research on pilgrimage began in earnest during the 1980s, the question as to who the pilgrims were was hardly ever asked and researchers were even less interested in the answers! As Karl Kramer observed (1960: 197), Andree's study still served as the model, while pilgrimage research in southern Germany and Austria was still grounded in the analysis of material culture (Brückner 1959: 123). Even those studies which, already at a very early stage, had focussed on those involved in pilgrimage, such as Brückner's research on Walldürn (1958), mainly illuminated a specific pilgrimage rather than look more broadly.

The studies of votive pictures, which dominated research on piety (see Kriss-Rettenbeck 1972), followed what Korff describes as the 'discipline

116 *Helmut Eberhart*

of context' (1986: 50) and were characterised by a stringent awareness of methodology and precise basic research (see also Ponisch 2008: 15). This approach was pursued in spite of the demand by such influential figures as Leopold Schmidt, the former director of the Austrian Museum of Popular Art, to take into account those involved in the pilgrimage cult (1948a: 102). He wanted researchers to look beyond the history of pilgrimage sites and studies on material objects, such as churches and votive offerings, to the wider cultural context. This research would include observing those undertaking pilgrimage, watching their rituals, dealing with the pilgrims' narratives after returning from their pilgrimage, etc. Schmidt also called for the inclusion of urban culture in pilgrimage research (1948a: 103), and with the benefit of hindsight, we can see that his suggestions and his approach to the discipline were amazingly forward looking.

Schmidt was well aware that his advice was future oriented. Even after a paradigm shift in European Ethnology and Folklore Studies around 1970 (see Brückner 1971, Bausinger et al. 1970), the Swiss scholar Iso Baumer got to the heart of the problem, when he stated that:

> nearly all scientific treatises on pilgrimage were at a disadvantage insofar as they were written from the viewpoint of the place of pilgrimage; not taking into consideration that the place itself was nothing more but a pilgrimage destination. However, the beginning and the end of a pilgrimage had their roots in the pilgrim's everyday life. That is why giving a complete account of a pilgrimage meant including the beginning and end in the description. (1977: 44)

RESEARCH ON PILGRIMAGE UNDER THE INFLUENCE OF A PARADIGM SHIFT

During the 1970s research began to focus more and more on both pilgrimage and the pilgrims.[2] This focus was informed by the paradigm shift in the humanities, which encouraged a more critical, less descriptive approach to cultural phenomena. It also marked the first step towards modern pilgrimage studies in the German-speaking world. The following three examples clearly show this change in approach:

1. In 1973 Helge Gerndt published a largely historical work on the *Vierbergelauf* [Four Mountains Run] in the Austrian state of Carinthia—a mediaeval pilgrimage tour, which still survives and takes the pilgrims in seventeen hours over four mountains with four churches on top. He followed the so-called Munich School, which tried to reconstruct the historical course of actions through a detailed and critical examination of sources. This was especially necessary with regard to the

From Religious Folklore Studies to Research of Popular Religiosity 117

Vierbergelauf because, even in the 1970s, this pilgrimage was still interpreted as a Celtic cultural survival. Gerndt discovered that the origin of this pilgrimage could be dated back to the late Middle Ages. He actually took part in this pilgrimage several times and not only produced a historical analysis, which is still considered to be exemplary, but also focussed on the pilgrims and their activities during the pilgrimage.

2. In 1984 the Bavarian national museum organised a major exhibition *Wallfahrt kennt keine Grenzen* [Pilgrimage knows no boundaries] and published a detailed catalogue (Kriss-Rettenbeck and Möhler 1984). It was the first time that the topic was discussed extensively and at an international level, even though Wolfgang Brückner's statement 'that over the past thirty years folklore studies has made abundantly clear that pilgrimage means the pilgrim's path and the pilgrim's experience of group dynamics' (1984: 104) was far too optimistic.

3. Another important study was co-written in 1985 by Martin Scharfe and others. He was lecturing at Tübingen and had already published a study, which originated from an undergraduate project at the Institute of Empirical Cultural Sciences. This study (Scharfe, Schmolze and Schubert 1985) is particularly important because the empirical research was carried out in 1983–1984, at a time when pilgrimages were visibly increasing but had by no means reached today's levels.

Scharfe and his fellow researchers acknowledged the increasing popularity of pilgrimage but objected to interpreting this development as the result of a growing need for spirituality (1985: 231–232). They argued that:

> Mary, the Mother of God, has always intervened in difficult circumstances— in cases of illness and droughts, hail, floods and accidents she has helped to solve school problems and pass driving tests. Why, therefore, should she not help to solve the problems of environmental pollution and of hardships in the Third World, nuclear armament and the military build-up of rockets? Everyone, who thinks like this (and supports this way of thinking), acts carelessly because they do not see the incomparability of the threats, and they do not realize that these are threats which are true for mankind as a whole—and man-made. Pilgrimage only helps to construct a wrong and dangerous continuity. (1985: 233)

In this quote the critical attitude of this group of researchers towards religion is made clear. Their belief that the perpetuation of pilgrimage in its traditional sense might lead to the construction of a dangerous continuity reflected the socio-critical attitudes of the humanities during the 1970s. They critiqued the belief among pilgrims that God's help could remedy any human inabilities regarding political concerns and any human carelessness in environmental concerns—always and worldwide.

118 *Helmut Eberhart*

Although some parts of their study may be considered outdated, its overall quality is undisputed because for the first time a study focussed on the agents themselves and the pilgrimage centre is pushed into the background. It deals exclusively with individuals who embark on this weary journey.

IN THE SEARCH OF NEW APPROACHES:
THE COMPENSATION MODEL

Classical research on pilgrimage had already provided us with an understanding of pilgrims' motives during the Middle Ages and the Early Modern period. The analysis of the various 'books of miracles' and *ex-voto* images revealed that illness, accidents and individual concern generated by wars were among the most common causes for people travelling in large numbers to Roman Catholic places of pilgrimage (see Schreiber 1938, Kramer 1951, Harmening 1966, Eberhart 1979, 1980, Janotta 1986, Schuh 1989). Heim's (1961) analysis of modern 'petition books' in Switzerland was the precursor for the rapid development of similar research in France, Germany, Austria and Hungary (see, for example, Nikitsch 1990, Herberich-Marx 1991, Kromer 1996, Ponisch 2001, Barna 2000, Eberhart and Ponisch 2000, Eberhart 2003, Berger-Künzli 2006). This research has enabled us to understand the diverse reasons for people going on contemporary pilgrimages, bound up with family, relationships, school problems and international peace to name a few. Everyday life has become a key theme in modern pilgrim petitions, and these petitions are not characterised by the same existential gravity as those revealed in older books of miracles (Eberhart and Ponisch 2000). The 'answers' to these petitions do not refer to exceptional events leading Peter Assion (1973) to coin the term 'trivial miracle'.

The resurgence of pilgrimage over the last thirty years has frequently been interpreted in terms of people's attempts to compensate for the collapse of social, temporal and spatial horizons. This process of social and cultural compensation was particularly associated with rapid urbanisation. Hermann Bausinger, for example, saw the trend towards fostering traditional folk culture (folk songs, folk dance, etc.) as evidence that these developments did not emerge from a continuous tradition but represented compensatory attempts at social and cultural renewal (Bausinger 1961: 108).

As long ago as 1983, Peter Assion had recognised the compensatory nature of pilgrimage and the importance of community experience. Yet like those working with Martin Scharfe, he did not explicitly deal with the compensatory theoretical models (Assion 1983). He stated that:

> all those factors mounted up to an experience which drew its appeal from the indifference and the cold business-like nature of 'ordinary' life to which pilgrimage formed a contrasting experience. . . . [It] also involved emotional needs, which could not be satisfied by our

From Religious Folklore Studies to Research of Popular Religiosity 119

achievement-oriented and consumer society nor could society permanently cover those emotional needs by offering alternatives. (1983: 10)

In this context the sociologist Alfred Lorenzer should also be mentioned because he observed a reduction of symbols and rituals and a 'destruction of sensuality' in connection with the Roman Catholic Church after the Second Vatican Council. He dispassionately detected the destruction of a culture that reached far beyond the Church, and he referred to this destruction as exemplary of a general 'societal process of destruction', which had to be examined carefully (Lorenzer 1984: 290). I am inclined to see this process as far more emotionally charged than Lorenzer does in his rather clinical and cautiously realistic approach. By simply commenting on the loss of sensibility and keeping it more or less in perspective, Lorenzer tends to misconceive the important consequences this loss has for people, who are in need of these sensual aspects of religion. This sense of loss was clearly seen in the context of pilgrimage.

I also interpret this need for symbols and rituals as a reaction to the ever faster pace of contemporary life, particularly in urban society; these cultural forms help to compensate for the loss of traditional ways of life. Odo Marquard also spoke of 'an acceleration in the change of reality in the modern and present-day world, which—in the end—requires compensation' (Marquard 1982: 25).

In 1962 the German philosopher Joachim Ritter had already published his thoughts on the obligations of the humanities and concluded that, amongst other things, they had undertaken the duty to compensate for the loss of values and the disorientation of modern societies through the pursuit of historical research (Ritter 1974). In the 1980s his students Odo Marquard and Hermann Lübbe introduced his ideas to the public arena (see Lübbe 1983, Marquard 1986), albeit with scant success. In 1990–1992, the German cultural scientist Martin Scharfe, whom I have already mentioned, introduced this model to our discipline when he explained the rapidly growing number of museums in the 1980s in terms of their compensatory nature (Scharfe 1992). Museums enable us to relive those cultural assets, which we have lost in our day-to-day living. Yet what some refer to as a museumification or musealisation of culture reaches far beyond the museums themselves. Paul Post, for example, notes: 'In part, I would like to interpret the pilgrims' accounts as an unmistakable sign of musealisation of religious (popular) culture' (Post 1994: 93).

The growth of museums, especially in the regions, was paralleled by the massive increase in the number of pilgrimages from the 1980s until around 2000. In my opinion, the current quest for meaning is mainly grounded in the cultural and spiritual shortcomings of our society. Over the past few years an oversupply of museums and shrines has emerged, which has caused even more disorientation. A growing number of spiritual guides, who offer to endow life with meaning, have entered the religious market to entice

120   *Helmut Eberhart*

those interested with a broad range of offers (see Krech 2011 for a recent exploration of the localisation of religion in modern societies). Religion and, in a broader sense, spirituality are used as vehicles for finding one's self.

However, there exists a major difference with regard to museums. Whereas small regional museums, in particular, played a compensatory role in modern society from the beginning of the twentieth century, industrialisation forced pilgrimage to withdraw for a time at least in Austria. The modernisation of society and its associated values seemed to counterbalance the loss of traditional culture. It was only in postindustrial society when this balance was lost and the new quest for post-secular meanings experienced its current boom.

The research, which I have carried out with my students and colleagues since the middle of the 1990s, has again and again confirmed these arguments concerning compensation. Interviews reveal vague longings for community and spirituality as key motives for going on pilgrimage. Yet although I have written about compensation theory several times (Eberhart 1999a, 1999b), it has become clear that this theoretical approach will not sufficiently explain all aspects of pilgrimage. Perhaps the desire for a change of the individual and collective life world plays an increasingly important role ?—we need to look beyond compensatory mechanisms, therefore.

During 1993–1994 I carried out two study projects with students from the Institute of European Ethnology and Cultural Anthropology at Karl Franzens University, Graz, which dealt with two themes—'Piety' and 'Piety: Mariazell as a Place of Pilgrimage'. After years of historically oriented pilgrimage research, I decided to focus on contemporary pilgrimage but still concentrated on the destination, i.e., Mariazell and the pilgrims' motives for going on pilgrimage (see Eberhart and Fell 1996). However, the evidence soon showed that it was imperative to change tack and reinforce research, which approached pilgrimage from the perspective of the particular groups and their places of origin. In the following years, this change of direction has been pursued—at least partially—and has led to interesting results. Yet the study of pilgrimage sites has not become obsolete; rather, approaches long ignored need to be explored. Furthermore, we should focus on the fact that the destinations of the pilgrimages, which emerged during the last twenty or thirty years, frequently do not have the same importance they used to have for their predecessors.

IN THE SEARCH OF NEW APPROACHES: BEYOND THE STUDY OF CONVENTIONAL PILGRIMAGE

In 1983 Wolfgang Brückner, one of the best-known experts on the history of piety in German-speaking Europe, had reproached Assion for ignoring the utopian notion of community, which has been the primary driving force behind a long-standing debate in official theology and ecclesiasticism.

From Religious Folklore Studies to Research of Popular Religiosity 121

The emotional and concrete experiences of today's pilgrimage, in the first instance, can only be interpreted as Christian experiences according to Brückner (1983). He pursued this theme in a 2006 publication, where he attempted an overview of German-speaking pilgrimage research produced during the twentieth century. Despite the range of studies on contemporary pilgrimage, he focussed exclusively on historical research. Furthermore, despite his call for an interdisciplinary and internationally comparative approach, in his introductory note to the report on the conference, which covered 728 pages and was printed in German and English, he still only discussed classical pilgrimage (Brückner 2006).

However, in my opinion, the development of the past twenty years has proved Assion right. In 1970, Gottfried Korff had already criticised the overly restrictive definition of the term 'pilgrimage', although he still did not consider pilgrimage (thus reflecting the debate around 1960) as something beyond religiously bound conceptualisations (Korff 1970: 142–143). Here is not the place for describing further counterexamples, but it would be remiss not to mention my former student Gabriele Ponisch, who, also in 2006, submitted her dissertation on contemporary pilgrimages in the Austrian state of Styria (Ponisch 2006–2008). This dissertation was based on a large project, which was carried out under my guidance between 2001 and 2003 and was financed by the Austrian Research Fund.[3] Ponisch tried for the first time to see pilgrimage in German-speaking Europe in the larger context of esoteric and spiritual movements, thus attempting to come closer to this highly topical phenomenon. She draws on English studies and refers, *inter alia*, to Steven Sutcliffe and Marion Bowman (2000), who also concluded that only recently have researchers acknowledged that current religious and spiritual developments were worthy of research (2008: 68; see also Badone 2014).

This leads us to a fundamental question, which has become more and more pressing over the past years: could pilgrimages—in extreme cases—any longer be religious at all? Iso Baumer, the Swiss researcher on pilgrimage, had already posed this question in 1978 at the beginning of the pilgrimage revival, but he answered in the negative (1978: 24). Today, this question must not only be posed anew and under different conditions, but it must also be expanded. We need to ask which visible symbolic actions are necessary (if they are necessary at all) in order to speak of pilgrimage. Perhaps public rather than academic discourse has already decided what pilgrimage is about.

In order to clarify this suggestion, I will refer to two examples which I have previously discussed (1999a and 1999b) and then look more closely at the public use of the term in different contexts. 'The starting signal for a pilgrimage of variety', wrote an Austrian daily at the beginning of an event held between September 7 and 8, 1996, which took place in Mariazell at the invitation of the Austrian Bishops' Conference *(Kleine Zeitung*, September 3, 1996).[4] The media were not interested in the term 'pilgrimage' but in

122 *Helmut Eberhart*

the fact that the future of the Roman Catholic Church in Austria would be discussed during this event. This 'pilgrimage of diversity' can be seen, therefore, as a metaphor for a pluralist way of thinking within a united Catholic Church. At the same time, the metaphor expresses a pluralist definition of the term 'pilgrimage', which, in this case, includes the fact that the bishops had invited all the faithful to take part in a dialogue about the future of the Austrian Church at the country's most famous place of pilgrimage. Thus, an event that could have taken place anywhere else was built up into a pilgrimage simply by the choice of the venue!

PILGRIMAGE REINTERPRETED

In June 1994 the Austrians had to vote on the entry into the European Union. At that time, Brigitte Ederer was a politician of the Social Democratic Party of Austria and State Secretary for EU matters. She promised to go on a walking pilgrimage from Vienna to Mariazell (following the traditional pilgrim route), if more than 51.5% of those entitled to vote would vote for entry into the European Union; eventually, 66.6% voted for entry (see Prettenthaler-Ziegerhofer 2010). On July 8, 1994, Brigitte Ederer set out for her pilgrimage. But was it really a pilgrimage? The journey was well staged to attract the attention of the media. Newspapers, radio and television stations took an interest in Ederer's 'walk to Mariazell', i.e., in the walk of a politician from Austria's highly secular Social Democratic Party!

Needless to say, she got the appropriate media coverage. A renowned daily ironically stated that all those had been wrong who had thought that it was easier for a camel to go through the eye of a needle than for a Social Democrat politician to go to Mariazell (*Der Standard*, July 9–10, 1994). Another daily simply refused to call this a pilgrimage and wrote about a bet, which Ederer had lost (*Kleine Zeitung*, July 10, 1994; see also Gabriel 1996: 278). Yet the formal framework conditions for a traditional pilgrimage seem to have been in place—namely the promise and making good on this promise by walking to a famous pilgrimage shrine and visiting the church there. If Ederer was criticised for a poor inner attitude or even for doing everything to get the appropriate media coverage, this would mean challenging pilgrimage itself.

I have deliberately chosen examples, which attracted the attention of the media rather than cases from everyday pilgrimages involving large numbers of 'ordinary' people. In my opinion, these high-profile examples clearly indicate a reinterpretation of pilgrimage, which is taking a variety of directions. Moreover, it is not only the Church that is giving the term 'pilgrimage' a new quality. In everyday discourse, we have become familiar with the phrase 'go on pilgrimage' in a secular context. (In German 'pilgern' and 'wallfahren', meaning 'to go on a pilgrimage', form a conceptual pair; the English archaic verb 'to pilgrim' and 'pilgern' have the same stem.) One just has to think of

From Religious Folklore Studies to Research of Popular Religiosity 123

the rituals in connection with the visits to Elvis Presley's grave in Memphis, U.S.,[5] or of Lady Diana's death and her grave in Althorp, Great Britain (see Bowman 2001, Daxelmüller 2003). Even a newspaper that belongs to the Roman Catholic Church used the headline: 'Althorp—Diana's grave has become a place of pilgrimage' (*Kleine Zeitung*, July 5, 1998). In an illuminating study, the German cultural scientist Christoph Daxelmüller examined the sacralisation of popular stars. Using the example of Lady Diana, he drew the conclusion that 'her apotheosis occurred at a time, when the saints the Church sanctioned as idols for moulding one's life lost their importance and took a back seat. The secular Holy Diana was a transparent and, therefore, an effective saint' (Daxelmüller 2003: 213).

It is not even necessary to refer to such an obvious example—our mundane daily routine will do. People come flocking (in German we use 'pilgern' instead of 'come') to a place, where there could be a highly popular venue, which is 'in' and the place mutates into a 'place of pilgrimage'. This sacralisation of the secular world escalates when religiously coined terms such as 'temple' and 'paradise' become deliberately constructed metaphors, such as consumption temple, or shopping paradise, and thousands of people undertake 'pilgrimage' to these venues.

The examples are numerous but I want to return Iso Baumer's question: whether pilgrimages—in extreme cases—may no longer be religious. He answered this question with an unequivocal 'no'. However, this answer requires further exploration. Over the past thirty years in German-speaking Europe the relationship between the religious and the secular in the context of pilgrimage has become complex. Equally distinct and also internationally recognised explorations of this relationship were made by John Eade and Michael Sallnow more than twenty years ago in their book *Contesting the Sacred* (1991). Their book was one of many, which showed the advantages of moving away from the exclusively ritual theoretical approach advocated by the Turners (1978). German research on pilgrimage needs to overcome its preoccupation with pilgrimage as an exclusively religious phenomenon (see Badone 2014). It is equally necessary to scrutinise the term 'pilgrimage' itself and redefine it.

The contributors to *Contesting the Sacred* also focussed on pilgrimage sites, but, in contrast to the Turnerian approach, going on a pilgrimage was seen more comprehensively and, therefore, depicted more realistically. When the book was advertised, one sentence put it in a nutshell: 'One person's holy site is another person's profit centre—and this mingling of the sacred and the profane is what makes the pilgrimage and their destination complex sites of exchange and conflict' (www.amazon.ca/Con testing-Sacred-ANTHROPOLOGY-CHRISTIAN-PILGRIMAGE/dp/0252069404).

Yet as others have argued, we have to go one step further. In my work I have sought to bring out the importance of the journey to a place of pilgrimage (see Harris 1937, Gerndt 1973, Scharfe, Schmolze and Schubert

124 *Helmut Eberhart*

1985, Dubisch 1995) and the changed semantic meaning of pilgrimage more clearly. In this respect, the idea of *communitas* as conveyed by Turner becomes important, especially with regard to walking pilgrimages. However, there appears to be a significant formal difference between traditional and new pilgrimages—at least in Austria. In the Austrian federal state of Styria, there are only a few pilgrimages, which invoke a centuries-old tradition—less than 10% of all activities (Eberhart 2007: 14). They are easily recognisable because in the procession the pilgrims follow a strict order and say the rosary while following a religious banner. This is not the case with modern pilgrimages, which developed from around 1980. On their way to the place of pilgrimage they frequently cannot be distinguished from ordinary hiking groups. Even if we take into consideration the differences between traditional groups of pilgrims and these groups, they share one key feature—they follow, at least temporarily, the idea of community. Hans Georg Soeffner's discussion of temporary groupings is particularly relevant here because he stated that individuals who temporarily meet for common action and experience may give this short-lived community the illusion of a relatively stable community (Soeffner 1992: 115).

SOME REMARKS ON RESEARCH ON PILGRIMAGE
BEYOND CATHOLIC PRACTICES OF PIETY

It is necessary to refer to another phenomenon, which has been observed for quite some time: pilgrimage in Protestantism. Luther condemned pilgrimage, and in his famous speech *An den Christlichen Adel deutscher Nation* [To Christian nobility of the German nation], which he delivered in 1520, he declared that in order to eradicate the seductive faith of simple-minded Christians, all pilgrimages ought to be banned. Pilgrimages know no commandments, no obedience, but only a vast number of causes for sin and for scorning God's commandments.[6]

Because of Luther's resounding rejection of pilgrimages, Protestant theologians face difficulties when arguing in favour of pilgrimage.[7] Nevertheless, the Protestant Church is strongly promoting pilgrimage and even runs pilgrim offices.[8] In order to be able to promote pilgrimage, Protestant theologians argue that Luther opposed pilgrimages only to Rome. Bernd Lohse supports this argument when quoting Luther's critique of pilgrimages to Rome: 'All pilgrimages to Rome should be stopped. . . . I do not want to say that pilgrimages are bad but at this very time it causes harm, because instead of giving a good example, it seems to be more a vain annoyance' (2012: 28).

Lohse's remarks shows that in Protestant northern Europe, the pilgrimage movement is extremely active. If we consider the background to these developments and activities, we come to the central motivation of current pilgrimages. A Protestant minister puts this motivation in a nutshell when he describes on a website titled 'Unchristian? No! Protestant!' his encounter

From Religious Folklore Studies to Research of Popular Religiosity   125

with a monk. The minister was driving to Santiago de Compostela, and on his way there he stopped in front of a monastery:

> When the monk saw the car, he considered this way of getting to Santiago unchristian. The minister, however, thought that this could be just as Protestant a feature as travelling the pilgrimage route the other way round. It is not the destination, in this case a presumed tomb of an apostle, which is important, but the freedom to discover one's own way off the beaten track in order to find the way to oneself.[9]

The term 'quest for the self' enables us to explain many of the current reasons for going on pilgrimage. It also points to the ways in which pilgrimage extends far beyond religious beliefs and people's increasing involvement in pilgrimage. This does not only apply to Christian churches, as was already shown in the exhibition *Unterwegs für das Seelenheil. Pilgern gestern und heute* [On the way for the salvation of one's soul: pilgrimage tours yesterday and today], which also dealt with the phenomenon of pilgrimage in Buddhism, Hinduism, Islam and Judaism.[10] In this context Europe-wide (rather worldwide) interreligious research projects to approach the phenomenon of pilgrimage are well overdue. As has become increasingly evident and as other contributors to this volume show, research on pilgrimage can no longer be ascribed to one discipline only—it requires interdisciplinary and international comparison too.

This seems to be even more important as it is becoming obvious that German-speaking sociology is already one step ahead of my discipline (in pilgrimage research) and has been paying more significant attention to English-speaking research (see Schützeichel 2012). German-speaking folklore studies/European ethnology has adhered to the topic of pilgrimage as a Roman Catholic tradition far too long. Not even the references to important research of the past thirty years can change this situation. In the meantime, however, there are clear signals that changes have taken place in the general understanding of this discipline. The extent to which European ethnology in German-speaking countries has met these new trends is indicated by the commission *Religiosität und Spiritualität* [Religiosity and Spirituality], which was founded in 2011 within the framework of the *Deutsche Gesellschaft für Volkskunde* [German Folklore Society]. The Society is eager to promote cooperation with other disciplines which also undertake research on piety and spirituality (see www.d-g-v.org/kommissionen/religiositaet-und-spiritualitaet). A conference scheduled for September 2014—*Reine Glaubenssache?* [Pure Matter of Faith?] will ask for new data in order to understand religious and spiritual phenomena more deeply in the context of secularisation. At this conference, lectures on 'Going on Pilgrimage' will be delivered by Lidija Vindis-Rösler and Barbara Sieferle in order to draw attention to pilgrimage beyond religious practices.

126   *Helmut Eberhart*

This raises the crucial relationship between pilgrimage and tourism (see, for example, Vindis-Rösler[11]). Tourism operators have discovered pilgrims as clients and have been working intensively on the question of how tourism could derive more benefit from this target group (e.g., Bliem 2012, Hofauer 2012). German-speaking research on pilgrimage has been dealing with this phenomenon for years (see Schwarz-Herder 2000, Leitner 2004, Stausberg 2010, Wunderlin 2013). At this point, it is not possible for me to go into detail; however, I want to point out that in the meantime the connection between pilgrimage and tourism has attracted the attention of the highest political bodies. In September 2014, the UNWTO (United Nations World Tourism Organisation) organised the 'First International Congress on Tourism and Pilgrimages' in Santiago de Compostela (see http://ethics. unwto.org/event/1st-unwto-international-congress-tourism-pilgrimages). This event clearly shows that an internationally comparative and interdisciplinary research on pilgrimage is becoming increasingly necessary. The German-speaking research on pilgrimage will certainly be able to make a major contribution to this topic.

CONCLUSION

In this chapter I have sought to outline the major developments within German-speaking research on pilgrimage. This might be seen as an ambitious endeavour given the limited number of pages. Of course, when looking more closely at German, Swiss and Austrian research, differences exist. However, I contend that research in these countries has basically been developing more or less in parallel.

The European ethnology and folklore studies tradition has long dominated this research, and it has been largely self-contained until recently. Early studies focussed on material artefacts, such as votive offerings, statues and records, and what went on at the pilgrimage destination. From the 1970s, however, attention began to be paid to the pilgrims' journeys and what motivated them to go on pilgrimage. This reflected a more general paradigm shift within German-speaking humanities and social sciences towards a phenomenological approach and the study of meaning. This approach sought to explain why, rather than dying away in the face of secular modernity, pilgrimage was flourishing. The number of local and regional museums was expanding too, strengthening the drive towards the preservation of cultural heritage including pilgrimage artefacts.

Explanations were provided through recourse to compensation theory—people were trying to compensate for the collapse of social, temporal and spatial horizons encouraged by urbanisation, in particular, through the creation of community, however temporary and mobile. Yet research by myself and others indicated that a wider focus needed to be developed. Research from the perspective of the particular groups and their places of

From Religious Folklore Studies to Research of Popular Religiosity   127

origin needed to be reinforced. Furthermore, the new pilgrimages, which have emerged over the last twenty or thirty years, frequently lack the same importance they had for their predecessors.

This research concentrated on Catholic pilgrimage but studies has now moved away from this narrow focus. In terms of religious pilgrimage Protestant hostility towards pilgrimage has weakened while global migration has also encouraged the emergence of non-Christian cults and shrines. Pilgrimage research has also moved far beyond the confines of religion. Hence, the chapter has discussed two cases where pilgrimage appeared to be defined in broader terms—the meeting convened by Austrian bishops at Mariazell and the walk by a prominent member of Austria's highly secular Social Democratic Party from Vienna to Mariazell along the traditional pilgrimage route. Pilgrimage was a term which could be applied to a variety of nonreligious activities such as visits to places associated with popular culture icons. What linked these activities to more traditional religious travels was both a quest for community and a search for an authentic self.

The growing diversity of pilgrimage evident elsewhere in Europe—the routes converging on Santiago de Compostela are a paradigmatic and well-studied example—requires a broad interdisciplinary and international approach. German-speaking sociologists are showing the way here through an engagement with Anglophone scholarship and debates, and some pilgrimage researchers are following suit, especially because pilgrimage and tourism have become intimately entwined at national and international levels.

One concluding remark: it is regrettable that research on current pilgrimage has not gained a wider profile within German-speaking European ethnology; sociologists show a keener interest than those working in our discipline. This is the more regrettable as—on an international level—not only pilgrimage itself but also research on pilgrimage has gained an enormous momentum. This extensive lack of relevant analyses explains why I have decided in this chapter to foreground my own findings as well as research carried out by my students.

NOTES

1. I will be drawing on papers that I published in the 1990s and after 2000; see Eberhart 1999a and 2007. It might be an ambitious endeavour to deal with German-speaking research on pilgrimage within a limited number of pages. Of course, when looking more closely at German, Swiss and Austrian research, differences exist, but research in these countries has basically been developing more or less in parallel. Hence, we can speak of a research within the German-speaking folklore tradition without having to deal with further differentiation.
2. Two fundamental studies belong to the most interesting exceptions: Assion 1982/83 and Brückner 1983. In both of these works the authors thematise the already evident revival of pilgrimage from different perspectives. Meanwhile,

128 *Helmut Eberhart*

in my opinion, Gottfried Korff's study—an early example for modern research on piety—which was influenced by the paradigm shift (and the paradigm shift in terms of our question), *also* can be considered a classic (Korff 1970: chapter 'Wallfahrt'/Pilgrimage).

3. The title of the project was 'Pilgrimage in Postmodernism'. It lasted between 2001 and 2003 and was funded by the Austrian Research Fund.
4. The following reflections on the term 'pilgrimage' (Mariazell has served as an example) are based on Eberhart (1999a, 1999b).
5. Ten years ago the sacralisation of Elvis Presley reached a new dimension, when his biography, written in the language of the Gospel of Matthew, was published (see Pollanz and Markart 2004).
6. The original text of 1520 is: *Solch falsch vorfurischen glauben der einfeltigen Christen außzurotten . . . solten alle wallefart nydergelegt werden, den es ist kein guttis nit drynnenn, kein gepot, kein gehorsam, sondern unzehlich ursach der sunden, unnd gottis gebot zur vorachtung* (Luther 1877: 42).
7. For the topicality of the debate, see also www.pfarrerblatt.de/text_378.htm; see also: www.eurovia.tv/home/content/view/162/205/lang,de/.
8. See the office in Hamburg, run by pilgrim priest Bernd Lohse, at www.jacobus.de/neu/deutsch/index_4_9.html.
9. See www.sonntagsblatt-bayern.de/news/aktuell/2012_04_11_02.htm.
10. This exhibition was conceptualised as a travelling exhibition, which started in the German Museum in Munich in 2010 (see the small catalogue, Hlatky, Gundler and Breitkopf 2010). Within the framework of this exhibition an additional symposium organised by the Protestant Church took place (2010 in Tutzing, Bavaria). This symposium dealt with pilgrimages as an opportunity for an interreligious dialogue and also provided a forum for speakers from different religious bodies.
11. The papers will focus the following topics: Barbara Sieferle: Zu Fuß auf dem Weg nach ('On foot to Mariazell: ethnographic observations on the physical practicew of pilgrimage'), Maria-Zell: Ethnografische Beobachtungen zur körperlichen Praxis des Pilgerns, and Lidija Vindis-Rösler: Mit Spiritualität im Rucksack. Pilgerwege als touristische Herausforderung im postkommunistischen Slowenien ('With spirituality in the backpack: the pilgrim's path as a touristic challenge in post-Communist Slovenia').

REFERENCES

Andree, R. (1904) *Votive und Weihegaben des katholischen Volkes in Süddeutschland: Ein Beitrag zur Volkskunde*, Braunschweig: F. Viehweg und Sohn.
Assion, P. (1973) 'Ein Kult entsteht. Zur Verehrung der Ulrika Nisch von Hegne am Bodensee', *Forschungen und Berichte zur Volkskunde in Baden-Württemberg, 1971–1973*: 43–63.
———. (1982/83) 'Der soziale Gehalt aktueller Frömmigkeitsformen', *Hessische Blätter für Volks-und Kulturforschung*, 14–15: 5–17.
Badone, E. (2014) 'Conventional and unconventional pilgrimages: conceptualizing sacred travel in the twenty first century', in A. Pazos (ed.) *Redefining Pilgrimage: New Perspectives and Contemporary Perspectives*, Farnham, UK, and Burlington, VT: Ashgate.
Barna, G. (2000) 'Gästebücher an Wallfahrtsorten, in Krankenhäusern und Hotels: Neue schriftliche Formen und Quellen ritualisierter Verhaltensweisen', in K. Kuti and B. Rásky (eds.) *Konvergenzen und Divergenzen: Gegenwärtige*

From Religious Folklore Studies to Research of Popular Religiosity 129

volkskundliche Forschungsansätze in Österreich und Ungarn, Budapest: Außenstelle Budapest des österreichischen Ost-und Südosteuropa-Instituts.

Baumer, I. (1977) *Wallfahrt als Handlungsspiel: Ein Beitrag zum Verständnis religiösen Handelns,* Europäische Hochschulschriften 14/12, Bern and Frankfurt am Main: H. Lang.

——. (1978) 'Gestalt und Sinn der Wallfahrt heute', in I. Baumer and W. Heim (eds.) *Wallfahrt heute,* Freiburg: Kanisius Verlag.

Bausinger, H. (1961) *Volkskultur in der technischen Welt,* Frankfurt am Main and New York: Campus Verlag.

——. et al. (1970) *Abschied vom Volksleben: Untersuchungen des Ludwig-Uhland-Instituts der Universität Tübingen* Vol. 7, Tübingen: Tübinger Vereinigung für Volkskunde.

Beitl, K. (1973) *Votivbilder: Zeugnisse einer alten Volkskunst,* Salzburg: Residenz Verlag.

Berger-Künzli, D. (2006) 'Lieber Gott, bitte hilf mir. Ich sterbe sonst weg.' *Analyse spätmoderner Religiosität am Beispiel von frei formulierten Gebetsanliegen und Fürbitten,* Bern: Peter Lang.

Bliem, G. (2012) 'Pilgrimage: View on an extraordinary, exciting market', in Diözese Graz-Seckau (ed.) *Pilgrimage in Europe: Cross-Border Routes Towards a Better Understanding and Faithful Cooperation.* Conference proceedings, Graz: Diözese Graz-Seckau.

Bowman, M. (2001) 'The people's princess: vernacular religion and politics in the mourning for Diana', in G. Barna (ed.) *Politics and Folk Religion.* Papers on the 3rd Symposium of SIEF Commission of Folk Religion in Szeged 1999, Budapest: Akademiai Kiado.

Brückner, W. (1958) *Die Verehrung des Heiligen Blutes in Walldürn: Volkskundlich-soziologische Untersuchungen zum Strukturwandel barocken Wallfahrtens,* Veröffentlichungen des Geschichts-und Kunstvereins 3, Aschaffenburg: Pattloch.

——. (1959) 'Wallfahrtsforschung im deutschen Sprachgebiet seit 1945', *Zeitschrift für Volkskunde,* 55: 115–129.

——. (1971) (ed.) *Falkensteiner Protokolle,* Frankfurt am Main: Selbstverlag.

——. (1983) 'Gemeinschaft—Utopie—Communio: Vom Sinn und Unsinn "sozialer" Interpretation gegenwärtiger Frömmigkeitsformen und ihrer empirischen Erfassbarkeit', *Bayerische Blätter für Volkskunde,* 10: 181–201.

——. (1984) 'Fußwallfahrt heute. Frömmigkeit im sozialen Wandel der letzten hundert Jahre', in G. Möhler and L. Kriss-Rettenbeck (eds.), *Wallfahrt kennt keine Grenzen: Themen zu einer Ausstellung des Bayerischen Nationalmuseum,* München: Schnell & Steiner.

——. (2006) 'Mentalitätsgeschichtliche Probleme moderner Wallfahrtsforschung: Eine diskursanalytische Besinnung', in D. Dolezal and H. Kühne (eds.) *Wallfahrten in der europäischen Kultur: Pilgrimage in European Culture,* Europäische Wallfahrtsstudien 1, Frankfurt am Main: Peter Lang.

Daxelmüller, C. (2003) 'Maria und Lady Di—Tradition und säkulare Religiosität', in W. Brunner (ed.) *Mariazell und Ungarn: 650 Jahre religiöse Gemeinsamkeit,* Veröffentlichungen des steiermärkischen Landesarchivs 30, Graz-Esztergom: Steiermärkisches Landesarchiv.

Dubisch, J. (1995) *In a Different Place: Pilgrimage, Gender, and Politics at a Greek Island Shrine,* Princeton: Princeton University Press.

Eade, J. and Sallnow, M. (1991) (eds.) *Contesting the Sacred: The Anthropology of Christian Pilgrimage,* London and New York: Routledge.

Eberhart, H. (1979) 'Der Mirakelzyklus in der Wallfahrtskirche Maria Freienstein', *Der Leobener Strauß,* 7: 61–102.

——. (1980) 'Das Mirakelverzeichnis von Maria Freienstein', *Der Leobener Strauß,* 8: 119–158.

130   Helmut Eberhart

———. (1999a) 'Aspects of and thoughts about pilgrimage today on the example of Mariazell', in A. Gustavsson and M. Santa Montez (eds.) *Folk Religion: Continuity and Change*. Papers Given at the Symposium of the Commission of Folk Religion in Portugal, September, Instituto de Sociologia e Etnologia das Religiões, Universidade Nova de Lisboa, Lisboa: Universidade Nova de Lisboa.

———. (1999b) 'Zwischen Vielfalt und Beliebigkeit: Zum Wandel des kulturellen Systems Wallfahrt in der postindustriellen Gesellschaft', in F. Grieshofer and M. Schindler (eds.) *Netzwerk Volkskunde: Ideen und Wege*, Festgabe für Klaus Beitl zum siebzigsten Geburtstag, Wien: Sonderschriften des Vereins für Volkskunde.

———. (2003) 'Von Lassing bis Kosovo: Aktuelle Ereignisse in Anliegenbüchern', in G. Barna (ed.) *Ritualisierung, Zeit, Kommunikation*, Bibliotheca Religionis Popularis Szegediensis 11, Budapest: Akadémiai Kiadó.

———. (2007) 'Überall ist Wallfahrt: Ein kulturwissenschaftlicher Blick auf ein wiederentdecktes Phänomen', *Heiliger Dienst*, 61: 7–25.

———. and Fell, H. (1996) (eds.) *Schatz und Schicksal*, Katalog zur Steirischen Landesausstellung in Mariazell, Graz: Kulturreferat.

———. and Ponisch, G. (2000) 'Hallo lieber Gott! Aspekte zu schriftlichen Devotionsformen in der Gegenwart', in K. Kuti and B. Rásky (eds.) *Konvergenzen und Divergenzen: Gegenwärtige volkskundliche Forschungsansätze in Österreich und Ungarn*, Budapest: Außenstelle Budapest des österreichischen Ost-und Südosteuropa-Instituts.

Gabriel, R. (1996) 'Viele Wege führen nach Mariazell', in H. Eberhart and H. Fell (eds.) *Schatz und Schicksal—Mariazell*, Beiträge zur Steirischen Landesausstellung, Graz: Kulturreferat.

Geramb, V. and Mautner, K. (1932–1935) *Steirisches Trachtenbuch* Vols. 1–2, Graz: Leuschner & Lubensky.

Gerndt, H. (1973) *Vierbergelauf: Gegenwart und Geschichte eines Kärntner Brauches*, Klagenfurt: Geschichtsverein für Kärnten.

Grabner, E. (1972) *Die Bilderwand zu Rattersdorf: Zu einem ikonographischen Programm einer burgenländischen Wallfahrt*, Eisenstadt: Burgenländisches Landesmuseum.

———. (2002) *Mater Gratiarum: Marianische Kultbilder in der Volksfrömmigkeit des Ostalpenraumes*, Vienna, Cologne and Weimar: Böhlau.

Gugitz, G. (1955–1958) *Österreichs Gnadenstätten in Kult und Brauch: Ein topographisches Handbuch zur religiösen Volkskunde in fünf Bänden* Vols. 1–5, Vienna: Brüder Hollinek.

Harmening, D. (1966) 'Fränkische Mirakelbücher', *Würzburger Diözesangeschichtsblätter*, 28: 25–240.

Harris, T. (1937) *The Unholy Pilgrimage*, New York: Round Table Press.

Harvolk, H. (1979) *Votivtafeln: Bildzeugnisse von Hilfsbedüftigkeit und Gottesvertrauen*, Munich: Callwey.

Heim, W. (1961) *Briefe zum Himmel: Die Grabbriefe an Mutter M. Theresia Scherer in Ingenbohl: Ein Beitrag zur religiösen Volkskunde der Gegenwart*, Schriften der Schweizerischen Gesellschaft für Volkskunde Vol. 40, Basel: Krebs.

Herberich-Marx, G. (1991) *Evolution d'une sensibilité religieuse: Témoignages scripturaires et iconographiques de pèlerinages alsaciens*, Strasbourg: PU Strasbourg.

Hladky, S., Gundler, B. and Breitkopf, B. (2010) *Unterwegs für's Seelenheil: Pilgerreisen gestern und heute*, Kurzführer durch die Ausstellung im Verkehrszentrum des Deutschen Museums, München: Deutsches Museum.

Hofauer, H. (2012) 'Altötting—touristic aspects of pilgrimage', in Diözese Graz-Seckau (ed.) *Pilgrimage in Europe: Cross-Border Routes Towards a Better Understanding and Faithful Cooperation*. Conference proceedings, Graz: Diözese Graz-Seckau.

From Religious Folklore Studies to Research of Popular Religiosity 131

Hugger, P. (1999) 'Pilgerschaft und Wallfahrt', in E. Halter and D. Wunderlin (eds.) *Volksfrömmigkeit in der Schweiz*, Zürich: Offizin Verlag.

Janotta, C. (1986) '(Die) Mirakelbücher', in J. Neuhardt (ed.) *Salzburgs Wallfahrten in Kult und Brauch*: *Katalog zur IX. Sonderschau des Dommuseums zu Salzburg*, Salzburg: Dommuseum zu Salzburg.

Korff, G. (1970) *'Heiligenverehrung in der Gegenwart'*, Untersuchungen des Ludwig-Uhland-Instituts der Universität Tübingen 29, Tübingen: Tübinger Vereinigung für Volkskunde.

———. (1986) 'Volkskundliche Frömmigkeits-und Symbolforschung nach 1945', in W. Brückner, G. Korff and M. Scharfe (eds.) *Volksfrömmigkeitsforschung*, Ethnologia Bavarica 13, Würzburg and München: Bayerische Blätter für Volkskunde.

Kramer, K. S. (1951) 'Die Mirakelbücher der Wallfahrt Grafrath', in T. Gebhart and H. Moser (eds.) *Bayrisches Jahrbuch für Volkskunde,* Regensburg: Josef Habbel.

———. (1960) 'Typologie und Entwicklungsbedingungen nachmittelalterlicher Nahwallfahrten', *Rheinisches Jahrbuch für Volkskunde*, 11: 195–211.

Krech, V. (2011) *Wo bleibt Religion? Zur Ambivalenz des Religiösen in der modernen Gesellschaft,* Bielefeld: Transcript.

Kretzenbacher, L. (1957a) 'Volkserinnerungen an die Reichs-Heiligtümer: Zum mittelalterlichen Wallfahrtstermin des "Dreinagelfreitags" im bambergischen Kärnten', *Carinthia*, 1/147: 803–828.

———. (1957b) 'Heimkehr von der Pilgerfahrt: Ein mittelalterlicher Legendenroman im steirisch-kärntischen Volksmund der Gegenwart', *Fabula: Zeitschrift für Erzählforschung*, 1: 214–227.

———. (1960) 'Pilgerfahrt nach Maria Luschari: Eine deutsch-slawische Legende aus der alten Untersteiermark', *Südostdeutsches Archiv*, 3: 87–100.

———. (1977) 'Kontrafakturen zur Jakobslegende in Slowenien', *Anzeiger für Slavische Philologie*, 9: 197–207.

Kriss-Rettenbeck, L. (1963) *Bilder und Zeichen religiösen Volksglaubens,* München: Callwey.

———. (1972) *Ex Voto: Zeichen, Bild und Abbild im christlichen Votivbrauchtum,* Zürich: Atlantis-Verlag.

———. and Möhler, G. (1984) (eds.) *Wallfahrt kennt keine Grenzen,* Themen zu einer Ausstellung des Bayerischen Nationalmuseums und des Adalbert Stifter Vereins, München and Zürich: Schnell & Steiner.

Kriss, R. (1953–1956) *Die Volkskunde der altbayrischen Gnadenstätten* Vols. 1–3, München and Passing: Filser.

———. and Kriss-Heinrich, H. (1955) *Peregrinatio neohellenika: Wallfahrtswanderungen im heutigen Griechenland und in Unteritalien,* Wien: Österreichisches Museum für Volkskunde.

Kromer, H. (1996) *Adressat Gott: Das Anliegenbuch von St. Martin in Tauberbischofsheim: eine Fallstudie zur schriftlichen Devotion in der Gegenwart,* Tübingen: Tübinger Vereinigung für Volkskunde.

Kurrat, C. and Heiser, P. (2012) 'Pilgern gestern und heute: Eine Einleitung', in P. Heiser and C. Kurrat (eds.) *Pilgern gestern und heute: Soziologische Beiträge zur religiösen Praxis auf dem Jakobsweg,* Berlin: Lit Verlag.

Leitner, M. (2004) *Wallfahrt und Tourismus zu Beginn des 21. Jahrhunderts am Beispiel von Mariazell*. Unpublished thesis, Graz.

Lohse, B. (2012) 'Meaning of pilgrim trails for the understanding between people and religions: using the case of northern Germany and Scandinavia', in Diözese Graz-Seckau (ed.) *Pilgrimage in Europe: Cross-Border Routes Towards a Better Understanding and Faithful Cooperation*. Conference proceedings, Graz.

Lorenzer, A. (1984) *Das Konzil der Buchhalter: Die Zerstörung der Sinnlichkeit: Eine Religionskritik,* Frankfurt am Main: Fischer.

132   Helmut Eberhart

Lübbe, H. (1983) *Zeit-Verhältnisse: Zur Kulturphilosophie des Fortschritts,* Herkunft und Zukunft 1, Graz: Styria.

Luther, M. (1877) *An den christlichen Adel deutscher Nation von des christlichen Standes Besserung,* Neudrucke deutscher Litteraturwerke des XVI und XVII Jahrhunderts 4, Halle a. S.: Max Niemeyer.

Marquard, O. (1982) *Krise der Erwartung—Stunde der Erfahrung: Zur ästhetischen Kompensation des modernen Erfahrungsverlustes,* Konstanzer Universitätsreden 139, Konstanz: Universitätsverlag Konstanz.

———. (1986) 'Über die Unvermeidlichkeit der Geisteswissenschaften', in O. Marquard (ed.) *Apologie des Zufälligen: Philosophische Studien,* Stuttgart: Reclam.

Nikitsch, H. (1990) 'Schreiben und Glauben. Anliegenbücher als Beispiel moderner Volksreligiosität', in H. Eberhart, E. Hörandner and B. Pöttler (eds.) *Volksfrömmigkeit. Referate der Österreichischen Volkskundetagung 1989 in Graz,* Buchreihe der Österreichischen Zeitschrift für Volkskunde, Neue Serie 8, Wien: Selbstverlag des Vereins für Volkskunde.

Pollanz, W. and Markart, T. (2004) *Das Buch Elvis: Aus den apokryphen Schriften,* Wies: Edition Kürbis.

Ponisch, G. (2001) *'Danke! Thank you! Merci!': Anliegenbücher als Möglichkeit zeitgenössischer schriftlicher Devotion am Beispiel Mariatrost bei Graz,* Grazer Beitrage zur Europäischen Ethnologie Vol. 9, Frankfurt am Main: Verlag Peter Lang.

———. (2008) *'daß wenigstens dies keine Welt von Kalten ist . . .': Wallfahrtsboom und das neue Interesse an Spiritualität und Religiosität,* Europäische Ethnologie 7, Münster: Lit Verlag.

Post, P. (1994) 'The modern pilgrim: A study of contemporary pilgrims' accounts', *Ethnologoa Europaea,* 24: 85–100.

Prettenthaler-Ziegerhofer, A. (2010) 'Brückenbauer Europas: Die österreichischen Bischöfe und der europäische Integrationsprozess', in H. Duchhardt and M. Morawiec (eds.) *Die europäische Integration und die Kirchen: Akteure und Rezipienten,* Veröffentlichungen des Instituts für Europäische Geschichte Mainz, Abteilung für Abendländische Religionsgeschichte und Abteilung für Universalgeschichte 85, Göttingen: Vandenhoeck & Ruprecht.

Ritter, J. (1974) 'Die Aufgaben der Geisteswissenschaften in der modernen Gesellschaft', in J. Ritter, *Subjektivität. Sechs Aufsätze,* Frankfurt am Main: Suhrkamp.

Röhricht, R. (1875) *Deutsche Pilgerreisen nach dem Heiligen Lande,* Gotha: Wagner'sche Universitätsbuchhandlung.

Scharfe M., Schmolze, M. and Schubert, G. (1985) (eds.) *Wallfahrt—Tradition und Mode: Empirische Untersuchungen zur Aktualität von Volksfrömmigkeit,* Untersuchungen des Ludwig-Uhland-Instituts der Universität Tübingen 65, Tübingen: Tübinger Vereinigung für Volkskunde.

———. (1992) 'Aufhellung und Eintrübung: Zu einem Paradigmen-und Funktionswandel im Museum 1970–1990', in S. Abel (ed.) *Rekonstruktion von Wirklichkeit im Museum,* Tagungsbeiträge der Arbeitsgruppe Kulturhistorische Museen in der Deutschen Gesellschaft für Volkskunde, Mitteilungen aus dem Roemer-Museum Hildesheim N.F. 3, Hildesheim: Deutsche Gesellschaft für Volkskunde.

Schmidt, L. (1948a) 'Volkskunde als Geisteswissenschaft', in L. Schmidt (ed.) *Handbuch der Geisteswissenschaften* Vol. 2, Wien: Bellaria-Verlag.

———. (1948b) *Die Bedeutung der Wallfahrt Maria Einsiedl auf dem Kalvarienberg bei Eisenstadt in den ersten Jahren ihres Bestandes,* Horn und Wien: Berger.

Schreiber, G. (1938) *Deutsche Mirakelbücher. Zur Quellenkunde und Sinngebung,* Forschungen zur Volkskunde 31/32, Düsseldorf: L. Schwan.

From Religious Folklore Studies to Research of Popular Religiosity   133

Schuh, B. (1989) 'Von vilen und mancherlay setlzamen Wunderzaichen': Die Analyse von Mirakelbüchern und Wallfahrtsquellen, Halbgraue Reihe zur historischen Fachinformatik, Serie A: Historische Quellenkunden 4, Göttingen: Max-Planck-Institut für Geschichte.

Schützeichel, R. (2012) 'Über das Pilgern: Soziologische Analysen einer Handlungskonfiguration', in P. Heiser and C. Kurat (eds.) Pilgern gestern und heute: Soziologische Beiträge zur religiösen Praxis auf dem Jakobsweg, Berlin: LIT Verlag.

Schwarz-Herder, K. (2000) 'Wallfahrt und Tourismus am Beginn des 21. Jahrhunderts', in H. Dikowitsch et al. (eds.) Die Via Sacra, Denkmalpflege in Niederösterreich 23, St. Pölten: Amt der niederösterreichischen Landesregierung.

Soeffner, H. G. (1992) Die Ordnung der Rituale, Die Auslegung des Alltags Vol. 2, Frankfurt am Main: Suhrkamp.

Stausberg, M. (2010) Religion im modernen Tourismus, Berlin: Verlag der Weltreligionen.

Sutcliffe, S. and Bowman, M. (2000) Beyond New Age: Exploring Alternative Spirituality, Edinburgh: Edinburgh University Press.

Tuchschaden, K. (2005) Die Wallfahrtsstätte Ptujska Gora. Unpublished thesis, Karl-Franzens-Universität Graz.

Turner, V. and Turner, E. (1978) Image and Pilgrimage in Christian Culture, Anthropological Perspectives, New York: Columbia University Press.

Wiebel-Fanderl, O. (1982) Die Wallfahrt Altötting. Kultformen und Wallfahrtsleben im 19. Jahrhundert, Passau: Verein für Ostbairische Heimatforschung.

Wunderlin D. (2013) (ed.) Pilgern boomt, Basel: Merian.

7 Exploring Jewish Pilgrimage in Israel

Nimrod Luz and Noga Collins-Kreiner

INTRODUCTION

In this chapter we wish to describe and analyse what we consider as Jewish pilgrimage and Jewish pilgrimage research. We believe that a *longue durée* approach is required in order to explain the changes in perceptions among Jews regarding pilgrimage and the emergence of a Jewish pilgrimage map linking the past and the present. This approach is particularly relevant if one wishes to understand current trends in pilgrimage within Israel and their relationship to religion and religiosity in the context of modernity and the nation-state.

We would like to begin with a rather intriguing observation recently made by Norman Solomon. While addressing the uniqueness of pilgrimage in Judaism, he claims that there is a stark difference between Judaism and other 'world religions', i.e. Christianity, Islam, Hinduism and Buddhism:

> If you were to pick a Christian at random in the street and ask what he or she could say about pilgrimage you could reasonably expect a coherent reply, maybe with a reference to Rome or Jerusalem or Santiago; a Muslim similarly button-holed might mention Mecca, a Hindu Varanasi. If you were to stop a Jew and pose the same question you would more likely get a puzzled look, perhaps a remark on the Pilgrim Festivals in Ancient Israel, or even a statement to the effect that 'we don't do pilgrimages'. Is this a difference of substance or just a difference of vocabulary? (2013: 42)

He certainly has a point, but the difference between Judaism and its counterparts (Christianity and Islam) in the region is not an essential one; rather, Judaism presents a different take or emphasis on the importance of ritual (Reiner, Limor and Frankel 2014). Furthermore, if a rejection of pilgrimage ever prevailed, it has long since succumbed to a plethora of pilgrimage sites and a dramatic rise in both its socio-political and religious importance. Thus, as in other religious perceptions, Jewish pilgrimage plays a key role

Exploring Jewish Pilgrimage in Israel 135

in the search for the holy and the maintenance of a community of believers (The Jewish Encyclopedia 1964, X: 35).

This role has become more complicated with the creation of the Israeli nation-state. A wide variety of pilgrimages has emerged across the whole country since Israel was established. Some 'sacred places' have become major sites of political mobilisation. Moreover, the long-established web of local shrines has considerably expanded through the immigration of Sephardic Jewish communities from N. Africa, in particular. Besides these religious pilgrimages, nationalism has encouraged the creation of secular pilgrimages, both inside and outside Israel, connected to memory and identity. Research by Israeli scholars on this diverse field has expanded but is still highly fragmentary. At the same time, traditional pilgrimage to Jerusalem has also become a key metaphor for the migration of Jews to the 'homeland'.

To explain these developments we believe that a longue durée approach is required. This approach will help us track changes in perceptions among Jews concerning pilgrimage and the emergence of a Jewish pilgrimage map linking past and present. It will put into perspective current trends in pilgrimage across Israel, and their relationship to religion and religiosity in the context of modernity and the nation-state. It will also help us to explain certain key factors, such as the centrality of the 'Temple' in the development of Jewish pilgrimage, and the consequences of its demise and the political and geographical implication of the terms *Aliyya Laregel* (ascending on foot), 'Holy Land', 'Eretz Israel' and 'Israel'. These concepts and terms are used interchangeably many times, and it is imperative to make some clarifications because they are not only relevant to the issues at hand but are responsible for some of the obscurities and misunderstandings in the field.

The next section will discuss, therefore, the main characteristics and sites of Jewish pilgrimage in the premodern periods, i.e., the Temple and the growth of a more nuanced and complex Jewish hagiographic map. We then consider the dramatic changes in Jewish pilgrimage during the modern period, particularly as part of the emergence of Jewish society within the State of Israel. While discussing pilgrimage and modernity we explore the national impacts of religious behaviour and how the two have altered the nature, volume and destinations of Jewish pilgrimage in contemporary Israel. The last part of the chapter expands on the different trends and main types of studies to be found in the vibrant and ever-changing field of Jewish pilgrimage research. We will conclude with a discussion which draws out the chapter's main insights.

HISTORICAL JEWISH PILGRIMAGE AND PILGRIMAGE IN JUDAISM: RUMINATIONS ON A RESEARCH TOPIC

Pilgrimage, as the move toward the sacred centre in order to be exposed to God's presence (Coleman and Elsner 1995), is located at the very core of belief within Judaism. The biblical text is unequivocal about the importance of this journey and the religious imperative to perform this ritual on both physical and metaphorical levels:

> Three times a year all your men must appear before the Lord your God at the place he will choose: at the Festival of Unleavened Bread, the Festival of Weeks and the Festival of Tabernacles. No one should appear before the Lord empty-handed: Each of you must bring a gift in proportion to the way the Lord your God has blessed you. (Deuteronomy 16: 16–17)

Following the ascendancy of Davidic traditions, Jerusalem and its religious centre (aka the Jewish Temple) became supreme and all other existing pilgrimage centres were shunned. Following the biblical creed, Jews were expected to 'appear before the Lord your God at the place he will choose'. According to the prevailing Jewish narrative, constructed by canonised texts that follow by and large Judean literature, after its inauguration by King Solomon (circa 970 BCE) the Jerusalem Temple became the most important and revered Jewish pilgrimage site. Although this narrative is under growing scrutiny (Finkelstein and Silberman 2001, Eliav 2005, 2008), there is ample evidence of the Jerusalemite temple's emergence as the focal point of Jewish pilgrimage Aliyya Laregel (literally, ascending on foot) during the Second Temple period (Eliav 2005). During the reign of King Herod (37–34 BCE) the compound underwent a massive and highly ambitious renovation and refurbishment project. A part of this unique project involved the construction of four gargantuan retaining walls. The western retaining wall became, after the massive Roman destruction, the most iconic Jewish pilgrimage site. This construction project transformed the temple into a separate urban entity known since then as the Temple Mount.

The ending of Jewish autonomy, symbolised mainly by the destruction of the sacred site in 70 CE, only intensified Jerusalem's symbolic role. The period of Jerusalem's ascendancy is crucially important because this pilgrimage map and imaginative geography served as the platform for pilgrimage made by Jesus himself, which culminated in his crucifixion. The Christian traditions regarding his death and resurrection established Jerusalem as a central pilgrimage shrine for Christians too, and added to the saturated hagiographic pilgrimage map of Jerusalem and the entire Holy Land (MacCormack 1990, Markus 1994).

The topocide of the central Jewish pilgrimage site and the cessation of the liturgy therein unleashed a lengthy philosophical debate regarding the status of the former temple and the pilgrimage to it (Feldman 2005, Urbach 1968). Initially, Jewish scholars were of the opinion, much like in early Christianity, that until the compound was restored to its former glory and function, Jerusalem and its temple were to be erased from the pilgrimage map. The biblical creed of *Aliyya Laregel* (literally, ascending on foot) to the house of

God was now null and void. However, this *axis mundi* was too strong to be ignored. It remained the ultimate object of yearning for Jews, the symbol of future redemption (*Geula*) and the end of the diaspora and a life in exile. Jews continued to come as pilgrims to Jerusalem and its environs with certain restrictions during the Roman period.

Over time the city, particularly the Wailing Wall (as the most important relic of the former temple), regained its mythic and central importance. Jews continued to come on pilgrimage to Jerusalem, which would culminate, political circumstances permitting, with a visit to the Wailing Wall (Prawer 1988). Thus, through a convoluted and meandering historical process, which originated in biblical times, began in earnest during the second Temple period and finalised after the Roman conquest in 70 CE, Jerusalem and its temple were transformed from ideas that symbolised the Jewish presence in Eretz Israel into spiritual and metaphysical symbols and the very essence of Jewish existence.

From Late Antiquity (the fourth to sixth centuries CE) Jewish pilgrims were no longer engaged with the canonical *Aliyya Laregel* but rather performed rituals which are better translated (and resemble) more the Latin term *peregrinatio* or 'pilgrimage' in English (Reiner 2014). After the Crusader period, especially during the Mamluk period (between the thirteenth and sixteenth centuries), Jews also went on pilgrimage to other sites in the Holy Land, which Jewish travelers and chroniclers referred to as *Eretz Israel* or the Land of Israel (Prawer 1988, Reiner 1988, 2014). The Galilee region in general and, more specifically, the Upper Galilee city of Safad, became a major Jewish sacred centre where new lunar months were announced (*Roshei Hodashim*). Galilee also emerged as an important centre for Jewish sages and poets, while Safad and Tiberius also emerged as two of the four Jewish holy cities. Another important development was the absorption of Christian and Muslim traditions and the embracing of non-Jewish sites as legitimate Jewish ones, such as the Tomb of David on Mount Zion and the Tomb of Rachel in Bethlehem (Limor 1988, 2007, Sered 1998). This process was shaped by periodic constraints imposed by local authorities, as well as by reaction to and contestation with the expanding number of Christian and Muslim sacred centres and traditions.

By the nineteenth century and the eve of the national struggle between Jewish and Arab communities, a wide range of Jewish pilgrimage sites and a highly variegated sacred map (hagio-geography) had emerged. This map became the blueprint against which the socio-political changes that ultimately led to the emergence of Israel as a Jewish state within the geographical setting of the biblical Holy Land. During the twentieth century, particularly after the creation of Israel in 1948, there was a dramatic growth in pilgrimage sites (whether old, new, or renewed) and the volume of Jewish pilgrims soared along with religious radicalisation and religious resurgence (Bar 2004, 2009, Goodman and Fisher 2004, Sered 1986, 1989, 1991, 1998,

Bilu 1998, 2010). This growth in Jewish pilgrimage has encouraged the emergence of a voluminous, varied and lively research field.

CONTEMPORARY JEWISH PILGRIMAGE: CONSECRATION AND VENERATION OF SAINTS IN THE NATIONAL AND MODERNISTIC JEWISH STATE

Israel, as the geo-political entity, which emerged from the Jewish ideological concept of the Holy Land or *Eretz Israel*, has undergone dramatic and riveting transformations, leading to a cornucopia of sacred sites and newly invented pilgrimage routes. These changes have involved the state's attempts to consecrate the land as part of the ongoing conflict with Palestinians from inside and beyond the Green Line, as well as religious resurgence and radicalisation within Israeli-Jewish society (Luz 2004, 2008, 2012). There has been a surge in traditional Jewish pilgrimage by religiously observant Jews from around the world, encouraged by the current geopolitical climate, Israel's control of traditional pilgrimage sites and the increasing ease of global travel.

Arguably, the Wailing Wall and its environs together constitute the most iconic landmark and the fulcrum of the processes, which have been involved in the increasing importance of the religious sphere in contemporary Israel (Reiter 2001). As we have seen, Jews yearned for and venerated the site for centuries before it became accessible again to Jewish pilgrims after the 1967 Six Days War. The state took an active part in transforming the site by changing its spatiality, including the demolition of a former Muslim neighbourhood. The changes were designed not only to produce a central pilgrimage site for Jews but also to reflect an emergent religio-nationalist understanding (Nitzan-Shiftan 2011). The centrality of this site and its canonic status as the most important national and pilgrimage icon has also to be understood in the context of Jewish Israeli everyday attitude toward a mythologised past, which was expressed through the geographical concept of *Eretz Israel* as the 'historical' foundation of modern Israel.

Today, the holy sites dating from historical periods consist primarily of the burial places of saintly figures (Sered 1998), among which we may mention the Tomb of Rachel the Matriarch in Bethlehem, the tomb of Maimonides in Tiberias, or the Cave of the Patriarchs in Hebron. It must be noted, however, that most of these sites are recognised as saintly graves based on later traditions and do not necessarily mark the saintly figure's (*zaddik*) exact burial location.

Eric Cohen's distinction between formal and popular pilgrimage centres (1992) is helpful here. Formal centres are usually more rigorous and are under the scrutiny of orthodox leaders. The rituals at these centres are highly formalised and decorous and are conducted in accordance with orthodox precepts. Although folkloric elements are present, they play a secondary role

Figure 7.1 Praying at the Wailing Wall—Jerusalem, Israel. (Photo: Guy Raivitz)

and sometimes are even suppressed by the authorities. At popular centres, on the other hand, folkloric activities are more important and may even take precedence over the more serious and sublime activities. The pilgrim's principal motive for the pilgrimage, if not just a pretext for recreation or entertainment, is typically a personal request or the fulfillment of a vow. Requests are often simple and concrete, such as the desire for success in business or luck in life and love, and supplications for good health or healing are the most common ones. Indeed, popular centres, rather than formal ones, often acquire a reputation for fulfilling requests and giving succour to individual worshippers.

While formal sites are growing and are well funded, popular shrines have also rapidly expanded. As we have seen, several of the Galilee sites became important pilgrimage centres when the Roman conquest prevented Jerusalem from functioning as a religious hub and the focal point of Jewish political-religious activity was forced to move northward to this mountainous region. Although these sites no longer serve as seats of political power, they continue to play a role as popular pilgrimage shrines. In terms of Israel's current socio-political structure, they can be seen as peripheral 'centres out there', even though they were not established as such, unlike the minor shrines, which emerged during the second half of the twentieth century and which will be discussed below.

The most important of these peripheral centres is the tomb of Rabbi Shimon Bar-Yochai, located on Mount Meron near Safad. Shimon Bar-Yochai lived in the second century CE and preached against the Romans. He is also believed to have written the *Zohar* ['The Book of Splendour'], the most important book of Jewish mysticism (Levy 1997) and to have performed miracles. Pilgrims visit the shrine throughout the year, but large-scale celebrations only occur during the festival of *Lag Ba'omer* (the thirty-third day after Passover). While around 1.5 million visit the shrine annually, it is estimated that approximately 500,000 people come for this one-day festival.[1] The site is also a major tourist attraction, drawing members from all levels of Israeli-Jewish society in the country and imbuing the site with a largely popular character. Other major popular pilgrimage centres on the margins include the tombs of Rabbi Yonatan Ben-Uziel near Safad, Rabbi Meir Ba'al Hanes near Tiberias, Rabbi Akiva in Tiberias, Honi Hameagel at Hatzor Haglilit in the Galilee region and Rabbi Yehuda Bar-Elaee near Safad (Collins-Kreiner 2006).

Since the 1980s, new Jewish saint shrines have been established or 'discovered' in several Israeli development towns (Epstein 1995). Sered (1986, 1989, 1991, 1998) forcefully argues that the development of these cults in contemporary Israel reflects, among other things, the popularity of devotions to holy men in North Africa, the role of the charismatic rebbe in Hasidic sects and a national wish to strengthen the sense of historical belonging to the land (1998: 28). Weingrod (1990, 1998), Ben Ari and Bilu (1992, 1997) and Bar (2004, 2009), for example, reflect on the reasons for this new kind of marginal site and conclude that the socio-cultural and political changes within Israeli society, influenced by the Jewish immigrants arriving during the 1950s primarily from Muslim North Africa, were the major factors leading to the emergence of these sites.

About ten of these new popular pilgrimage sites currently exist across Israel, and their numbers are growing. Most have only a limited following, but some are popular throughout the entire country and attract a large number of visitors throughout the year, especially on Jewish holidays and the *hillulot*, which are marked by a gathering at the saint's grave on the anniversary of his death. The most popular site of this kind is the Tomb of Baba Sali in the town of Netivot, located in the Negev desert region of southern Israel. A similar pilgrimage site is Rabbi Chaim Chouri's Tomb in Beer Sheva (Weingrod 1990). Many sites located in North Africa—in Morocco, Tunis, the island of Djerba and Egypt—also attract visitors, who visit them as pilgrims (Ben-Ari and Bilu 1992, Carpenter-Latiri 2012). Recently, Stadler and Luz have been exploring newly emerging popular sites in their charismatic stage through a comparison between the three dominant religions in Israel (see http://sacredplaces.huji.ac.il; Stadler and Luz 2014, forthcoming).

Figure 7.2 Pilgrims at the Baba Sali annual festivities—Netivot, Israel. (Photo: Guy Raivitz)

After 1948, and particularly from the 1970s, the Jewish pilgrimage map has dramatically changed (Bar 2008). Along with the revitalization, renovation and reconstruction of established official sites, new popular shrines have been constructed, mythologised and appropriated. Part and parcel of this process is the growing connection among Zionism and pilgrimage. While Zionism is a highly secular-modern ideology, it has from the beginning targeted the Land of Israel as its platform for national resurrection solely on the basis of the Jewish collective memory of *Eretz Israel*. Moreover, the highly religious concept of *Aliya Laregel* was adopted as a creed, which meant mostly Jews returning to their homeland. Thus, the highly venerated historical pilgrimage sites have been joined by new mythologised nationalistic sites to create a voluminous secularist-cum-religio-nationalistic pilgrimage map (Abu al-Hajj 2001). These sites and map reflect the way that Israel as a state, which faces more than its fair share of challenges, is involved in a concentrated effort to construct a national collective memory (Schuman, Vinitzky-Seroussi and Vinkur 2003).

The most notable site, which commemorates the remote (mythical) Jewish past is Masada—a secluded mountain in the Judean desert where,

142 *Nimrod Luz and Noga Collins-Kreiner*

according (only) to Jewish history, Jewish rebels resisted the might of the Roman army for three years until the bitter end (Zrubabvel 1995, Ben Yehuda 1995). Another site is intimately linked to the commemoration of the Holocaust. Yad Va-Shem (literally, a memorial and a name) was inaugurated in Jerusalem in juxtaposition to Mt Herzel, the national burial site of fallen soldiers. This mountain also hosts the commemoration site of the National Leaders Memorial Park. The close proximity between the sites is intentional and reflects the most foundational myth of modern Israel as the manifestation of Jewish nationalism, the hardship of the past and both resilience and resurrection in the present. Students of all levels as well as groups and individual citizens visit the site all the year round, especially during the official commemoration days, which are part of Israel's national holidays (Feldman 2007a).

A recently added site to the evolving national sacred pilgrimage geography is the commemoration site of the former Israel Prime Minister, Yitzhak Rabin, who was assassinated during a peace rally in Tel Aviv on November 4, 1995. This highly significant national *lieu de mémoire* has emerged very quickly as one of the most important nationalistic memorial sites (Schuman, Vinitzky-Seroussi and Vinkur 2003). Vered Vinitzky-Seroussi, who has studied the various manifestations of Rabin's commemoration for more than a decade, describes the highly nuanced and somewhat conflictual socio-political process surrounding this site and associated ritual observed around Israel and argues that it reflects the fragmentation of Israeli-Jewish society (Vinitzky-Seroussi 2010).

In recent years, amid a widespread religious resurgence in Jewish-Israeli society, intriguing links have been forged between Zionism as a national-secularist theory and various Jewish religious manifestations. Thus, Aliya interpreted as a movement towards the land of Israel has acquired a new meaning among religious Zionists circles. It is used as an umbrella term for various activities which aim at reconstructing the ruined temple and performing pilgrimage there (Chen 2014). The number of pilgrims has continually increased, and new platforms are being used to increase public knowledge and awareness about this burgeoning practice. Social media, Internet forums and websites of specific sites and for general information are becoming widespread. This indicates not only the proliferation and rise in the number of pilgrimage sites but also the more general religious resurgence throughout Israel.

RESEARCHING JEWISH PILGRIMAGE
AS PART OF GLOBAL TRENDS

As the opening chapter to this volume has shown, international debates surrounding the definition of pilgrimage and other terms have intensified over the years, especially since the 1990s, when a number of scholars

Exploring Jewish Pilgrimage in Israel   143

began to generate new knowledge regarding secular sites and the nonreligious factors involved in pilgrimage (Eade 1992, Badone and Roseman 2004, Coleman and Eade 2004, Margry 2008, Badone 2014). The subjects explored and the kinds of sites analysed in contemporary pilgrimage studies have transcended the 'officially sacred'. This development shows the influence of the perspective advanced by Eade and Sallnow (1991), which highlighted the heterogeneity of pilgrimage and introduced a new basis for comparing pilgrimages throughout the world, anchored in an understanding of pilgrimage as an arena for competing religious and secular discourses.

Contemporary studies on pilgrimage also reflect a tendency towards differentiation between different mobilities, with many researchers claiming that the differences between pilgrimage, secular pilgrimage, tourism and other mobilities are narrowing (Bilu 1998, Frey 1998, Ebron 1999, Digance 2003, 2006, Collins-Kreiner 2010). Dedifferentiation also appears to have penetrated the study of pilgrimage through multidisciplinary collaboration. Sometimes the disciplinary cross-currents have grown so strong that it is difficult to distinguish the contribution of one discipline from the others. Geographers have engaged most closely with the field of anthropology (Kong 2001), but there have also been convergences with sociology, history, religious studies and, most recently, leisure and tourism research. Researchers have found common ground in the assumption that pilgrimages are products of the culture in which they were created; hence, they tell us 'stories' infused with political, religious, cultural and social meaning. The question remains whether these convergences have had an effect on current Jewish pilgrimage research and, if so, in what way.

As we have seen, Israel—as the geographical extension of a mythical Holy Land—enjoys a well-developed and highly complex pilgrimage tradition. However, until recently the word 'pilgrimage' was not used very much by scholars to refer to people visiting Jewish holy sites, shrines, or tombs. Nevertheless, the rising demand for sites; the marked growth in visitor numbers; and the cultural, social and political trends that have prevailed in Israeli society since the 1980s have all encouraged scholars to address pilgrimage directly. As a result, new insights have been developed, primarily through the application of anthropological and sociological tools.

The studies that have been published on Jewish pilgrimage make for a very diverse field of inquiry. They have been produced across a wide range of disciplines ranging from historical and cultural geography (Bar 2004, 2009, Goldberg 1997, Collins-Kreiner 2006, 2010) to anthropology and sociology (Sered 1986, 1989, 1991, 1998, Bilu and Ben Ari 1987, 1995, Bilu 1998, 2010, Feldman 2007b) to the more politically oriented Weingrod (1990, 1998). They are not only varied in their perspectives but also represent a wide spectrum of methodologies. By and large they are highly accessible internationally because Israeli scholars tend to publish in English

Figure 7.3 Women at Rachel's Tomb—Jerusalem/Bethlehem, Israel. (Photo: Guy Raivitz)

due to various constraints shaped by academic promotion policies and the limited market of Hebrew readers. Eventually, most of the important studies in this somewhat fuzzy field of Jewish pilgrimage research in Israel will be available and internationally disseminated.

Here we have focussed mostly on the social sciences and only discuss what we deem to be the more general and important aspects. However, we also need to emphasise that for those who are mostly interested in the historical aspects of Jewish pilgrimage, there is a plethora of studies on such issues. Overall, then, an impressive body of work has been produced on such topics as pilgrimage centres; the political, nationalist, folkloric and ethnic aspects of pilgrimage; pilgrimage sites associated with deceased cultural heroes; the tourist dimensions of pilgrimage; educational visits to sacred and historical locations; and pilgrimage for the sake of travel.

THE STUDY OF POPULAR PILGRIMAGE IN CLOSER FOCUS

As we have seen, considerable academic interest has been shown in the growth of Jewish 'popular pilgrimage'. However, its early beginnings in Israel

Exploring Jewish Pilgrimage in Israel 145

were rather humble. The dominance of secularisation theory in the fields of sociology and anthropology of religion was reflected in the meagre research conducted on religious phenomena, in general, and pilgrimage and the veneration of saints, in particular. This dearth was not only due to the dominance of secularisation theory but also to the prevailing Israeli secular-cum-national ethos, which failed to accept or even acknowledge the existence of marginalised narratives of religiosity.

Against this backdrop the pioneering studies of Ben-Ami, Bilu and Sered represent a dramatic change. This transformation was the outcome of the realisation on their part that the secularisation model was not applicable to sections of Israeli society. Modernisation and secularisation processes were accompanied by a plethora of activities and social processes, which could only be described as religious resurgence.

Issachar Ben-Ami, an ethnologist and Middle Eastern scholar, painstakingly collected for more than a decade folkloristic data on Moroccan Jewish saints and religious ceremonies (1984, 1998). His work denotes a real change and marks a new turn within Israeli anthropology of pilgrimage. As a member of the Hebrew University's Folklore Research Centre, he examined the interrelationship among belief, custom and narrative in Moroccan Jewish folklore as an insider. Susan Sered also pioneered the study of cults surrounding female saints and pilgrimage sites dedicated to female figures. In her numerous publications she demonstrated how processes of religious resurgence and consecration of the Israeli landscape that predate the proclamation of the state of Israel had intensified dramatically after the large influx of Jews from Middle Eastern and Islamic states (1986, 1989, 1991, 1998).

Yoram Bilu, a psychological anthropologist, was arguably the most prominent scholar to realise that the Israeli periphery (where many new immigrants from Middle Eastern and Muslim-majority countries were settled by the state) encouraged the strengthening of magic, spiritualistic and Kabalistic tendencies in Israel. He revealed not only the cultural codes characterising a large portion of the immigrants in question but also the individual and collective difficulties they faced in moving from traditional to modern society in Israel. Bilu's book *The Saints' Impresarios* (2010) examines the striking revival of saint worship in contemporary Israel ignited by Moroccan Jews, who came to Israel during the 1950s and 1960s. Between 1986 and 1989, he carried out fieldwork with Eyal Ben-Ari in the town of Netivot (Bilu and Ben-Ari 1987, 1995, 1997, Ben-Ari and Bilu 1992), the burial place of the renowned Jewish Moroccan rabbi Israel Abu Hatzeira (known widely as the Baba Sali) and a major centre of activity for the thriving cults of saint worship among North African Jews in Israel. Bilu and Ben-Ari sought to document and analyse the development of this holy site and to compare its rise with similar places on Israel's periphery.

Bilu and Ben-Ari's research was part of the critical and innovative wave of Israeli sociological scholarship that began to emerge in the early

146 *Nimrod Luz and Noga Collins-Kreiner*

1990s against the background of a relative void, which had prevailed until that point in time. As part of this maturation of the field, Bilu shed light on the difficulties of contending with the immigration waves at the micro level and dealt extensively with the Jews from the Middle East and North Africa.

In *The Saint of Beersheba* (1990), Alex Weingrod also developed an anthropological study of the emergence of a new Jewish saint or *zaddik* in Israel and the annual pilgrimage to his grave by thousands of North African Jews. In a later paper titled 'The Saints Go Marching On' (1998), he provided a more general account of the pilgrimage by Jews of Moroccan descent to the graves of saintly figures across Israel. The paper depicts the immigrants' adaptation to life in Israel, despite the impact of their bitter experiences in the country during its first decades. It was only in the 1970s that the ideal of the melting pot began to give way to the notion of ethnic pluralism. Some of Weingrod's studies expressed criticism of the Israeli establishment and its methods of absorbing immigrants during the period in question and helped spark a change in its absorption and settlement policies. From this perspective, his studies also belong to the realm of applied anthropology.

The study of sacred sites in terms of their development and spatial dynamics has also contributed to Jewish pilgrimage research. Avi Sasson is one of the few who has written extensively on the development of specific sites. In one of his studies (2002), he offers a classification of sites based on their stage of development. Doron Bar (2004, 2009) also explores the emergence of new sacred spaces in Israel in recent decades, maintaining that 'one of the more prominent geographical testimonies of religious expression is sacred space' (Bar 2009: 267). Collins-Kreiner highlights the mounting convergence of old-fashioned pilgrimage and current tourism (2006) and emphasises the expanding nexus of holy sites, society, politics, ideology and culture (2010).

Bar (2009) shows that while North African Jews (*Mizrahim*) participated in rituals at the older and more established holy places, they also tended to adopt and develop holy places near their new settlements and where only hints of ancient Jewish sanctity were to be found. This process emerged mainly on Israel's social and geographical periphery, i.e., in regions and places where most immigrants were settled by the Israeli establishment during the 1950s and 1960s.

This social scientific research on Jewish pilgrimages frequently involved scholars who approached the traditions of ethnic groups in terms of the groups' 'otherness'. Their attitudes range from scepticism and criticism of the 'primitive' nature of the phenomenon to an effort at relativism and, perhaps more notably, an attempt to protect the beliefs of the participants, who typically come from with low socio-economic backgrounds, from the condemnation of the authorities.

CONCLUSION

Contemporary research on Jewish pilgrimage has undoubtedly been influenced by the major trends in international pilgrimage studies, such as the expanding fields of research, the movement towards dedifferentiation, the gradual waning of an integrative approach and multidisciplinarity.

The movement towards dedifferentiation in the Israeli context can be understood in the shifting focus of attention away from the formal sites at Jerusalem to the new popular sites, which, as we have seen, have been the subject of most of the research. Jewish studies also reveal the emergence of a more integrated way of viewing formal and popular pilgrimage. Furthermore, although the position of Jerusalem as the holy 'centre of the world' for Jews remains unchallenged, new important sites have emerged. We can understand these old and new sites in terms of a scale-based Jewish typology shaped by the changing relative emphasis of each kind of pilgrimage. Thus, in addition to Jerusalem as a pivotal centre, other 'formal' locations have appeared, and as time passed these have become more structured, organised and orthodox. At the same time new popular sites have appeared throughout Israel which not only gain more and more scholarly attention but also tell a fascinating story on current socio-political and surely religious processes among Jewish communities in Israel.

Scholars currently engaged in the study of Jewish pilgrimage also speak of 'interpretations', seeking meanings based on the assumption that new Jewish pilgrimages are products of the culture in which they were created. In this way, they tell us 'stories' that are infused with political, religious, cultural and social meaning (Bar 2009, Collins-Kreiner 2010). These pilgrimages are not only products of the norms and values of social tradition, order and culture, but they also play a meaningful role in shaping them.

Jewish pilgrimage research also reflects the multidisciplinary nature of pilgrimage research in general. A careful reading of most of the current literature on Jewish pilgrimage reveals that the main theoretical focusses of pilgrimage research outside the religious realm currently originate from sociology and anthropology. More and more studies are dealing with the development of sacred sites and space, the sanctification of space, location, patterns of movement, cultural impacts on space and the convergence with tourism (Collins-Kreiner 2006 2010, Bar 2009). Most research still addresses specific case studies and is based on close examination of their respective stories. The result is a mosaic of analyses of histories, politics, cultures and traditions devoid of any one systematic theoretical framework.

Despite the diverse array of the forms assumed by Jewish pilgrimage activity and the millions of Jewish pilgrims who circulate among destinations not only inside Israel but also elsewhere, particularly in North Africa and in Uman, Ukraine and the equally complex vocabularies they generate,

Jewish pilgrimage has yet to be widely recognised as a topic of research within Israeli social sciences. We suggest that in addition to the Jewish religion's lack of a formal definition of pilgrimage, this ongoing tendency to overlook pilgrimage can also be explained by the phenomenon's 'primitivist' image, at times coupled with an aversion towards forms of popular religiosity that are not connected to institutional Judaism.

The reemergence of rituals surrounding the tombs of saintly figures is but one of many forms of mobilities that may be collectively understood as the sanctification of space in Israel. Such phenomena encompass prominent elements of traditional and civil religion alike and include a diverse range of commemoration and memorial sites, from saintly tombs to military monuments.

In this chapter we have sought to examine the ways in which Jewish pilgrimage has been studied mostly by social scientists. While in the past research has typically considered Jewish pilgrimage solely from a religious perspective, recent studies have been more innovative and explored other aspects of Jewish pilgrimage. This process may continue with regard to the scholars engaged in the topic and the attributes of the phenomenon itself. We are fully aware that in this short survey we only discussed what we considered to be the most relevant, central and important issues and research projects. However, new sites are being explored, new directions are being pursued and new methodologies are being implemented, which all makes for a vibrant and viable field of Jewish pilgrimage research in both the historical and contemporary Israel.

NOTE

1. These numbers can only be an ephemeral estimation, as they keep rising along with the deepening of religious resurgence of the Jewish society in Israel.

REFERENCES

Abu al-Hajj, N. (2001) *Facts on the Ground: Archaeological Practice and Territorial Self-Fashioning in Israeli Society,* Chicago: University of Chicago Press.
Badone, E. (2014) 'Conventional and unconventional pilgrimages: conceptualizing sacred travel in the twenty-first century', in A. Pazos (ed.) *Redefining Pilgrimage: New Perspectives on Historical and Contemporary Pilgrimages,* Farnham, UK, and Burlington, VT: Ashgate.
———. and Roseman, S. (eds.) (2004) *Intersecting Journeys: The Anthropology of Pilgrimage and Tourism,* Champaign: University of Illinois Press.
Bar, D. (2004) 'Re-creating Jewish sanctity in Jerusalem: the case of Mount Zion and David's Tomb between 1948–1967', *The Journal of Israeli History,* 23 (2): 233–251.
———. (2009) 'Mizrahim and the development of sacred space in the state of Israel, 1948–1968', *Journal of Modern Jewish Studies,* 8 (3): 267–285.
Bar, G. (2008) 'Reconstructing the past: the creation of Jewish sacred space in the state of Israel, 1948–1967', *Israel Studies,* 13 (3): 1–21.

Exploring Jewish Pilgrimage in Israel 149

Ben-Ami, I. (1984) *Saint Veneration among the Jews in Morocco*, Jerusalem: Magnes (in Hebrew).

———. and Bilu, Y. (1987) 'Saints' sanctuaries in Israeli development towns: on a mechanism of urban transformation', *Urban Anthropology*, 15 (2): 243–272.

Ben Ami, I. (1998) *Saint Veneration among the Jews in Morocco*, Detroit: Wayne State University Press.

Ben-Ari, E. and Bilu, Y. (1992) 'The making of modern saints: manufactured charisma and the Abu-Hatseiras of Israel', *American Ethnologist*, 19 (4): 672–687.

———. (1997) *Grasping Land: Space and Place in Contemporary Israeli Discourse and Experience*, New York: State University of New York.

Ben Yehuda, N. (1995) *The Masada Myth: Collective Memory and Mythmaking in Israel*, Madison, WI: University of Wisconsin Press.

Bilu, Y. (1998) 'Divine worship and pilgrimage to holy sites as universal phenomena', in R. Gonen (ed.) *To the Holy Graves: Pilgrimage to the Holy Graves and Hillulot in Israel*, Jerusalem: The Israel Museum, Jerusalem (in Hebrew).

———. (2010) *The Saints' Impresarios: Dreamers, Healers and Holy Men in Israel's Urban Periphery*, Israel: Academic Studies Press.

———. and Ben-Ari, E. (1995) 'Modernity and charisma in contemporary Israel: the case of Baba Sali and Baba Baruch', *Israel Affairs*, 1 (3): 224–236.

Carpenter-Lahiri, D. (2012) 'The ghriba on the island of Jerba or the reinvention of a shared shrine as a metonym for a multicultural Tunisia', in G. Bowman (ed.) *Sharing the 'Sacra': The Politics and Pragmatics of Intercommunal Relations around Holy Places*, Oxford and New York: Berghahn Books.

Chen, S. (2014) 'Visiting the Temple Mount: Taboo or Mitzvah', *Modern Judaism*, 34 (1): 27–41.

Cohen, E. (1992) 'Pilgrimage centers: central and excentric', *Annals of Tourism Research*, 19 (1): 33–50.

Collins-Kreiner, N. (2006) 'Graves as attractions: pilgrimage-tourism to Jewish holy graves in Israel', *Journal of Cultural Geography*, 24 (1): 67–89.

———. (2010) 'Researching pilgrimage: continuity and transformations', *Annals of Tourism Research*, 37 (2): 440–456.

Coleman, S. and Elsner, J. (eds.) (1995) *Pilgrimage: Past and Present in the World Religions*, Cambridge, MA: Harvard University Press.

———. and Eade, J. (eds.) (2004) *Reframing Pilgrimage: Cultures in Motion*, London and New York: Routledge.

Digance, J. (2003) 'Pilgrimage at contested sites', *Annals of Tourism Research*, 301: 143–159.

———. (2006) 'Religious and secular pilgrimage', in D. Timothy and D. Olsen (eds.) *Tourism, Religion and Spiritual Journeys*, London and New York: Routledge.

Eade, J. and Sallnow, M. (eds.) (1991) *Contesting the Sacred: The Anthropology of Christian Pilgrimage*, London and New York: Routledge.

———. (1992) 'Pilgrimage and tourism at Lourdes, France', *Annals of Tourism Research*, 19: 18–32.

Ebron, P. (1999) 'Tourists as pilgrims: commercial fashioning of transatlantic politics', *American Ethnologist*, 26: 910–932.

Eliav, Y. (2005) *God's Mountain: The Temple Mount in Time, Space, and Memory*, Baltimore, MD: Johns Hopkins University Press.

———. (2008) 'The Temple Mount in Jewish and early Christian traditions: a new look', in T. Mayer and S. Mourad (eds.) *Jerusalem: Idea and Reality*, London and New York: Routledge.

Epstein, S. (1995) 'Inventing a pilgrimage: ritual, love and politics on the road to Amuka', *Jewish Folklore and Ethnology Review*, 17 (1–2): 25–32.

Feldman, J. (2005) 'The experience of communality and the legitimation of authority in Second Temple pilgrimage', in O. Limor and E. Reiner (eds.) *Pilgrimage: Jews, Christians, Muslims*, Rananna: Open University/Yad Ben Zvi.

———. (2007a) 'Between Yad Vashem and Mount Herzl: changing inscriptions of sacrifice on Jerusalem's "Mountain of Memory"', *Anthropological Quarterly*, 80 (4): 1145–1172.

———. (2007b) 'Constructing a shared Bible Land: Jewish-Israeli guiding performances for Protestant pilgrims', *American Ethnologist*, 34 (2): 349–372.

Finkelstein, I. and Silberman, N. (2001) *The Bible Unearthed: Archaeology's New Vision of Ancient Israel and the Origin of Its Sacred Texts*, New York: Simon and Schuster.

Frey, N. L. (1998) *Pilgrim Stories: On and Off the Road to Santiago*, Berkeley, CA: University of California Press.

Goldberg, H. E. (1997) 'Gravesites and memorials of Libyan Jews: alternative versions of the sacralization of space in Judaism', in Ben-Ari and Bilu, op. cit.

Goodman, Y. and Fisher, S. (2004) 'Towards an understanding of secularism and religiosity in Israel: the secularisation theory and possible alternatives', in Y. Yona and Y. Goodman (eds.) *Maelstrom of Identities: A Critical Look at Religion and Society in Israel*, Tel Aviv: Van Leer Institute and Hakibbutz Hameuchad Publishing House.

Kong, L. (2001) 'Mapping "new" geographies of religion: politics and poetics in modernity', *Progress in Human Geography*, 25: 211–233.

Levy, A. (1997) 'To Morocco and back: tourism and pilgrimage among Moroccan-Born Israelis', in Ben-Ari and Bilu, op. cit.

Limor, O. (1988) 'The origins of a tradition: King David's tomb on Mt. Zion', *Traditio*, 44: 453–462.

———. (2007) 'Sharing sacred space: holy places in Jerusalem between Christianity, Judaism and Islam', in I. Shagrir, R. Ellenblum and J. Riley-Smith (eds.) *Laudem Hierosolymitani: Studies in Crusades and Medieval Culture in Honour of Benjamin Z. Kedar*, Aldershot, UK: Ashgate.

Luz, N. (2004) *Al-Haram Al-Sharif in the Arab-Palestinian Public Discourse in Israel: Identity, Collective Memory and Social Construction*, Floersheimer Institute for Policy Study, Jerusalem: Achva Press [Hebrew].

———. (2008) 'The politics of sacred places. Palestinian identity, collective memory, and resistance in the Hassan Bek mosque conflict', *Society and Space: Environment and Planning D*, 26 (6): 1036–1052.

———. (2012) 'The Islamic movement and the lure of the sacred: the struggle for land through sacred sites', in E. Rekhess and A. Rudnitzky (eds.) *Muslim Minorities in non-Muslim Majority Countries: The Test Case of the Islamic Movement in Israel*, Tel Aviv: Eyal Press.

MacCormack, S. (1990) 'Loca sancta: the organization of sacred topography in Late Antiquity', in R. Oustershout (ed.) *The Blessed of Pilgrimage*, Urbana and Chicago: University of Illinois Press.

Margry, P. (ed.) (2008) *Shrines and Pilgrimage in the Modern World: New Itineraries Into the Sacred*, Amsterdam: Amsterdam University Press.

Markus, R. (1994) 'How on earth could places become holy? Origins of the Christian idea of holy places', *Journal of Early Christian Studies*, 2/3: 257–271.

Nitzan-Shiftan, N. (2011) 'Stones with a human heart: on monuments, modernism and preservation at the Western Wall', *Theory and Critic*, 38–39: 65–100.

Prawer, J. (1988) *The History of the Jews in the Latin Kingdom*, Oxford: Oxford University Press.

Reiner, E. (1988) *Pilgrimage and pilgrims to Eretz-Yisrael 1099–1517*. PhD dissertation, The Hebrew University of Jerusalem.

Reiner, E. (2014) 'Jewish pilgrimage to Jerusalem in Late Antiquity and the Middle Ages', in O. Limor, E. Reiner and M. Frankel (eds.) *Pilgrimage: Jews, Christians, Muslims*, Rananna: The Open University of Israel Press.

Exploring Jewish Pilgrimage in Israel 151

Reiter, Y. (ed.) (2001) *Sovereignty of God and Man: Sanctity and Political Centrality on the Temple Mount,* Jerusalem: The Jerusalem Institute for Israel Studies.

Sasson, A. (2002) 'Movement of graves: the passage of the hegemony of holy graves from north to south', in M. Cohen (ed.) *Sedot-Negev: Man, Environment and Heritage,* Jerusalem: The Regional Council Sdot-Negev & Makom Ltd.

Schuman, H. Vinitzky-Seroussi, V. and Vinkur, A. D. (2003) 'Keeping the past alive: memories of Israeli Jews at the turn of the millennium', *Sociological Forum,* 18 (1): 103–136.

Sered, S. (1986) 'Rachel's Tomb and the Milk Grotto of the Virgin Mary: two women's shrines in Bethlehem', *Journal of Feminist Studies in Religion,* 2 (2): 7–22.

——. (1989) 'Rachel's Tomb: societal liminality and the revitalization of a shrine', *Religion,* 19: 27–40.

——. (1991) 'Rachel, Mary, and Fatima', *Cultural Anthropology,* 6 (2): 131–146.

——. (1998) 'A tale of three Rachels, or the cultural history of a symbol', *Nashim: A Journal of Jewish Women's Studies & Gender Issues,* 1: 5–41.

Solomon, N. (2013) 'Jewish pilgrimage and peace', in A. Pazos (ed.) *Pilgrimages and Pilgrims as Peacemakers in Christianity, Judaism and Islam,* Farnham, UK, and Burlington, VT: Ashgate.

Stadler, N. and Luz, N. (2014) 'Sacred sites in contested regions', available at http://sacredplaces.huji.ac.il) last accessed 19 August 2014).

——. and Luz, N. (2014) 'The veneration of womb tombs: body-based rituals and politics at Mary's Tomb and Maqam Abu al-Hijja'. *Journal of Anthropological Research,* 70 (2): 183–205.

——. and Luz, N. (forthcoming) 'Two venerated mothers separated by a fence: iconic spaces and borders in Israel: Palestine', *Journal of Religion & Society.*

Urbach, E. (1968) 'Earthly Jerusalem and heavenly Jerusalem', in *Jerusalem through the Ages; The 25th National Conference for the Study of Israel,* Jerusalem: Magnes.

Vinitzky-Seroussi, V. (2010). *Yitzhak Rabin's Assassination and the Dilemmas of Commemoration,* New York: SUNY Press.

Weingrod, A. (1990) *The Saint of Beersheba,* New York: SUNY Press.

——. (1998) 'The saints go marching on', in O. Abuhab et al. (eds.) *Local Anthropology,* Tel Aviv: Cherikover (in Hebrew).

Zerubavel, Y. (1995) *Recovered Roots: Collective Memory and the Making of Israeli National Tradition,* Chicago: The University of Chicago Press.

8 Italian Studies on Pilgrimage

Beyond Folklore Towards a National Anthropological Tradition and the International Circulation of Ideas

Elena Zapponi

Italy contains the largest number of Roman Catholic shrines, established over many centuries. This chapter concentrates on research undertaken primarily by Italian scholars from the nineteenth century and the focus on pilgrimage in Southern Italy and popular religion after the Second World War. Non-Italian researchers are also contributing to the ethnographic literature, especially through networks between Italian and French institutions, while Italian researchers are studying pilgrimage outside the country. Pilgrimage in Italy is also changing through its intimate relationship with tourism, the promotion of cultural heritage and individualised spirituality.

INTRODUCTION

Pilgrimage has played a crucial role in Italian national history, culture and tradition. All over the country, sanctuaries and pilgrimage places attract a wide range of people motivated by both spiritual and worldly considerations. More than simply an escape from everyday life, pilgrimage has played a traditional role in shaping people's individual identity, affirming local identity and resolving controversies and issues, such as political claims for territory or the defence of regional boundaries. Even today hundreds of pilgrimages across the country express local devotion to a particular patron saint or the Virgin in the shadow of the Roman Catholic official presence.

Over the last decades some of these events, which reflect traditional rhythms of local life, have been adopted by political supporters of regional cultural heritage. Pilgrimages have been reinterpreted as representing a path for individual regeneration in an age of uncertainty and providing political agency for imagined communities. Local and regional pilgrimages have been revived through the tourism industry and with political support, especially from the middle class, for the promotion of regional history and cultural heritage. As other contributors to this volume have noted, this development has been associated with a shift away from the category of the 'religious' towards an individualised spirituality.

The study of pilgrimage in Italy has a new role, therefore—an analysis of the local reappropriation of cultural heritage. This chapter, which does not claim to be exhaustive, seeks to place this role within the context of the development of Italian pilgrimage research and international circulation. The chapter begins by considering the national folk studies tradition, which dominated the ethno-anthropological research landscape during the second half of the nineteenth century and focussed particularly on cultural traditions in Southern Italy.

PILGRIMAGE IN ITALIAN FOLK STUDIES

During the nineteenth century, Italian folk studies was shaped by regional traditions and focussed on local practices, costumes, beliefs and festivals as well as cults surrounding particular saints and shrines. The research reflected a historical and philological perspective and was often very detailed and exhaustive. A prime example is the study undertaken by Giuseppe Pitrè (1841–1916) on Sicilian popular tradition. As professor in the History of Popular Tradition at Palermo and then chairman in 'demopsychology',[1] Pitrè produced a twenty-five-volume *Library of Sicilian Popular Traditions*, an impressive collection of popular songs, nonsense, proverbs, stories, plays and medicinal recipes, which also included a rich repertoire of deeply rooted traditions.

Pitrè's preservation of popular beliefs and practices gave voice to local people at a time when the idea of *ethnos* and nation was being vigorously debated (see Cocchiara 1941). His work distinguishes him from other contemporary commentators because he created a method for the systematic study of folk tradition,[2] which combined philological and ethnographic approaches; archival study was completed by personal experience and participant observation. His approach emerged at a time when anthropology was developing as an academic discipline. Charles Darwin's theories had opened up new perspectives on species evolution through natural selection and social scientists, especially in France and Britain, were generating hypotheses concerning the development of social institutions, such as the family, the state, or the transformation of religious systems and social technologies: a debate which saw traditions as the product of cultural survival in modern European societies. The first university chair in anthropology, held by Paolo Mantegazza in 1869 in Florence, was founded on the idea of combining the study of natural history and human beings. In this context, the 'contemporary primitives' were a new subject for research, and Pitrè's approach to Sicilian popular traditions and popular tradition, in general, pointed to the active role played by the folk in history—a role largely neglected by folklore studies until then (see Pitrè 2002).

A large part of Pitrè's study is devoted to symbolic and religious systems (Pitrè 2005). Beliefs and religious practice emerge from his analysis of legends, beliefs and devotional objects, such as *ex votos* or festival sweets. In

154 Elena Zapponi

this context, pilgrimage and local processions, in particular, were (and still are) intimately connected with patron saints and the cult of the Virgin. Pitrè underlined the importance of the sacred journey in Sicilian folk culture: from the Santa Rosalia procession across Palermo to the St Peter procession in Modica, to the widespread belief in the pilgrimage which souls of the dead should make to St James's shrine at Santiago de Compostela in order to pass to a new eternal life (Pitrè 2002: 249).

Pilgrimage was less important than local processions, however, reflecting the need to control space and time in order to purify the community and renew a sense of belonging. In these processions collective participation involves walking a short distance through the main village streets and squares and past the church. A central element is the intimate, physical relationship between the devotees and the statue of the saint or the Virgin—an expression of a lived religion characterised by intense devotion.

Pitrè's comparative study introduces a historical shift where local traditional history is incorporated in a national history, which he seeks to fix in the collective memory. Nevertheless, his approach is primarily philological; a deeper anthropological analysis of the social function of religious beliefs, pilgrimages and processions appears half a century later, thanks to the work of Ernesto De Martino. As we will see later, even if De Martino did not focus on pilgrimage, in order to understand the Italian pilgrimage studies tradition it is necessary to consider the turning point introduced by his analysis of religious rituals and their symbolic systems. This innovative overview opened new avenues for research and provided new instruments for the analysis of Italian pilgrimages and shrine cults.

During the nineteenth century attention was mainly paid to national rural customs and festive performances. The Romantic and Risorgimento approaches towards folklore largely ignored popular devotion. The Risorgimento intelligentsia was mostly interested in popular tales, histories, songs and poetry, even if these were seen as generally superstitious (Cirese 1992: 134–138). These genres were considered an expression of the folk inner protest and impulse towards resistance and were celebrated as the 'spontaneous' expressions of the 'national soul' (1992: 16–17). Scant attention was paid to local pilgrimages, which reflected the vitality of popular devotion during a period when new national and international Marian cults were developing (Fattorini: 55–66). Unlike popular song or poetry, they were a part of the national tradition that did not fit within the project of modern nation building, promoted in a anticlerical, liberal climate of hard-fought battle with the Vatican (Pace 2007: 40). At a time when nation building operated like a 'secular religion' (Luzzatto 2011), popular devotion—and, therefore, local pilgrimage—was considered to be a sort of superstitious subculture.

Colonial policy, promoted by the Fascist regime after the First World War, did not substantially alter this trend. The development of colonial studies was encouraged by the publication of books and the organisation of exhibitions (Labanca 1992), but the emphasis was on celebrating the regime rather than understanding 'primitive' culture. The main subject of ethno-historical research continued to be the traditional life of the peasantry, whose picturesque repertory helped to sustain a myth of the new nation's folk foundations (see Labanca 2002). No specific attention was paid here to popular devotion. Italian anthropology of 'exotic cultures' was scarce and mainly focussed on a rhetorical and apologetic vision of colonial cultures, which the Fascist regime used to contrast with the 'new' Italian nation (Del Boca 1991).

A NEW ANTHROPOLOGICAL PERSPECTIVE ON POPULAR CULTURE AND RITUAL: ERNESTO DE MARTINO AND HIS COLLABORATORS

After the Second World War Italy's colonial adventure was ignored. While some scholars such as Raffaele Corso changed their racist positions and encouraged a sort of applied ethnology for the study of non-European societies (Dore 1980), research continued to focus on the history of popular traditions. However, during the 1950s thanks to a new Italian anthropological approach, influenced by Gramsci, attention began to be paid to popular beliefs and local devotion as an expression of a subaltern culture, which indirectly contested the hegemonic social order. This 'magico-religious culture' of Southern Italy, including rituals and practices concerning the evil eye and spells, for example, attracted a new generation of scholars. This generation was politically left-wing and committed to reporting and denouncing the miserable conditions experienced in the South.

Ernesto De Martino (1908–1965) introduced the idea, drawn from Soviet ethnology, of a 'progressive folk culture', which required urgent study. This new positive outlook towards an 'archaic' rural world and pagan-Christian syncretism was influenced by Antonio Gramsci's view that folklore was a culture of resistance and opposition (Gramsci 1950: 215–221; Cirese 1992: 10–17) and demonstrated how the subaltern sees the world (see Crehan 2002). In a national context of intense political fervour when Carlo Levi (1990), Antonio Gramsci, Rocco Scotellaro (2012) and Pier Paolo Pasolini looked to Southern Italy as a new space of investigation, De Martino organised several interdisciplinary surveys, which sought to study traditional forms of magico-religious rituals. 'Popular culture' was to be studied through an analysis of the gap between popular knowledge and customs, on the one hand, and official Catholicism and hegemonic history, on the other. Local behaviour and beliefs were no longer interpreted as an expression of irrationality or barbarism but as historical products, manifesting specific needs and social desires.

This interest in southern Italian culture grew from De Martino's political engagement first in the Italian Socialist Party and then in the Communist

156   Elena Zapponi

Party. He went beyond Naples, where he was born, to a deeper south where he met a humanity, officially called 'primitive':

> I entered Puglia peasants' homes as a 'companion', searching for people and forgotten human histories, at the same time spying and controlling my own humanity, wanting to make myself a participant, together with the people I met, in the foundation of a better world, where we would both become better. (quoted in Angelini 2008: 53–54)

Through field research on such topics as the magical world conception (1948, 1959), lamenting (1975), or 'tarantism' (1961)—an ancient ritual, which was still alive in the 1950s and which sought to liberate through music and dance the individual bitten in a mythic tarantula attack during harvest time—De Martino inaugurated an Italian scholarly ethnographic approach, which was ideologically left-wing and secular. Two of his most important research students and collaborators at the University of Cagliari, Sardinia, where he taught the History of Religions and Ethnology, were Alberto Mario Cirese and Clara Gallini. He also worked with Vittorio Lanternari (1918–2010) on what they described as an 'ethnographic humanism', which entailed a cultural revolution—the inclusion within official history of the subaltern and marginal classes (Lanternari 1994, 1997, 2003).[3]

Even if De Martino did not pay a lot of attention to pilgrimage, his studies of religion and local beliefs deeply influenced those who directly studied this topic. Because he was a historian of religion, his approach towards religion particularly encouraged a multidisciplinary perspective, which renewed the Italian discipline of ethnology. Hence, the team researching tarantism in Puglia in 1959 included an anthropologist (Amalia Signorelli) and those studying medicine, psychology, ethnomusicology (Diego Carpitella) and visual anthropology (Franco Pinna). De Martino's promotion of visual anthropology made a lasting impact on Italian symbolic anthropology studies, while the study of religion and pilgrimages also benefitted from this approach (see Gallini and Faeta 1999). It is also important to mention the focus on the social position of women, which De Martino's research introduced. He considered women's religious and symbolic practices to be a central feature of popular religion and rituals, such as tarantism, revealing utopian spaces and the contestation of socially passive roles.

Annabella Rossi (1933–1984) was another researcher who worked with De Martino on tarantism and made a significant contribution to Italian pilgrimage studies. Her pioneering study, *Le feste dei poveri* (1986), examined southern Italian pilgrim devotion to saints as a 'culture of sorrow' (see also Rossi 1970). The need for the saint's patronage, the production of ritual objects, such as *ex votos* or saint's costumes, the walk to the sanctuary, the practice of sleeping nearby and the celebration of the patronal feast represent moments of regeneration from the hardships of everyday life and typify both traditional popular culture and a new consumerist popular culture.

Rossi shows how visits to local sanctuaries reveal the subaltern class's permanent state of precariousness and its search for symbolic spaces where life is better and more secure. Offerings and *ex votos* express the devotee's desire to be free from the sense of oppression, disease and evil imposed by living conditions in the South. The sense of participation in these social conditions expressed by *Le feste dei poveri* is highly innovative. Rossi draws on both quantitative and qualitative data to dismiss the idea that popular devotion was a cultural survivor of a primitive age and explores the social and economic reasons for religious beliefs and the performance of pilgrimage. The book can also be seen as anticipating the recent focus on lived religion within international pilgrimage studies through its analysis of the devotees' bodily engagement in saints' festivals and pilgrimage.

Annabella Rossi also played a major role in promoting Italian visual anthropology and its contribution to pilgrimages studies. Her position at the National Museum of Arts and History of Popular Tradition in Rome allowed her to conspicuously enrich the museum's photographic and documentary archive, collaborating with several other documentarians. One of them, Michele Gandin, was her companion and also studied the South's magico-religious folk culture (Esposito 2003). Because this point will be considered later, it is time to consider others who worked with De Martino.

Clara Gallini is an anthropologist who was also trained in the history of religion. Along with her theoretical and methodological works and her editions of De Martino's books (De Martino 2002, 2005), Gallini has examined the changes affecting Italian Catholicism since the 1960s, particularly in the context of popular Catholicism and folk culture in Sardinia (Gallini 2007, 2009). One of her most important works on this topic is *Il consumo del sacro: feste lunghe di Sardegna* (1971), which studied several local nineday pilgrimages during the summer season. These events were characterised by the walk to a rural sanctuary where different groups met and lived together in the open country as a temporary festive community. In a deeply pastoral and isolated society, these annual events fostered social communication and were important psychologically because they created new social ties and renewed those already established.

Gallini analyzed the nine-day rituals in both their sacred and consumerist aspects (1971). She identified the middle-class interest in these traditional pilgrimages, which date back to the fifteenth century and the impact of new bourgeois applications of 'popular' religion. She emphasised the 'neo-rustic model' that was altering these pilgrimages, i.e., Sardinia's 'long festivals' were becoming a sort of annual family holiday destination.

Besides the devotional aspect and the focus on *ex votos* and supplications for intercession, she showed the importance of economic processes. Pilgrimage was an analytical key, therefore, to understand the social life of pastoral society during a particular moment of change from a precapitalist model to an industrial and more 'Western' way of life. Gallini also opened a window into the transformation of traditional religious ritual

158 Elena Zapponi

into cultural heritage, sponsored and valorised by tourism, as well by historical and anthropological research. She mapped out a new itinerary for the Italian study of pilgrimage, viz. the study of the search for authentic traditions and the local community's desire to preserve an inalienable 'homeland identity'.

Two decades later Gallini returned to the topic of pilgrimage, this time looking beyond Italy and her long-lasting study of popular culture to undertake an ambitious analysis of Lourdes. She devoted two articles and one book to this subject (1993, 1994, 1998). The topic is approached from an original perspective, drawing on both an ethnographic study of miraculous healing and a rereading of Emile Zola's novel *Lourdes* (1894). She pursues this by juxtaposing the viewpoints of Zola's main characters with her own critical voice. This choice of methodology is not neutral because Zola anticipated arguments currently central to debates within the anthropology and sociology of religion: the collapse of rationalist utopias, the return of the sacred and the search for individual salvation from modern crises. The story of the journey of the protagonist, Pierre (Zola's alter-ego), who constantly wonders about the reasons for his journey, is a sort of reflection on the crises afflicting science and its triumphalist promises of salvation and on the mass demand for future miracles. Hence, the Grotto at Lourdes appears as the place where a mysterious force of consolation, hope and life acts on bodies and creates a process leading to healing.

One of these Lourdes reflections—*Il miracolo e la sua prova. Un etnologo a Lourdes*—also explores the hermeneutics of pilgrimage and acknowledges the difficulty of interpreting the pilgrims' devotion and faith. The pilgrim's perspective clashes with the positivist-rational view, and Gallini places herself between rational 'truth' and belief. Her writing portrays the research journey and talks of suffering and pleasure, the moments of crisis and the hope for salvation.

In a national research landscape marked by a preoccupation with folklore and the divide between hegemonic and subaltern culture, Gallini's approach is very innovative. She introduces a new perspective towards the Gramscian notion of 'culture gap' (Gramsci 1950: 215–221) for Italian studies on pilgrimage. She does not see the gap as solely the product of a specific social class but a more general social fact, which lies beyond folklore and subaltern history and involves a strong phenomenological dimension—miracle, vision, collective prayers and hierophany. Furthermore, she contends that this gap deserves to be analysed by drawing on social history, sociology and psychology as well as anthropology.

Gallini's work points to two closely aligned paths, which have been pursued not only by Italian anthropological research generally but also by pilgrimage studies, more specifically, during the 1970s and 1980s. One follows the Gramscian concept of hegemonic and subaltern culture, while the other adapts this tradition by examining the reinvention of popular culture. These two approaches have informed the work of Alberto Maria Cirese, who was

Italian Studies on Pilgrimage   159

influenced by De Martino as a young researcher and became the father of a more recent generation of ethnologists, folklorists and anthropologists. Cirese's impressive output was stimulated by his realisation that the notion of popular culture has to be reconsidered in order to understand the impact of the Italian industrial revolution on rural tradition. This shift can be illustrated by mentioning one of Cirese's most well-known works, *Cultura egemonica e culture subalterne. Rassegna degli studi sul mondo popolare tradizionale* (1973), and the studies produced three decades later, which affirmed the anachronistic character of the notion of an 'internal cultural gap', the search for local identity in a global world (2003) and the urgent need to preserve the nonmaterial heritage of traditional culture (2007).

Cirese also shows that consideration needs to be paid to those who did not particularly study pilgrimage because they opened up new avenues and provided new instruments for participant observation and critical analysis. From the 1970s as Italy rapidly changed socially and economically, pilgrimages and patronal festivals became markers of identity for local communities. Although traditional rituals were modified by scientific 'progress', it became clear that the transformation of local Italian pilgrimages required a new analytical approach as anthropologists critiqued the dated and ambiguous notion of 'popular culture'. This critique was encouraged, for example, by Cirese's research student, Pietro Clemente (2001, 2004), and the publishing house, Meltemi, and is well represented by Fabio Dei's book, *Beethoven e le mondine. Ripensare la cultura popolare* (2002). Anthropologists moved away from seeing pilgrimage as a folkloric phenomenon and towards exploring its involvement in the reinvention of archaic rituals, the individualisation of belief, multiculturalism, identity politics and cultural heritage.

PILGRIMAGE IN ITALIAN VISUAL ANTHROPOLOGY

As already mentioned, visual anthropology made a significant contribution to the study of local Italian pilgrimages after the Second World War. Three films in particular stand out—*La taranta* (1961) by Gianfranco Mingozzi, *Processioni in Sicilia* (1964) by Michele Gandin and *La Madonna del Pollino* (1971) on a Calabrian pilgrimage by Luigi di Gianni. Between 1950 and 1970 these ethnographic filmmakers contributed, with others, to a really fertile period of documentaries, which focussed on magical-religious culture. Despite the lack of funding and the very precarious national identity of ethnographic movies, these filmmakers represented a cinematographic current, which was known in Italy as 'cinematografia demartiniana' because they were strongly influenced by De Martino and focussed on similar subjects, i.e., southern Italian magical-religious folklore, especially pilgrimages, festivals, patron saint celebrations and magical-religious rituals, and they shared a common stylistic language (see Carpitella 1981, Gallini 1981). The filmmakers also worked closely with anthropologists, who

160 Elena Zapponi

often wrote the texts of the documentaries. De Martino was the scientific consultant for Michele Gandin's *Lamento funebre* (1953), for example, while Annabella Rossi worked as a scientific consultant or scriptwriter for Di Gianni's *La Madonna del Pollino, La Madonna di Pierno, Il male di San Donato, La possessione, Morte di Padre Pio, La Potenza degli spiriti*; M. Gandin's *Luciano Morpurgo, fotografo dei poveri*; and G. Mingozzi's *Sud e Magia*.

While the demartinian documentary marks an important step in Italian ethnographic research on religion, it had one limitation, which Clara Gallini has pointed out: there was a sharp division between the viewpoint of the anthropologist and the filmmaker, often revealed through the contrast between the narrator and the visual dimension. This gap is evident in Di Gianni's movies, which visually represent S. Italian culture as eternal, cyclic and timeless, while insisting textually on a specific historical dimension and on a history told from below.

Two decades later a more integrated approach towards visual and textual representation was introduced by researchers, such as Francesco Faeta and Antonello Ricci (1997, 2003, 2012), but the main field of research was still Southern Italy, particularly Campania, Calabria and Sicily. Since the 1960s the ethnomusicologist Diego Carpitella has also encouraged the development of visual anthropology and worked with Annabella Rossi on a documentary film festival, MAV (Materials of Visual Anthropology), from the 1980s. The festival is still being held and provides an important platform for the presentation of new authors' ethnographic work.

ANTHROPOLOGICAL STUDIES ON PILGRIMAGE: DEVELOPMENTS SINCE THE 1990s

The study of Italian pilgrimage does not constitute a compact body of research. Moreover, unlike the French or Anglo-Saxon traditions, there is no 'father' figure like Alphonse Dupront (1987) or Victor Turner (1978) and no powerful theory about pilgrimage, which provides a starting point for challenge or validation through subsequent investigations. Pilgrimage is more of a latent and fertile subject for those, who are not just interested in the study of religion and symbolic systems but seek to understand history as told from below and the realities of power, as well as the history of women, sainthood, or the anthropology of tourism.

Indeed, if we compare this fragmentary and work-in-progress situation with research on pilgrimage in Britain, the U.S., France and northern Europe and the Anglophone academic publishing industry devoted to pilgrimage topics, it may be more accurate to refer to 'Italian studies on pilgrimage' rather than 'Italian anthropological pilgrimage studies'. To make this suggestion more concrete it is worth considering those who have been working on pilgrimage since the 1990s.

Italian Studies on Pilgrimage 161

An important theoretical contribution has been made by L. M. Lombardi Satriani. He has undertaken a series of studies in Southern Italy informed by folk studies from the late nineteenth century, the work by Pitrè and De Martino and a wide contemporary national and international bibliography. He has focussed particularly on Calabrian or Sicilian regional traditions, where pilgrimage is long established and secular charismatic ritual operators are central in the wider cultural context of an individual search for well-being. He has studied local healers and 'magicians', who derive their charisma from claims to a privileged relation with the Christ, the Virgin, or the local saint. These charismatic figures have also become vectors in the demand for social and economic change, which still reveals the urgency of the 'Southern question'. Satriani further shows that pilgrimage can also be a metaphor for understanding Southern Italy's culture of death. In *Il ponte di san Giacomo* (1996) he explores traditional Sicilian beliefs in pilgrimage as a bridge, which allows the dead to pass to eternal life, and uses the metaphor to consider the traditional ritual work of symbolic reorganisation demanded by death and the process of mourning.

Southern Italy, especially the region of Naples, has again been the focus of anthropological research by Paolo Apolito. On May 1985, in the village of Oliveto Citra, a group of children claimed to have seen the Virgin and Apolito draws on his local fieldwork to analyse the collective construction of visions and a transcendent symbolic universe. This insight into the construction of a 'heaven on earth' allows him to reflect more generally about visions and modern apparitions at Lourdes, Fatima and Medjugorije. His analysis refers once more to the South's subaltern culture and links to Clara Gallini's approach and her reflection on miraculous healing and medical proof. The boundary between rational truth and collective belief is here the central topic, and the pilgrimage to the Virgin Mary emerges as a symbolic space where life and the world are connoted by a 'baroque harmony of enchanted signs' (Apolito 1992: 227–228).

The issue of visions and miracles has also attracted Franca Romano, who investigates a social event which intrigued the media and public opinion at the end of the millennium: the weeping of three statues of the Virgin in central and northern Italy, associated with the phenomenon of miracles (1997). Her book reveals the direct relation established by devotees with the Virgin beyond the Church's control, but she also analyses the development of a miracle industry, which both criticises and lives on media discourse.

The publications by Apolito and Romano, together with Gallini's *Lourdes Il miracolo e la sua prova*, represent a new, strongly ethnographic approach to Italian studies on pilgrimage. They reveal an engagement with N. American interpretive anthropology and the 'Writing Culture' approach but are not translated and, therefore, not known widely abroad. Nevertheless, the long tradition of exchange and dialogue between French and Italian research, encouraged by conferences and reviews, has influenced Élisabeth

162 Elena Zapponi

Claverie's investigation of Medjugorije apparitions over many years (2003). This encounter between academic traditions has also been encouraged by institutions such as *L'école française de Rome*, which was established during the late nineteenth century. These institutions have promoted pilgrimage and religious studies and, before the Internet era, they facilitated the circulation of theories about pilgrimages and devotional itineraries by authors such as Alphonse Dupront, Dominique Julia, Pierre-Antoine Fabre and Daniel Fabre.

Many Italian scholars working on sociology of religion or anthropology have benefited from these traditional links through study at French universities. For example, Giordana Charuty, an Italian in origin and a European ethnologist, has been working in France for many years on the study of popular devotion, pilgrimage and Catholicism more generally in the Mediterranean area (1992, 1997, 2001, 2005). She has also helped to spread knowledge about Italian ethnological studies abroad (Charuty and Severi 1999, Charuty 2009). Dionigi Albera's research reveals a constant interest in devotional changes taking place across the Mediterranean area. He approaches pilgrimage through the lens of multiculturalism and the shared sacred space at shrines (2009/2012), analysing in particular a Marian shrine in Provence, which attracts both Catholic and Muslim pilgrims (2005, 2012) and circulating ideas about pilgrimage studies through his publications in French, Italian and English.

New insights are being developed by a younger generation of Italian researchers thanks to education abroad and a growing attention to international research and debates. For example, Anna Fedele's *Looking for Mary Magdalene: Alternative Pilgrimage and Ritual Creativity at Catholic Shrines in France* (2012) is an ethnographic account of the new spirituality surrounding Mary Magdalene's shrine in southern France, which draws on debates concerning corporeality and sexuality stimulated by Élisabeth Claverie, William Christian (2012) and Nancy Frey (1998). My own research on walking pilgrimages (Zapponi 2010, 2011a) has been strongly influenced by both Italian research and the French sociology of religion, especially studies on the individualisation of belief (De Certeau 2003, 1990, 1974, Hervieu-Léger 1993, 1999) and recent religious ethnographic approaches by E. Claverie, Albert Piette, Yves Lambert and Marc Augé, for example. In *Marcher vers Compostelle. Ethnographie d'une pratique pèlerine* (2011a) I explore the spiritual reasons, which encourage pilgrims to walk to Compostela through an ethnographic perspective. The journey attracts not only Catholics but also those who pursue a nondogmatic spirituality and are uninterested in conventional Catholic shrines, such as Lourdes, Fatima and Medjugorie. The idea of walking and the quest for identity are key motives for setting out along the *camino* to Santiago (see Frey 1998). It provides space and time for a large number of people, who are looking for a spiritual experience based on the shift from external regulation of truths and rites to subjective emotions and beliefs.

The participation by pilgrims from different cultural backgrounds has been the central point of Elisabetta Di Giovanni's 2009 study of Roma pilgrimage to Monte Pellegrino outside Palermo and her research on the Santa Rosalia pilgrimage (2010). The ways in which local Sicilian devotion to Santa Rosalia is changing are explored by Giuseppe Burgio (2007) in the context of the arrival of Tamils, who believe but do not, as yet, belong. Furthermore, my recent research in Rome on a Filipino Catholic transnational movement, *Banal Na Pag-Aaral*, reveals the ways in which new forms of religious syncretism are being generated through transnational migration (2011c). The procession across Rome by an Our Lady of Fatima statue—'Mama Mary', as she is familiarly called by Roman Filipinos—from one family place to another, seems to involve a symbolic strategy of both integration and disintegration in the immigration context; 'Mama Mary' encounters 'Mama Roma'.[4] My research has also explored the reinvention of pilgrimage practice in the Rio de La Plata region, especially in Buenos Aires and Montevideo. After the 2001 economic crisis, new forms of pilgrimage were born in both cities, expressing the sudden flourishing of the cult of Saint Expedito—a saint who responds to urgent needs (2012). Every Thursday the Mothers of the Plaza de Mayo in Buenos Aires march in front of the Casa Rosada, renewing each week their brand of lay pilgrimage (2011b).

Although this new interest in multicultural pilgrimage or ethnic pilgrimage in the context of transnational migration context is making a significant contribution to Italian pilgrimage research, the long-established local character of pilgrimage is still being studied. For example, during the last few decades there has been growing support from institutions involved in heritage politics, which has been encouraged by the 2003 UNESCO Convention for the Safeguarding of Intangible Cultural Heritage.[5]

PILGRIMAGE IN SOCIOLOGICAL AND HISTORICAL ITALIAN STUDIES

Sociologists have often approached the topic of pilgrimage but through a more quantitative approach than anthropologists. They have collected statistics concerning pilgrimage participation and details of the religious geography as well as developing models and typologies. They range from Franco Ferrarotti, a pioneer of Italian sociology studies, to more recent scholars as Maria I. Macioti (2000) and Roberto Cipriani (2002, 2012), Carmelina Chiara Canta (2004), Renato Grimaldi (2012) and Enzo Pace (1989, 2007). These studies, compared with the Italian anthropology of pilgrimage, concentrate on the general characteristics of pilgrimage, its universal as well as its national character and relevance to the international history of pilgrimage. They also consider questions of theory and method, demonstrated through book annexes, which include survey questionnaires, quantitative

164 *Elena Zapponi*

or qualitative interviews and questions concerning research methods and epistemology.

The Roman Jubilee of 2000 represented a peak of interest for sociologists, as the publications by M. Immacolata Macioti (2000) and Roberto Cipriani (2002, 2012), among others, demonstrate. This event not only provided the opportunity for a detailed analysis of a Roman jubilee but also inspired researchers more generally to investigate the experience of sacred journeys. This perspective is evident in both Macioti's *Pellegrinaggi e giubilei* and Franco Ferrarotti's *Partire, Tornare. Viaggiatori e pellegrini alla fine del millennio*, a small literary-style book for a big subject, viz. the boundary between pilgrimage and travel, the pilgrimage goal and the philosophical question of *how* to return home.

While anthropological research emerged from the Italian 'history of popular traditions' approach of the late nineteenth century, Italian sociology only developed after the Second World War. It was less homogeneous and less influenced by the subaltern/hegemonic model and the focus on folklore. Differences in theory and method have led some anthropologists to be highly critical of the sociological guided interview method. Yet the sociological approach has made an important contribution to understanding why people participate in pilgrimage and, unlike the folk tradition in anthropological studies, has been quick to engage with analyses of international pilgrimages, enabling researchers to study different national religious traditions.

The international circulation of ideas has further been encouraged by sociological associations and the promotion of conferences and joint publications. Engaging with Anglophone university networks is now strongly encouraged, although collaboration between Italy and France continues to be promoted as demonstrated by the University of Trento Sociology Department's link with the Ecole Hautes Etudes de Science Social in Paris. This collaboration has encouraged the research by Salvatore Abbruzzese (1995, 1999, 2010) on the relation between Church, territory and individual creativity and by Giovanna Rech on the development of a local religious industry. Rech's work underlines the strong pilgrimage presence in N. Italy, especially its revival through the interaction between faith and tourism in the mountain region (2010, 2011).

Historians have also made an important contribution to Italian pilgrimage studies. Many have focussed on local cults of saints and relics, the economic and social life of shrines and the relationship between the Church and popular religion. Emma Fattorini has studied pilgrimage at Marian shrines between the nineteenth and twentieth centuries and changing devotional beliefs and practices (1999, 2012), Lucetta Scaraffia (1999) has studied Roman jubilees, while Paolo Caucci von Saucken (1995) has specialised on the history of the pilgrimage to Santiago de Compostela. His interest in this subject has not only been academic because he has supported the Italian confraternity of St James and the restoration of a Romanesque pilgrimage hostel near Burgos.

Sergio Luzzato (2009) has made an important contribution to pilgrimage study through his study of pilgrimage to Padre Pio's shrine in southeast Italy. He reveals the significance of local politics, how the growing trend of right-wing nationalism dovetailed with Padre Pio's cult (encouraged by Padre Pio himself) and how this political tendency was important in campaigns to overthrow socialist councils across Southern Italy. Luzzato provides one of the finest in-depth studies not just of the dynamics of a shrine but of its saint.[6] These and other Italian historians have also sought to engage with researchers outside their discipline. Sofia Boesch Gajano, a mediaeval historian, has played a crucial role here, encouraging the circulation of ideas through her promotion of multidisciplinary conferences (Boesch Gajano 2000) and her publications (see Boesch Gajano 1999, for example).

THE LIMITATIONS IN THE CIRCULATION OF IDEAS AND THE REINVENTION OF TRADITIONS: NEW PILGRIMS, OLD SHRINES AND NEW ACADEMIC PERSPECTIVES

During the last few decades pilgrimages have been studied with regard to two specific dimensions: a strong collective participation and the reinterpretation of popular beliefs and practices. In the context of lived religion pilgrimage represents an extraordinary sensory experience, which attracts both the conventionally religious and nonconventional, free-style believers (see Badone 2014). While shrines and the social practices and beliefs surrounding them have been studied for a long time, researchers have recently turned towards pilgrimage routes, the journey and the individual dimensions of pilgrimage. Moreover, this anthropology of experience approach is beginning to place long-established shrines within the context of an increasingly multicultural society where those from migrant communities come in significant numbers as believers rather than belongers. Traditional boundaries are breaking down to some extent, and some Italian researchers are realising that this process must also extend to academic disciplines. To understand the complexity of contemporary pilgrimage a more integrated, interdisciplinary approach is required where historians, sociologists and anthropologists can learn from one another and from their colleagues outside Italy.

The dissemination of Italian research on pilgrimage in the international academic arena has been limited by the preoccupation with small-scale shrines, local saint cults and communities and the social construction of charismatic leaders across Southern Italy. Moreover, these studies have usually been published in Italian and are rarely translated into other languages. When translations are undertaken—in the case of certain publications by Gallini and De Martino, for example—they have usually been in French because of the historic ties between Italy and France. As international flows of knowledge increase and global competition between universities becomes more intense, the circulation of publications abroad, especially in

166   Elena Zapponi

English, has become more urgent. Yet Anglophone researchers also need to pay attention to studies in languages other than English. As this examination of Italian studies on pilgrimage has indicated, the international arena could be considerably enriched by accessing the rich array of empirical work and the variety of theoretical insights developed outside the Anglophone world.

NOTES

1. Italian History of Popular Traditions Studies was later called 'demologia'. The prefix 'demo', from the Greek 'demos' (folk) referring to popular culture, is still currently used in academic and scientific context to define a specific area of research—the 'demo-ethno-anthropological' area—and university departments. The term was institutionalised during the 1970s to reduce the use of the word 'folklore', which was associated commonsense perceptions about media commercialisation of popular culture (see Cirese 1992: 62–63).
2. Pitrè is also the author of a first accurate bibliography on national popular traditions; see Pitrè (1984).
3. Lanternari extended the study of subaltern culture to contexts beyond Europe. His work on new religions/religious movements of the 'oppressed', such as 'cargo cult' type movements, represents a new field of investigation, pioneering for the day; see Lanternari (1994 and 2003).
4. Valentina Napolitana is also working on transnational Catholics in Rome (Latin Americans) and publishing mainly in English (2015).
5. See, as an example, the research project conducted by the Istituto Centrale del Catalogo e della Documentazione on Vallepietra pilgrimage (Lazio). The project focusses on the historical-anthropological evolution of the pilgrimage and on its intangible and tangible heritage, involving pilgrimage songs and visual expressions, for example (see Simeoni 2006).
6. Anglophone researchers have also contributed to this literature, e.g., McKevitt (1991) and Di Giovine (2009).

REFERENCES

Abbruzzese, S. (1995) *La vita religiosa. Per una sociologia della vita consacrata,* Rimini: Guaraldi.
———. (1999) 'Catholicisme et territoire: pour une entrée en matière', *Archives de Sciences Sociales des Religions,* 107: 5–21.
———. (2010) *Un moderno desiderio di Dio. Ragioni del credere in Italia,* Soveria Mannelli: Rubbettino.
Albera, D. (2005) 'La Vierge et l'Islam. Mélange de civilisations en Méditerrannée', *Le Débat,* 137: 134–144.
———. (2009) 'Pellegrinaggi misti e devozioni condivise nel Mediterraneo', in G. Filoramo (ed.) *Le religioni e il mondo moderno,* Torino: Einaudi.
———. (2012) 'The Virgin Mary, the sanctuary and the mosque: interfaith coexistence at a pilgrimage centre', in W. Jansen and C. Notermans (eds.) *Gender, Nation and Religion in European Pilgrimage,* Farnham, UK, and Burlington, VT: Ashgate.

Angelini, P. (2008) *Ernesto De Martino*, Roma: Carocci.

Apolito, P. (1992) *Il cielo in terra. Costruzioni simboliche di un'apparizione mariana*, Bologna: Il Mulino.

Badone, E. (2014) 'Conventional and unconventional pilgrimages: conceptualizing sacred travel in the twenty-first century', in A. Pazos (ed.) *Redefining Pilgrimage: New Perspectives on Historical and Contemporary Pilgrimages*, Farnham, UK, and Burlington, VT: Ashgate.

Boesch Gajano, S. and Petrucci, E. (1999) *La santità*, Bari: Laterza.

——. (2000) *Santi e culti del Lazio: istituzioni, società, devozioni. Atti del Convegno di studio, Roma, 2–4 maggio 1996*, Roma: Società romana di storia patria.

Burgio, G. (2007) *La diaspora interculturale. Analisi etnopedagogica del contatto tra culture: Tamil in Italia*, Pisa: Edizioni ETS, available at www.academia.edu/5119143/Tra_Ganesh_e_S._Rosalia._La_comunita_dei_tamil_a_Palermo (last accessed 2 February 2014).

Canta, C. (2004) *Sfondare la notte. Religiosità, modernità e cultura nel pellegrinaggio notturno alla Madonna del Divino Amore*, Milano: Franco Angeli.

Carpitella, D. (1981) 'Pratica e teoria nel film etnografico italiano: prime osservazioni', *La ricerca Folklorica*, 3: 5–22.

Caucci von Saucken, P. (1995) *Guida Del Pellegrino Di Santiago. Libro quinto del Codex Calistinus secolo XII*, Milano: Jaca Book.

Certeau, M. de (1990) *L'invention du quotidien*, Paris: Gallimard.

——. (2003) *La faiblesse de croire*, Paris: Seuil.

——. and Domenach, J.-M. (1974) *Le christianisme éclaté*, Paris: Seuil.

Charuty, G. (1992) 'Le vœux de vivre. Corps morcelés, corps sans âme dans les pèlerinages portugais', *Terrain*, 18: 45–60.

——. (1997) 'Le pèlerin et ses doubles', *Ateliers*, 18: 75–80.

——. (2001) 'Du catholicisme méridional à l'anthropologie des sociétés chrétiennes', in D. Albera, A. Blok and C. Bromberger C. (eds.), *L'anthropologie de la Méditerranée*, Paris: Maisonneuve Larose, MMSH.

——. (2005) 'La Vierge en action. Entretien avec Elisabeth Claverie', *Terrain*, 44: 153–160.

——. (2009) *Ernesto de Martino. Les vies antérieures d'un anthropologue*, Marseille: Éditions Parenthèse.

——. and Severi, C. (eds.) (1999) 'Ernesto De Martino: un « intellectuel de transition »', *Gradhiva*, 26: 1–7.

Christian, W. (2012) *Divine Presence in Spain and Western Europe 1500–1960*, The Natalie Zemon Davis Annual Lectures, Budapest: Central European University Press.

Cipolla, C. and Cipriani, R. (2002) *Pellegrini del Giubileo*, Milano: Franco Angeli.

Cipriani, R. (2012) *Sociologia del pellegrinaggio*, Roma: Franco Angeli.

Cirese, A. (1992) *Cultura egemonica e culture subalterne. Rassegna degli studi sul mondo popolare tradizionale*, Palermo: Palumbo.

——. (2003) *Tra cosmo e campanile. Ragioni etiche e identità locali*, Siena: Protagon.

——. (2007) *Beni volatili, stili, musei*, Prato: Gli Ori.

Claverie, É. (2003) *Les guerres de la Vierge. Une anthropologie des apparitions*, Paris: Gallimard.

Clemente, P. (2004) 'La pattumiera e la memoria. La civiltà Contadina come epoca', in *Il terzo principio della museografia. Antropologia, contadini, musei*, Roma: Carocci.

——. and Mugnaini, F. (2001) *Oltre il folklore. Tradizioni popolari e antropologia nella società contemporanea*, Roma: Carocci.

Cocchiara, G. (1941) *Giuseppe Pitrè e le tradizioni popolari*, Ciuni: Palermo.

168 Elena Zapponi

Crehan, K. (2002) *Gramsci, Culture and Anthropology*, Berkeley and Los Angeles: University of California Press.

Dei, F. (2002) *Beethoven e le mondine. Ripensare la cultura popolare*, Roma: Meltemi.

Del Boca, A. (ed.) (1991) *Le guerre coloniali del fascismo*, Bari: Laterza.

De Martino, E. (1948) *Il mondo magico. Prolegomeni a una storia del magismo*, Torino: Bollati Boringhieri.

———. (1959) *Sud e magia*, Milano: Feltrinelli.

———. (1961) *La terra del rimorso*, Milano: Il Saggiatore.

———. (1975) *Morte e pianto rituale. Dal lamento funebre al pianto di Maria* (Introduction by C. Gallini), Torino: Bollati Boringhieri.

———. (2002) *La fine del mondo. Contributo all'analisi delle apocalissi culturali*, in C. Gallini (ed.), Introduction by C. Gallini and M. Massenzio, Torino: Einaudi.

Di Giovanni, E. (2009) 'Ritualità rom e dinamiche di dis-identità. La festa di Djurdjevdan/Herdelezi a Palermo', *Religioni e Sette nel mondo*, 1: 62–72.

Di Giovine, M. (2009) 'Re-presenting a contemporary saint: Padre Pio of Pietrelcina', *Critical Inquiry*, 35 (3): 481–492

Dore, G. (1980) 'Antropologia e colonialismo italiano. Rassegna di studi di questo dopoguerra', *La Ricerca Folklorica*, 2: 129–132.

Dupront, A. (1987) *Du sacré. Croisades et pèlerinages*, Paris: Gallimard.

Esposito, V. (ed.) (2003) *Annabella Rossi e la fotografia. Vent'anni di ricerca visiva in Salento ed in Campania*, Napoli: Liguori.

Faeta, F. (2003) *Strategie dell'occhio. Saggi di etnografia visiva*, Milano: Franco Angeli.

———. (2012) *Representing the Past. Social Anthropology and History of Art in a Holy Drama in Northern Italy*, Columbia University-Italian Academy for Advanced Studies in America, New York: Fellows Publications.

———. and Ricci, A. (eds) (1997) *Lo specchio infedele. Materiali per lo studio della fotografia etnografica in italia*, Roma: Edizioni del Museo nazionale delle Arti e Tradizioni Popolari.

Fattorini, E. (1999) *Il culto mariano tra Ottocento e Novecento. Simboli e devozione: ipotesi e prospettive di ricerca*, Roma: Franco Angeli.

———. (2012) *Italia devota. Religioni e culti tra Otto e Novecento*, Roma: Carocci.

Fedele, A. (2012) *Looking for Mary Magdalene: Alternative Pilgrimage and Ritual Creativity at Catholic Shrines in France*, Oxford: Oxford University Press.

Frey, N. (1998) *Pilgrim Stories: On and off the Road to Santiago. Journeys Along an Ancient Way in Modern Spain*, Berkeley and Los Angeles: University of California Press.

Gallini, C. (1971) *Il consumo del sacro: feste lunghe di Sardegna*, Bari: Laterza.

———. (1981) 'Il documentario etnografico "demartiniano"', *La Ricerca Folklorica*, 3: 23–31.

———. (1993) 'Le soglie del dolore dai racconti di guarigione di Lourdes', *Etnoantropologia*, 2: 8–31.

———. (1994) 'Lourdes e la medicalizzazione del miracolo', *La Ricerca Folklorica*, 29: 83–94.

———. (1998) *Il miracolo e la sua prova. Un etnologo a Lourdes*, Napoli: Liguori.

———. (2005) *Ernesto de Martino e la formazione del suo pensiero. Note di metodo*, Napoli: Liguori.

———. (2007) *Croce e delizia. Usi, abusi e disusi di un simbolo*, Torino: Bollati Boringheri.

———. (2009) *Il ritorno delle croci*, Roma: Manifestolibri.

———. and Faeta, F. (eds) (1999) *I viaggi nel Sud di Ernesto De Martino* (Photos by A. Zavattini, F. Pinna and A. Gilardi), Torino: Bollati Boringhieri.

Italian Studies on Pilgrimage   169

Gramsci, A. (1950) 'Osservazioni sul folclore', in *Letteratura e vita nazionale*, Einaudi: Torino.

Grimaldi, R. and Cavagnero, S. (2012) *Il pellegrinaggio in trasformazione*, Roma: Aracne.

Hervieu-Léger, D. (1993) *La religion pour mémoire*, Paris: Cerf.

——. (1999) *Le pèlerin et le converti. La religion en mouvement*, Paris: Flammarion.

Labanca, N. (ed.) (1992) *L'Africa in vetrina. Storia di musei e di esposizioni coloniali*, Treviso: Pagus.

——. (2002) *Oltremare. Storia dell'espansione coloniale italiana*, Bologna: Il Mulino.

Lanternari, V. (1994) *Medicina, magia, religione e valori*, Napoli: Liguori.

——. (1997) 'Da Carlo Levi a Ernesto De Martino. Verso la nuova antropologia', in *La Mia alleanza con Ernesto De martino e altri saggi post-demartiniani*, Napoli: Liguori.

——. (2003) *Movimenti religiosi di libertà e di salvezza dei popoli oppressi*, Roma: Editori Riuniti.

Levi, C. (1990) *Cristo si è fermato ad Eboli*, Torino: Einaudi.

Luzzatto, S. (2009) *Padre Pio. Miracoli e politica nell'Italia del Novecento*, Torino: Einaudi.

——. (2011) *La mummia della repubblica. Storia di Mazzini imbalsamato*, Torino: Einaudi.

Macioti, M. (2000) *Pellegrinaggi e giubilei. I luoghi del culto*, Bari: Laterza.

McKevitt, C. (1991) 'San Giovanni Rotondo and the shrine of Padre Pio', in J. Eade and M. Sallnow (eds.) *Contesting the Sacred: The Anthropology of Pilgrimage*, London and New York: Routledge.

Napolitana, V. (2015) *Migrant Hearts and the Atlantic Return: Humanitas and the Challenge of Transnationalism to the Roman Catholic Church*, New York: Fordham University Press.

Pace, E. (1989) 'Pilgrimage as spiritual journey: an analysis of pilgrimage using the theory of V. Turner and the resource mobilization approach', *Social Compass*, 36 (2): 229–244.

——. (2007) 'Religion as communication: the changing shape of Catholicism in Europe', in N. Ammerman (ed.) *Everyday Religion: Observing Modern Religious Lives*, Oxford: Oxford University Press.

Pitré, G. (1984) *Bibliografia delle tradizioni popolari d'Italia*, Palermo: Clausen.

——. (2002) *La famiglia, la casa, la vita del popolo siciliano* (ed. T. Tentori), Palermo: Documenta.

——. (2005) *Feste patronali in Sicilia* (ed. A. Amitrano Savarese), Palermo: Documenta.

Rech, G. (2010) 'Religious tourism and local pilgrimages in a mountain region: opportunity for local development or reinvention of local traditions?', in D. Picard and C. Amaral (eds.) *Tourism and Seductions of Difference*. Proceedings of the TOCOCU 1st Biennial Conference (Lisbon, Portugal, 9–12 September), Sheffield, UK: TOCOCU.

——. (2011) 'Le Trekking du Christ pensant dans les Dolomites: narrations de la création d'un Lieu', in F. Bakkar and S. Berlière (eds.), *Entreprise et sacré: regards transdisciplinaires*, Paris: Actes de la Journée de recherche du Propédia, Cimeos, CHERPA, Paris Groupe IGS.

Romano, F. (1997) *Madonne che piangono. Visioni e miracoli di fine millennio*, Roma: Meltemi.

Rossi, A. (1970) *Lettere da una tarantata*, Bari: De Donato.

——. (1986) *Le feste dei poveri*, Palermo: Sellerio.

Scaraffia, L. (1999) *Il Giubileo*, Bologna: Il Mulino.

170 *Elena Zapponi*

Scotellaro, R. (2012) *L'uva puttanella. Contadini del sud,* Bari: Laterza.
Simeoni, P. (ed.) (2006) 'Ministero per i beni e le attività culturali—Istituto Centrale per il Catalogo e la Documentazione', *Fede e tradizione alla Santissima Trinità di Vallepietra. 1881–2006,* Roma: Artemide.
Turner, V. and Turner, E. (1978) *Image and Pilgrimage in Christian Culture: Anthropological Perspectives,* Oxford: Blackwell.
Zapponi, E. (2010) 'Le pèlerinage vers Saint-Jacques-de-Compostelle', *Archives de Sciences Sociales des Religions,* 149: 73–87.
———. (2011a) *Marcher vers Compostelle. Ethnographie d'une pratique pèlerine,* Paris: L'Harmattan/AFSR.
———. (2011b) 'La seconda vita di una madre. Il movimento delle Madri della Plaza de Mayo e la cultura della memoria', *Studi Storici, Rivista Trimestrale dell'Istituto Gramsci,* 2 (52): 423–425.
———. (2011c) 'La pratica religiosa come strategia di resistenza culturale nel processo migratorio. Il caso della comunità cattolica filippino-romana *Banal Na-Pag-Aaral,' Religioni e Società,* 71: 106–110.
———. (2012) 'La transmission de la mémoire. Générations croyantes à Buenos Aires et Montevideo', in C. Béraud, F. Gugelot and I. Saint-Martin I. (eds.) *Catholicisme,* Paris: Éditions de l'École des Hautes Études en Sciences Sociales.

9 From Cryptic to Critique
Early and Contemporary French Contributions to the Study of Pilgrimage

Anna Fedele and Cyril Isnart

Our inventory includes even pilgrimages that are, if not exactly clandestine, at least anarchic, derived from a grave and powerful, albeit elementary, folklore. These pilgrimages, conducted in a mentality that might be described as 'pre-logical' can obviously not be properly understood by our investigative methods. The solution resides in defining, together with ethnographers, an adequate exploration to create two parallel inventories: one dedicated to official pilgrimages, and the other to examine their obscure, even cryptic, counterparts.

(Dupront 1964–1965)

Arnold Van Gennep's analysis of rites of passage lies at the heart of contemporary pilgrimage studies thanks to the influential study by Victor and Edith Turner, but other French authors have received little attention from non-French scholars. It is impossible to summarise in a single chapter the entire French tradition of pilgrimage studies, and we have, therefore, decided to offer a panoramic view of French approaches to the study of pilgrimage. We begin with religious historians and folklorists like Arnold Van Gennep, Robert Hertz and Alphonse Dupront and then explore their relationship to more contemporary anthropological and sociological approaches to pilgrimage (Danièle Hervieu-Léger, Élisabeth Claverie, Giordana Charuty and Dionigi Albera).

Even if France has been one of the earliest European centres for the social scientific study of religion, scant attention was paid to pilgrimage before the second half of the twentieth century. Early French scholars such as folklorists, philologists and sociologists focussed on the peripheral practices surrounding pilgrimage, describing the divinities and their genealogies, the sites and their use, or the human relations to the saint rather than offer a theoretical framing of pilgrimage itself. Hence, between 1880 and 1960 anthropologists or historians discussed pilgrimage not as an object *per se*, but as one of the ways of experiencing religion. However, if we pay close attention to the place given to pilgrimage in this literature we can see the major trends in religious studies at the time, evaluate the weight of major concepts in the analysis of religion and identify some alternative paradigms and surveys,

172 *Anna Fedele and Cyril Isnart*

which have opened the path for innovative approaches to pilgrimage. We will focus in particular on two interconnected *fils rouges* (red lines) that emerge from the French tradition of pilgrimage studies: 1) the sometimes violent, sometimes balanced opposition between clerical and spontaneous devotion (Sébillot, Hertz, Van Gennep) and 2) Alphonse Dupront's descriptive category of 'cryptic', which addresses all those elements related to pilgrimage that escape and sometimes even oppose the rigid and generalised cults and rituals defined by religious institutions. Both of these themes emerge in more recent French approaches to pilgrimage that we will analyse in this chapter, even if they are not always explicitly referred to.

Part I: The Genealogy of the Cryptic Paradigm

Early French Approaches to Pilgrimage (1880–1960)

In the early stage of French religious studies we can identify three moments or movements, which gave a different role to pilgrimage within their theoretical paradigms and descriptive tools:

- The study of folklore, characterised by a quest for the survivals of a lost European paganism, a focus on folk gestures at a specific shrine (Sébillot), the elaboration of a directory of peculiar popular forms of religious practices and the inscription of pilgrimage within a structural analysis of ritual activity (Van Gennep).
- The Durkheimian School, mainly represented by Robert Hertz, who published the sole monograph based on fieldwork practice on a local pilgrimage in the Alps. While this text represents an early keystone in the French sciences of religion, it also provides an innovative perspective on Durkheim's theory of the sacred and is still considered an important example of the anthropological analysis of religion.
- The work of the historian Alphonse Dupront and his colossal inventory of pilgrimages in Europe in the early 1960s. Although he led one of the few experiments in studying pilgrimage as an object *per se*, most of his work is still unpublished. It demonstrates not only a continuity with previous French approaches but also an original perspective on the supernatural elements and the practical arrangements operating at European pilgrimage sites.

THE FOLKLORE OF PILGRIMAGE AT THE TURN OF THE TWENTIETH CENTURY: PAUL SÉBILLOT AND ARNOLD VAN GENNEP

In France the development of religious studies is marked by a long phase of institutionalisation, a slow stabilisation of boundaries between disciplines and a gradual specialisation on certain research topics. The study of folklore, as a science focussing almost exclusively on the culture of European peasants,[1] coexisted with the ethnography of far-flung locations and the history of ancient religions. Although bridges were built between these disciplinary traditions,[2] they were often created by strong academic personalities, who were not very representative of the ethnographic work conducted within those disciplines. The study of folklore at the turn of the twentieth century in France is marked by two major authors, Paul Sébillot and Arnold van Gennep, who both explored cultural practices in the wake of nineteenth-century romantic folklore and attempted to establish a science of religions (see also Pierre Saintyves 1907). Their analyses emphasise the paradigms of survival and premodern civilisations and focus on divinities, locations and ritual forms that could be integrated within the scheme of cultural evolutionism.

Sébillot's (1843–1918) most important publications are his impressive four volumes, each five hundred pages, published between 1904 and 1907 under the title *Le Folk-lore de la France* and organised around specific themes (*The Sky and the Earth*, *The Sea and Fresh Water*, *Fauna and Flora*, *Peoples and History*). Pilgrimage is not analysed as a particular object, but there are around fifty references to the terms 'pilgrimage', 'pilgrim', or 'sanctuary' in each volume. Broadly speaking, pilgrimage is mentioned in two different contexts: 1) in folk literature pieces that tell the story of a pilgrim or a saint who is faced with some difficulty during his journey and 2) when describing a ritual, a cult or a specific pilgrimage site (in this context ethnographic descriptions are more numerous and more accurate).

Sébillot draws on secondhand testimonies and makes a point of collecting and describing heterodox practices, bizarre rituals, or unchanged features of ritual acts throughout France. He does not attempt to construct a model of pilgrim devotion or establish an inventory of active sites—rather, he wants to uncover the ancient forms of pagan religions that underlie popular rituals.

According to Sébillot's interpretative model of religious survival, clerical devotions are created through the transformation of pagan devotions. However, these devotions still survive in the spontaneous, popular, or nonauthorised rituals of the peasants. Here we can already find one of the key themes that provide the axes for our analysis of the French pilgrimage study tradition. Sébillot pays special attention to the relationship between the rituals' pagan and Christian elements, which are sometimes violently opposed or, more frequently, balanced with some degree of harmony. There is no formal theorisation of pilgrimage, but he provides a model of cults that involves a form of religious journey, typical of the folk.

This model becomes particularly evident when Sébillot analyses the cult of healing fountains. He argues that these cults involve both journeys by the believers and a relationship with local supernatural powers (water) and miracles coming from ancient local religions. Pilgrimage ensures, thereby, the survival of pagan elements in Christianised cults. To support his thesis,

174   *Anna Fedele and Cyril Isnart*

Sébillot focusses on the range of ritual acts, the categories of sites and the divinities celebrated during rituals at the fountains:

> In many cases, [. . .] the acts performed at the fountain are often preceded or followed by devotion at the sanctuary that contains the statue or the shrine of the Saint to whom the source is dedicated. In some cases it is a fusion of the cults; the rituals by the fountain retain vestigial traces of paganism that are sometimes very apparent, whereas inside the chapels, the rituals are generally far more Christianised. (Sébillot 1905: 218–219)

His discussion sometimes leads towards a social analysis of practices, for example, when he describes 'professional pilgrims', who carry out the journey and rituals on behalf of others (1905: 234) or when he mentions the intellectual aristocracy's disapproval of abortion rituals (Ibid: 234).

Arnold Van Gennep (1873–1957) belongs to another generation. Less concerned with the theory of survival, he is ambivalent towards Sébillot's approach to folklore. An independent and controversial figure in the world of twentieth-century academia, Van Gennep is well known for his comparative essay on rites of passage (1909), which inspired Victor Turner (among others) to formulate his pilgrimage theory. However, Van Gennep also produced original ethnographies and developed a methodical and comparative analysis of the ethnography of France. His unfinished *Manuel de folklore français contemporain* (1937–1958) is an attempt to use his theory about rites of passage to analyse life cycle rituals, collective ceremonies and agricultural customs in France. The *Manuel* is more than five thousand pages long and is divided into four volumes and nine parts (including 'Introduction'; 'From the Cradle to the Grave'; 'Periodic, Cyclic and Seasonal Customs'; 'Questionnaires'; 'Bibliography'; and 'Index').

He is not particularly interested in pilgrimage but rather searches for an authentic popular and folk religion based on the rites of passage paradigm and opposed to church and aristocratic devotions (see Van Gennep 1973 for the theorisation). Hence, in the *Rites de passage* only a page and a half are dedicated to this pilgrimage as such, which is relegated to a section named 'Other Categories of Rites of Passage' (1909: 263–264). The subject is occasionally mentioned in the lists of folkloric facts categorised according to the 'From the Cradle to the Grave' cycle, the Carnival-Lent-Easter cycle of the *Manuel* and in certain of his regional monographs. The pilgrimages are primarily related to vows for health and requests for a good life. The *sanctuaires à répit* provide an interesting case of the way in which pilgrimage and rites of passage are connected. If babies die before they are baptised, parents can bring their bodies to these sanctuaries to have them resurrected for a short time and baptised, thereby allowing their souls to enter the kingdom of heaven (1998: 123). Here pilgrimage to a shrine is essential to performing baptism and achieving the passage from life to death.

From Cryptic to Critique   175

Van Gennep also dedicates five pages to pilgrimages that take place towards the end of the Easter cycle, sometimes replaced by simple outings and picnics (1999: 1375–1395). Most of these practices seem to him to be authentic folk customs and help to pass from one season to another. Also in his study on the cycle of May and Saint John, pilgrimages and processions of an agricultural or healing nature take the centre stage (1999: 1696–1701). Sometimes the evolutionist interpretation of the survival of spring cults or, more broadly, the functionalist interpretation of healing practices return. Yet once again, the focus on rites of passage and autonomous folk devotions, especially those belonging to the calendar cycle, take precedence over a sociological analysis of pilgrimage.

In his work on Algerian ethnography (1913: 41–58, cf. Sibeud 2004), Van Gennep describes his participation in a Jewish pilgrimage in the Tlemcen region. He analyses the rites performed by Jewish believers around the tomb of a Spanish rabbi and takes scrupulous notes on the elements he can attribute to rites of passage. He provides some ethnographic details that speak of the religious originality of this pilgrimage, its plural dimensions (the saint's tomb is visited by Algerian and Moroccan Jews but also Muslims and Catholics), the relativity of beliefs (a local female informant comments on her personal adaptation of the rituals and refers to the variability of devotions) and the ways in which social and sexual hierarchies were expressed through lived ritual (Van Gennep mentions the gender divide which shapes ritual and devotion, emphasising the local garments worn by Jewish women unlike the men who dress according to Western fashion, and the specific nature of the female vows to the saint, often related to bearing children and getting married).

ROBERT HERTZ: TOWARDS A DURKHEIMIAN READING OF PILGRIMAGE

During the first decade of the twentieth century Arnold Van Gennep and the group gathered around Émile Durkheim (Robert Hertz, Henri Hubert, Marcel Mauss and later Maurice Halbwachs) created a very dynamic academic landscape, but they also represented a very competitive and often mutually exclusive approach within the emerging sociological study of religion. Durkheim's group largely ignored pilgrimage, and Durkheim only mentions it on three occasions in his classic text, *Les formes élémentaires de la vie religieuse/The Elementary Forms of the Religious Life* (1912: 332, 534, 550). The term is used when referring to tattooing practices used by Catholic pilgrims or when describing in a metaphor the journey undertaken by the Arunta during totemic ceremonies. He did not intend to explicitly associate the Western term and Australian practices in a conceptual manner. Rather, the episodes implicitly link monotheist pilgrimage to the saints to the more general cult of ancestors and to an evolutionist genealogy that establishes the continuity of the totemic explanatory scheme.

176 *Anna Fedele and Cyril Isnart*

Durkheim's lack of interest in pilgrimage was challenged by Robert Hertz's study of an Alpine Catholic cult (1913).[3] Hertz (1881–1915) is better known for his contributions to the reformulation of Durkheimian themes concerning the sacred, the purity and their transgressions (Hertz 2014). However, his 1913 text is the first French sociological analysis of a cult dedicated to a saint, as well as a firsthand ethnographic description of a European pilgrimage. The study made little impact at first. It was despised by Durkheim and Mauss, poorly understood by Hertz's contemporaries and only rediscovered in France during the 1970s. It is now regarded as a classic text in French religious studies, and its fame has extended beyond French-speaking circles, thanks to its translation into English by Stephen Wilson. Jeremy MacClancy and Robert Parkin (1997), who revisited Hertz's field-work during the 1990s, sought to include him in the genealogy of pilgrim-age theoretical debates (MacClancy 1994) and provided a fine-grained introduction to his work, the issues it raises and the scientific context of its production (Parkin 1996). More recently, several French sociologists and anthropologists have furthered this analysis by reviewing research archives and records, broadening the comparative field, or conducting fieldwork on modern pilgrimages (see Isnart 2009 and 2014a).

Unlike many of his contemporaries, Hertz stays close to ethnographic facts, but, even so, a theoretical and sometimes moralising perspective emerges in the introduction and conclusion to his study. Right at the beginning of his text he draws on Durkheim's notion of the invisible, albeit powerful, religious force as the interpretative key to the reasons why local people engage in the pilgrimage. In a European context, therefore, Hertz shows how the Durkheimian theory of the sacred can be transformed by a specific local context. He also describes the journey as a source of suffering and a conscious gift to the saint and uses the concept of sacrifice previously analysed by Hubert and Mauss (1899). He uses this notion of sacrifice once more when describing the system of offerings at the sanctuary, which is crucial to the economy and moral dimensions of the organisation of the pilgrimage.

By examining the appearance of the saint in historical sources, by confronting various hagiographic texts and by describing the ritual as he saw it performed, Hertz reconstructs the intersecting dynamic of the political usage and popular representations of St Besse. When he bypasses the theory of survival of rituals and sacred theories (only to return to it at the end of his text) by introducing it into Durkheim's theory of social integration, Hertz reveals the sociological dimension specific to this pilgrimage. He is careful to reveal the political dimensions of religion, to describe some details of the ritual and to relate to the local meanings in an ethnographic and interpretative synthesis.

Another original feature of Hertz's work is his systematic attention to the scale of the community, which becomes more focussed and complex in the course of the analysis. The discussion of the small group of St Besse devotees is strongly influenced by Durkheim's religious and sociological interpretation, which sees religion as playing a major role in social integration. Yet while Durkheim defends a systematic and equivalent relationship between religious groups and social cohesion, Hertz argues that the definitions of the community can change or evolve through time and according to political manoeuvring.

Rather than engaging directly with current ethnographic discussions about totemism or explicitly offering a theory on pilgrimage and methodological guidelines to investigate it, Hertz makes the Durkheimian model more complex and receptive to local and specific conditions and provides some innovative paths for the exploration and analysis of pilgrimage as a social phenomenon. However, it is probably when Robert Hertz, the sociologist, or even Arnold Van Gennep, the folklorist, were able to experiment and consider the pilgrimage from a personal standpoint that the relevance of the object emerges from the theories.

Approaching pilgrimage through their own experience and feelings surely implied another kind of knowledge that was very different from the 'armchair anthropology' of the nineteenth-century historians of religion, and this tendency anticipates the late-twentieth-century development of reflexivity in Anglophone anthropology. Probably, folk/church competition around the cult of St Besse and the discrete and unofficial practices in Algeria would not have been so clear without the experience of the fieldwork by Hertz and Van Gennep. The examination of the third scholar of the early studies on pilgrimage in France will provide new evidence concerning this point.

ALPHONSE DUPRONT—AN ALTERNATIVE APPROACH TOWARDS PILGRIMAGE?

From the end of the First World War until the Turners' study (1978), pilgrimage research in France was limited. The only exception was provided by the historian Alphonse Dupront (1905–1990). A specialist on the Crusades, which he considered to be the ultimate and most extreme form of pilgrimage, he published papers on two Marian shrines—Lourdes (1958) and Rocamadour (1973)—as well as a general synthetic article (1985). As a founder of the Université Paris-IV and director of studies of the École Pratique des Hautes Études (1959), he also led one of the most extensive surveys on European pilgrimages ever attempted. The study failed to produce many publications, and most of the data remains unused and archived at his research centre (Centre d'Anthropologie Religieuse Européenne). Nevertheless, the data nourished his more theoretical work, especially in the last book, *Du sacré* (1987), and in his contribution to the *Encyclopedia Universalis* (Julia 2008). These texts express his belief that pilgrimage involved both a 'sacred site', structuring the material elements of pilgrimage, and a spiritual effusion produced through the encounter with the divine.

He also agrees with one of the central themes of French pilgrimage studies: the separation between ecclesiastical and popular experiences of pilgrimage. His detailed research revealed that behind the Marian cults, which local churches were trying to spread, there was an older cult, dedicated to healing saints. Little-known pilgrimages and sacred sites provided the best examples of this more authentic approach towards the divine (1987: 33). Dupront called for a combination of a sociology of pilgrimage, which analysed how people make the shrine and what they do there, and an experiential approach towards what and how people feel at the shrine (1987: 41). The place, and particularly its topography, natural elements and religious devices (including buildings and sacred images), constitute the foundations on which religious feelings and authentic perceptions of the divine can be experienced.

Dupront then calls for a type of research into the forms of pilgrimage, which he describes as 'cryptic': a new descriptive category, which he opposes to the rigid and generalised cults defined by the Church (Dupront 1968–1969, in Julia 2008). Following the paths of Rudolph Otto (sacred as supernatural experience) and Carl Jung (collective unconscious, archetypes), he explores how certain structures of human religious thought, defined by him as universal, primitive and prelogical, resist institutional frameworks and find their expression through healing practices and vows. Hence, contemporary pilgrims can experience a cryptic type of encounter with the divine that remains within the limits of the Church's structure but does not need to be mediated by an institution. Dupront uses specific psychological or emphatic vocabulary ('sacral', 'telluric', 'dark forces', 'cosmic', 'chthonian', 'panic', 'immemorial', 'eschatological', 'depth feeling', 'exorcism of the inescapability of the cosmic') to describe the human universal feelings produced by the apparition of the sacred ('le sacral'). Considering it as intrinsically human, he assumes that the cryptic perception and representation of the sacred is present in all forms of pilgrimage but is more vivid and visible in what he identifies as the archaic, simple and grassroots versions.

1950s Lourdes was for Dupront, therefore, a typically authentic and cryptic sacred site, which was entirely constructed through the faith of ordinary people. It combined places clearly organised around a Catholic cult, with emblematic natural elements (water, fields, cavern, fertility) and highly commercialised zones, which sharply contrasted with the spaces controlled by the Church. This entanglement of institutional and popular places and practices created the 'real purity of Lourdes' (1987: 346), as a totally grassroots, folk, primitive and cryptic religious site. For Dupront real pilgrimage is to be found in these cryptic shrines, where the Church has little influence and where psychological and essential patterns of religious experience can survive.[4]

Dupront was a regular pilgrim to Lourdes, and in 1958 he drew on his own religious experience to uncover what he saw as a perfect example of a cryptic process, which provides access to perceptions of more universal religious feelings. Once again, it seems that only empirical research can reveal the negotiated, complex and deeper aspects of pilgrimage. This is a lesson that all modern anthropologists accept today, but it is worth remembering that during the first half of the twentieth century, fieldwork was not seen as vital to the pursuit of anthropological research in France.

Dupront died soon after the publication of his masterpiece, *Du sacré* (1987), but his research centre has continued to support the field of pilgrimage studies. His students have investigated popular religion, modern devotional changes and pilgrimage sites, often focussing on French religious traditions or on French historical regions. For reasons of brevity we cannot detail here the important research done on the history of pilgrimage, but we would like to cite the study by Philippe Boutry and Michel Cinquin of the nineteenth-century devotion to the Curé d'Ars (1980) and Marie-Hélène Froeschlé-Chopard's extensive research on modern religious life in Provence, which is partly dedicated to local pilgrimages (1994, 2002). Thanks to the French-Italian traditional academic connections supported by the Ecole Française de Rome, many surveys and colloquia have been held to continue and/or renew Dupront's approach. Two inventories of French and Italian pilgrimage sites have been undertaken, and important volumes on pilgrimage, vows and religious itineraries have been published by Philippe Boutry, Pierre-Antoine Fabre and Dominique Julia (Boutry and Julia 2000, Boutry, Fabre and Julia 2000), while Serge Brunet (2001, Brunet and Lemaître 2005) and Sofia Boesche Gajano and Lucetta Scaraffia (1990) have studied sacred sites in mediaeval and modern times.

The American scholar William A. Christian has also participated in some of these conferences and contributed to the debates. Drawing mainly on history and anthropology, he has shared his profound knowledge not only of the Anglophone authors but also of French, Italian and Spanish authors studying Marian apparitions, pilgrimage and vernacular religion, in general. Publishing mainly in English (1972, 1981, 1992, 1996), he has introduced Anglophone researchers to the new developments in French research. Other Anglophone religious scholars, such as John Eade (1991, 1992, 2012) and Ellen Badone (2007, 2008), have helped to popularise French studies on pilgrimage and religious devotion through their own work. Despite their mutual interests, Anglophone and Francophone researchers have not engaged with each other very much until recently, largely due to linguistic and disciplinary boundaries.

During the last four decades researchers have continued to work on pilgrimage and contemporary religion. Since the middle of the twentieth century and Dupront's investigations, Lourdes has become one of Europe's biggest shrines and functions as a paradigm of what a pilgrimage site can be. Other Marian shrines have also gained in importance, and the study of pilgrimage has become a key theme within the anthropology of religion. Ethnographies in France, but also around the Mediterranean, foster, combine and mix the heritage of the early masters with current religious and social

180 *Anna Fedele and Cyril Isnart*

dynamics. Despite these developments it appears that the themes of church/ folk rivalry and the cryptic side of the pilgrimage still structure the domain.

Part II: Critical Approaches to Pilgrimage

Modern and Contemporary French Authors[5]

DANIÈLE HERVIEU-LÉGER: SECULARISATION, MEMORY AND MOBILITY

During the 1970s and 1980s those studying religion followed the international trend by focussing on secularisation and the decline of institutionalised religions. Hence, scant attention was paid to contemporary forms of pilgrimage. Danièle Hervieu-Léger was an exception to this rule. Working sometimes together with her husband, Bertrand Hervieu (1973, 1983), she has had an important influence on French scholars studying pilgrimage. She was one of the first scholars to study secularisation and religious modernity and in 1993 co-founded the Centre d'Etudes Interdisciplinaires des Faits Religieux. She also became the first female president of the Ecole des Hautes Etudes en Sciences Sociales (2004–2009) and is one of the few French sociologists of religion whose texts have been published in English. Her collaboration with Grace Davie (1996) helped to deepen her impact on Anglophone debates in the sociology of religion.

After *La religion pour memoire* (1993, translated as *Religion as a Chain of Memory*, 2000) Hervieu-Léger used the emblematic figures of the practising Christian, the pilgrim and the convert to illustrate modern 'religion in movement' (1999). The practising Christian observes an obligatory, fixed and repetitive practice; follows the norms established by institutions; and is attached to a certain territory. The practitioner represents a kind of religiosity that has been inherited in contrast to the convert. In between these two poles the pilgrim represents a more complex identification with the religious because it is not as radical as that of the convert and allows the individual to access the religious at a historical moment when the intergenerational transmission of religion seems to have lost its power. The pilgrim is more involved in religious practices, which are voluntary, autonomous, changeable, individual, mobile and exceptional. Hence, for Hervieu-Léger the pilgrim represents a Catholicism in movement that offers a possible answer to the crisis of institutionalised religions because it provides a mobile religiosity that responds to the modern need for religious individualism. These three ideal types of involvement with the religious do not exclude each other: an individual may well start as a convert and gradually become a practitioner; there can also be pilgrims with routinised attitudes similar to those of the practitioners.

The way in which Hervieu-Léger sets the figure of the pilgrim apart from more institutionalised figures within Christianity reminds us of the two central themes we have identified in this chapter. She develops this opposition between institutionalised religion and lived pilgrimage practices further, portraying the pilgrim as a mobile and, we might add, cryptic figure who infuses Christianity with the kind of dynamism it needs in order to survive in an increasingly secularised society.

In her ethnography of the pilgrimage to Santiago de Compostela, Elena Zapponi (2011) draws on Hervieu-Léger's approach to explore the ways in which pilgrims create their own *bricolage* of theories and practices along the way. Her research also shows the close relationship between French and Italian research on pilgrimage mentioned earlier and discussed by Zapponi elsewhere in this volume.

GIORDANA CHARUTY: FOLKLORE AND RELIGIOUS FOOLISHNESS

Giordana Charuty represents another figure of French academia who fruitfully developed the dialogue with the Italian tradition. She has managed to blend the tradition of the French and Italian ethnographers and folklorists from the late nineteenth and early twentieth centuries with more Foucauldian approaches.

After initial research on the medical and folk conceptualisation and treatment of mental illness (1985), Charuty explored the different ways in which madness was addressed in Christian contexts in rural European societies (1997). She shows how certain forms of mental illness, described by biomedicine as hysteria or epilepsy, were considered in particular rural societies as a failure to go through certain rites of passage; they therefore represented a potential danger for the social order. She describes the complex symbolic systems through which these cases of failure were ritually addressed and analyses in detail some specific cases. These mental disorders are often identified with the name of a saint (e.g., the illness of Saint Donato in Umbria, Italy) and are said to be healed through pilgrimages to shrines related to that specific saint.

Analysing different types of 'curative pilgrimage' (1997: 16), Charuty demonstrates that the efficacy of this ritual treatment relies upon the equivalence that exists between pilgrimage on Earth and pilgrimage through which the Christian soul reaches paradise. Drawing upon this parallelism Charuty argues that the mortification rituals made during these pilgrimages, e.g., the simulation of funerals in Portugal and the weighing and measuring of souls in Italy, replicate on Earth the itinerary of the dead in the other world, thereby allowing the healing of the body and establishing the person's eligibility for marriage.

Charuty further describes how the final sequences of these pilgrimages serve to assess the mental and sexual status of the pilgrim healed by the saint. The dances and the fairs that conclude the pilgrimage experience have

182 Anna Fedele and Cyril Isnart

always been condemned by the ecclesiastical authorities (1997: 303–310) eager to control and to banish the sexualised and ostentatious displays of virility or femaleness that took place. These curative pilgrimages endow the mentally ill pilgrims with a gender identity and allow them to become members of society through the ritual of marriage. The ritual reinforces and legitimates the social structure and allows individuals to strengthen their position within their society.

Charuty is one of the major researchers of Catholicism in southern Europe (Charuty 2001). She forms part of a generation influenced by Claude Lévi-Strauss's structuralism and has provided detailed descriptions of the multiple and often contradictory practices related to rural lived religion in Europe. This generation has drawn on the research of European folklorists since the eighteenth century, as well as the medical literature of these periods, and has blended this historical data with rich ethnographic data gathered in different countries across southern Europe.

Charuty also builds on the analysis of the social construction of gender developed by other French researchers, such as Yvonne Verdier or Daniel Fabre. Verdier compared the three figures of the midwife, the female cook and the woman in charge of the preparation of corpses in French peasant society (Verdier 1974), while Fabre explored rituals of male initiation through practices related to particular sites of pilgrimage (1986a), practices related to the mythical figure of the savage (2005), or the custom of taking young birds from their nests (1986b). These authors thus show how people are embedded in a specific ritual and symbolic system that forms the framework of their religious and gender experience.

Cyril Isnart (2008) has been influenced by this generation of anthropologists.[6] Like them he does not situate pilgrimage at the centre of his research, but some of the rituals he describes form part of a specific pilgrimage tradition. He offers a detailed ethnography of the feasts and pilgrimages related to early Christian military saints known in small localities in Italy and France and shows how the images of the saints and their hagiographies are used in each local context as the basis for the construction of different performances of masculinity for the young generations.

ÉLISABETH CLAVERIE: CRITIQUE, METHODOLOGICAL THEISM AND MARIAN CONFLICTS

Élisabeth Claverie's ethnography *Les Guerres de la Vierge: une anthropologie des apparitions* (2003) offers an innovative approach to understanding international pilgrimages to the contested Marian apparition site of Medjugorje. She applies the methodology of the *sociologie de la critique* (also described as *sociologie pragmatique*), developed by Luc Boltanski, Laurent Thévenot, Bruno Latour and Claverie herself, as well as by other sociologists clustered around the Groupe de Sociologie Politique et Morale. French pragmatic

From Cryptic to Critique   183

sociology emphasises the critical capacity of social actors and examines particularly the ways in which people analyse and justify their choices (e.g., Boltanski 1990, 2009, 2011, Boltanski and Thévenot 1991, 1999).

Claverie describes how the different actors at Medjurgorje make assertions and critical statements about the visionaries, who assert that the Virgin Mary appeared to them and continues to appear every month to one of them and once a year to the others. Claverie develops a fine-grained analysis of the experience of the French pilgrims, whom she accompanied, by dividing the first chapter into sequences (airport, bus, arrival at Medjugorje, etc.). These sequences mark their process of learning to become a pilgrim and their growing involvement with the apparition site, while paying attention to the different strategies to express, negotiate and neutralise criticism in an ongoing movement from belief to critique and back. Claverie shows how the pilgrims find themselves entangled in a web of different and often conflicting worlds, where political tensions related to the postwar context in the Western Balkans and local disputes between villages and debates related to Marian devotion go hand in hand. She explains how in this context the Durkheimian opposition between sacred and profane is of little use.

Claverie also describes the historical process through which different political and ecclesiastical authorities sought to test the veracity of the apparitions, and the reader can follow the gradual transformation of a place into a sacred site. She captures the opposition between spontaneous and clerical devotion, following attentively the passage from a formative period of the pilgrimage, with a relative lack of religious routines and restrictions, towards a well-structured international pilgrimage site.

Claverie takes her informants seriously when they say that they are in the presence of a meta-empirical being, and with an audacious methodological experiment, she decides to give this being an analytical status, considering it like a social actor. Referring to her as 'she' (*elle*), Claverie analyses what the Virgin makes appear and carefully unpacks a painful scenario where the apparition allows the public acknowledgement of two different massacres in 1941 and 1945. This 'methodological theism', developed by Claverie together with Albert Piette (2003), offers an interesting alternative to the often implicit agnostic or atheist approach of social scientists dealing with pilgrimage, in particular, and religion, in general. Their approach pushes the anthropologist's intent to take informants seriously to its extremes but also opens up new interpretative frameworks.

Claverie's focus on the critical dimension of pilgrimage appears as a further development of Dupront's category of the cryptic, addressing the tensions between lived pilgrimage and its institutional dimension. It also builds upon and expands Eade and Sallnow's model of pilgrimage sites as arenas for competing discourses by offering a detailed analysis of the wide range of discourses present at Medjurgorje. Claverie moves some steps further, however, by showing how belief and uncertainty are dynamic processes and are never fully established, not only in the context of pilgrimage but also

184 *Anna Fedele and Cyril Isnart*

more generally through other religious experiences (see also Claverie and Fedele 2014).

Several scholars studying pilgrimage have been influenced by Claverie's focus on criticism and have put to work the methodological theism in different contexts. In her ethnography of two Palestinian pilgrimage sites in Cisjordan (West Bank), Emma Aubin-Boltanski (2007) analyses the political dimension of the pilgrimage feasts celebrated yearly to honour the prophet Moses and the prophet Sâlih. She shows how between 1997 and 2000 the Palestinian authorities encouraged these two festivities, transforming these two saints into the symbols of a newly reconstituted Palestine. Her work is particularly interesting because she manages to combine different approaches to the study of pilgrimage that have often been presented as being in conflict with each other—the Durkheimian and Turnerian models, the model proposed by Eade and Sallnow (1991) and Claverie's approach discussed above. Aubin-Boltanski presents the pilgrimages as collective phenomena related to the creation of a national identity, but she also shows how the pilgrims visiting the two sites of Nabî Mûsâ and Nâbi Sâlih are drawn by a desire for *communitas*. They want to experience a common belonging to the Palestinian nation and the ideal community they can relate to. Yet she also carefully describes the obstacles the pilgrims find in their quest for *communitas* and the strategies put into place by the pilgrims themselves or by those in charge of the sites to overcome these obstacles or to deal with failure. Aubin-Boltanski also highlights the tensions existing between the different religious and political discourses articulated at each site.

In more recent research Aubin-Boltanski (2010) analyses a Lebanese interreligious pilgrimage that originated during 2004 through a Marian apparition at Beshouat, a Catholic Maronite village in the Bekaa valley. She offers a fine-grained analysis of the intersection of different discourses elaborated by politicians, clerics and intellectuals in a complex and fragile scenario where the Virgin Mary emerges as a vehicle for reconciliation between Christians and Muslims.

Other scholars influenced by Claverie's approach have also analysed this complex intertwining of religion, politics and society. Katia Boissevain's monograph on the cult of a frontier female saint in contemporary Tunisia (2006) explores rituals performed at rural and urban sanctuaries, but she also analyses the pilgrims outside the sacred place, describing the gender division of the cult and the complementarity among folk devotions and a more institutionalised religion. Anna Poujeau (2014), in a detailed ethnography of Christian devotion in Syria, examined the ways in which various monasteries and shrines negotiate their presence within the context of local and national life. She uncovers the entanglements of politics and religious activity by following pilgrims from different denominations as well as those living in local Christian communities.

In her *Looking for Mary Magdalene: Alternative Pilgrimage and Ritual Creativity to Catholic Shrines in France* (2013) Anna Fedele draws on

Claverie's approach to study a kind of pilgrim whom social scientists often have trouble taking seriously. The pilgrims she accompanied came from Italy, Spain, Britain and the U.S., were influenced by the international Goddess spirituality movement and did not consider themselves as practising Christians, even if they came from Catholic or Protestant backgrounds. Fedele describes their pilgrimages to Mary Magdalene or dark Madonna shrines as 'critical journeys' (2012), where they could express their criticisms of patriarchy. They particularly criticised the 'Church', which to their mind had appropriated 'power places' where pagan deities had previously been venerated. Through their devotions to Mary Magdalene they were able to get in touch with the 'healing energy' at work at the shrine and come to terms with issues related to incest, abortion, stillbirths and sexual abuse.

Fedele follows the pilgrims' life narratives and analyses in particular their passage from their parents' religion towards a feminist spirituality. She finds that they took a pragmatic approach, continually testing the theories and rituals proposed in books or by the pilgrimage leaders. The pilgrims were also voracious readers, especially in religious studies and anthropology, and were well acquainted with theories of pilgrimage and ritual (Fedele 2013: 248–252, 2014). Although Fedele refers to her interlocutors as pilgrims, she found the pilgrim-tourist divide, which is still prevalent in many pilgrimage studies, unhelpful to understanding their beliefs and practices, especially with regard to the 'energy', which the pilgrims saw as pervading the world (2009, 2012, 2013, 2014; see also Badone and Roseman 2004 and the first chapter of this book).

Valérie Kozlowski is another scholar who draws on Claverie's approach, in her study of the Greek Catholic community associated with St Volodymyr Cathedral in Paris (2008). She paid special attention to the pilgrimage by members of this community to Lourdes. Analysing the relationship between collective remembrance of the motherland and pilgrimage, Kozlowski describes these journeys as rites of passage that help newcomers from Ukraine to become part of the diaspora. Following Claverie's lead, she pays special attention to the process whereby the pilgrims gradually interiorise the discourses about Lourdes, which they hear from the group leader. They learn to experience Lourdes as their French motherland—a place that allows them to establish a link between Ukraine and their new French homeland.

DIONIGI ALBERA: THE 'APPEAL' OF RELIGIOUS OTHERNESS AND RELIGIOUS EXPERIMENTATION IN MIXED MEDITERRANEAN COMMUNITIES

In dialogue with both the Franco-Italian academic world and Anglophone pilgrimage studies, the Italian anthropologist Dionigi Albera has focussed on the religious life of Mediterranean communities, developing his research at the Institut d'Ethnologie Méditerranéenne, Européenne et Comparative,

186 Anna Fedele and Cyril Isnart

Aix-en-Provence. Working with other specialists in the anthropology of the Mediterranean (Albera, Blok and Bromberger 2001, Albera and Tozy 2005), he has explored interreligious cults and pilgrimages related to the Virgin Mary, which attract both Muslims and Christians. His interest in the shared and complex usage of this central figure within Catholicism, who is also recognised by the Islamic tradition, has led him to broaden his research (2005a) and study the shrine of Notre-Dame de Santa Cruz in Nîmes (2005b), which represents a replica of a homonymous shrine in Oran, Algeria. Founded in the 1960s by Algerian repatriates, this shrine also attracts Muslims from the Maghreb. Albera has also studied with Benoît Fliche a similar shrine based at the church of Saint Anthony of Padua in Istanbul (Albera and Fliche 2012). Drawing on his encyclopaedic knowledge about shared shrines in the Mediterranean area and the ethnographic data he has gathered, Albera analyses the ways in which religious actors cross religious borders and transgress norms, revealing thereby the permeability of religious frontiers.

He has also collaborated with Maria Couroucli (2009) to bring together those researching shared shrines across the Balkans, Turkey, Syria, Egypt and Morocco (see, for example, Bowman 2011, Hayden 2002) as well as those who are studying texts concerning interreligious relationships across the Mediterranean since Hasluck in 1929. The 2009 volume addresses, in particular, the ritual practices of devotees who do not belong to the religious majority at the shrines. In his conclusion to the volume, Albera argues that these ethnographic approaches challenge uniconfessional conceptualisations of pilgrimage and reveal aspects of the religious experience that are not easy to grasp in other contexts. The ways in which the devotees manage to ignore rules, their pragmatic strategies, and their use of the ritual elements appear to be particularly evident at mixed shrines. Albera also shows that practices of religious sharing do not eliminate differences or lead to ritual syncretism but rather represent cases of border crossing, which do not question the religious affiliation or heritage of the devotees. The very existence of these sharing practices testifies to a certain degree of critique by pilgrims of official teachings and reveals the somewhat anarchical nature of pilgrimage sites, which are inspired by forces that extend far beyond the bureaucratisation of beliefs and practices of religious institutions.

Influenced by Albera's approach, several researchers have also examined confessional plurality at different Mediterranean pilgrimage shrines. In his research on the Catholic community in Rhodes (2014b), Cyril Isnart has shown how this minority living in a Greek Orthodox territory encouraged and valorised interconfessional practices around the figure of Saint Anthony of Padua, especially during the weekly blessing of the bread and during the yearly feast of the saint. The Catholic Church has also encouraged religious border crossing, allowing Greek Orthodox members of mixed families to venerate their Catholic parents' corpses according to certain Orthodox ritual norms and to bury them in the Catholic cemetery. As with the mixed cults discussed above, confessional borders are not erased but simply crossed for a particular occasion.

In Rhodes the religious institution remains more influential than in the cases analysed in Albera and Couroucli (2009), and Manoël Pénicaud (2011) found a similar situation at the pilgrimage shrines dedicated to the Seven Sleepers in the Mediterranean area. Following in footsteps of the renowned French Orientalist, Louis Massignon, who made the Seven Sleepers into a symbol of the dialogue between Christians and Muslims during the second part of the twentieth century by reactivating a pilgrimage site in Brittany, Pénicaud examines the ways in which the institutionalisation of interconfessional practices (Catholic and Muslim) is organised at these shrines.

CONCLUSION

In this chapter we have explored French approaches to pilgrimage studies, focussing first on early authors such as Van Gennep, Sébillot, Hertz and Dupront and their links to later French authors. We have detected two leading themes that in our opinion keep emerging and that seem to represent a sort of French legacy to pilgrimage studies: the opposition between clerical devotion and spontaneous devotion and Dupront's descriptive category of 'cryptic', which seeks to encompass all those elements of pilgrimage that do not conform to institutionalised religion. We have seen how the discovery of these two main elements gradually led French religious scholars to realise that the kind of unexpected and unofficial religiosity expressed during pilgrimage can only be effectively grasped by those who have participated in its intense rituals or experienced the religious feelings associated with it. More recent authors such as Hervieu-Léger, Charuty, Claverie and Albera have further developed the theories associated with these leading themes by analysing the ways in which pilgrimage provides spaces for religious controversies, ritual experimentation and social criticism. An interesting element in this context is that Lourdes, a site that always played an important role in French pilgrimage studies and tends to be presented today as the reference model for institutionalised Catholic pilgrimage, was presented by Dupront as the cryptic pilgrimage site *par excellence*!

If we broaden our perspective and look beyond national borders, we can see that the opposition between vernacular and orthodox conceptions and Dupront's cryptic dimensions of pilgrimage appear again as central themes in the now classic volume *Contesting the Sacred: The Anthropology of Christian Pilgrimage* (Eade and Sallnow 1991), as well as in other more recent debates such as the intersections of pilgrimage and tourism (Badone and Roseman 2004), the centrality of gender and corporality (Frey 1998, Jansen and Notermans 2012, Fedele 2013), interconfessional pilgrimage (Albera and Couroucli 2012, Coleman 2013), or New Age pilgrimage (Bowman 1993, 2000, Fedele 2013, 2014). Hence, while French research

188 *Anna Fedele and Cyril Isnart*

about pilgrimage has not always received the attention it deserves by Anglophone scholars, the central findings of early French folklorists, religious historians and anthropologists have found, at least indirectly, their way into the international pilgrimage literature.[7]

NOTES

1. In the nineteenth-century French literature, the term *ethnographie* was mainly used to describe non-European cultures, whereas *folklore* was taken to describe European populations. Under Anglo-Saxon influence, the term *folklore* was sometimes also taken to describe non-European populations. In the second part of the twentieth century, the term *folklore* was abandoned by the French and replaced by *ethnologie* and by *anthropologie* in the twenty-first century.
2. For example, *The Golden Bough* by Frazer (1890) indiscriminately cites sources from Antiquity, exotic locations and folklore, and Henri Hubert and Marcel Mauss referred to facts from Indian, Native American, Celtic, or Classical cultures (for instance, see Hubert and Mauss 1899).
3. For the latest English version, see Hertz (2009).
4. See Boutry's review of the 1987 book (Boutry 1989), and for a more critical approach of Dupront's views, see Albert 2000.
5. For reasons of brevity there is no discussion here of research in Francophone European countries such as Belgium or Switzerland.
6. Another scholar who has been influenced by these scholars is Deborah Puccio-Den (2009).
7. This work was supported by the Portuguese Foundation for Science and Technology [grant number PEst-OE/SADG/UI4038/2014].

REFERENCES

Albera D., Blok, A. and Bromberger, C. (eds.) (2001) *L'anthropologie de la Méditerranée*, Paris: Maisonneuve et Larose.
———. (2005a) 'La Vierge et l'Islam. Mélanges de civilisations en Méditerranée', *Le Débat*, 37: 134–144.
———. (2005b) 'Pèlerinages mixtes et sanctuaires 'ambigus' en Méditerranée', in S. Chiffoleau and A. Madoeuf (eds.) *Les Pèlerinages au Maghreb et au Moyen-Orient*, Beirut: IFPO.
———. and Couroucli, M. (2009) *Religions traversées: lieux saints partagés entre chrétiens, musulmans et juifs en Méditerranée*, Arles: Actes sud. (Published in English (2012) as *Sharing Sacred Spaces in the Mediterranean: Christians, Muslims, and Jews at Shrines and Sanctuaries*, Bloomington, IN: Indiana University Press.)
———. and Couroucli, M. (eds) (2012) *Sharing Sacred Spaces in the Mediterranean: Christians, Muslims, and Jews at Shrines and Sanctuaries*, Bloomington and Indianapolis: Indiana University Press.
———. and Fliche, B. (2012) 'Muslim devotional practices in Christian Shrines: the case of Istanbul', in Albera and Couroucli, *op. cit.*
———. and Tozy, M. (eds.) (2005) *La Méditerranée des anthropologues. Fractures, filiations, contiguïtés*, Paris: Maisonneuve et Larose.
Albert, J.-P. (2000) 'Des lieux où souffle l'esprit', *Archives de sciences sociales des religions*, 111: 111–123.

From Cryptic to Critique 189

Aubin-Boltanski, E. (2007) *Pèlerinage et nationalisme en Palestine. Prophètes, héros et ancêtres,* Paris: Éditions de l'EHESS.
——. (2010) 'Fondation d'un centre de pèlerinage au Liban: Notre-Dame de Béchouate', *Archives de Sciences Sociales des Religions,* 151: 141–160.
Badone, E. (2007) 'Echoes from Kerizinen: pilgrimage, narrative and the construction of sacred history at a Marian shrine in northwestern France', *Journal of the Royal Anthropological Institute,* 13 (2): 453–470.
——. (2008) 'Pilgrimage, tourism and the da Vinci code at Les-Saintes-Maries-De-La-Mer, France', *Culture and Religion,* 9 (1): 23–44.
——. and S. Roseman (eds.) (2004) *Intersecting Journeys: The Anthropology of Pilgrimage and Tourism,* Champaign, IL: University of Illinois Press.
Boesch, G. and Scaraffia, L. (1990) *Luoghi sacri e spazi della Santità,* Torino: Rosenberg et Sellier.
Boissevain, K. (2006) *Sainte parmi les saints. Sayyda Mannûbiya ou les recompositions culturelles dans la Tunisie contemporaine,* Paris: Maisonneuve & Larose.
Boltanski, L. (1990) *L'amour et la justice comme compétences: trois essais de sociologie de l'action,* Paris: Éditions Métailié.
——. (2009) *De la critique: précis de sociologie de l'émancipation,* Paris: Éditions Gallimard.
——. (2011) *On Critique: A Sociology of Emancipation,* Cambridge: Polity Press.
——. and Thévenot, L. (1991) *La justification,* Paris: Gallimard.
——. and Thévenot, L. (1999) 'The sociology of critical capacity', *European Journal of Social Theory,* 2 (3): 359–377.
Boutry, P. (1989) 'Alphonse Dupront. Du sacré. Croisades et pèlerinages. Images et langages, Paris, Gallimard, "Bibliothèque des Histoires", 1987, 541 p.', *Annales ESC,* 5: 1245–1248.
——. and Cinquin, M. (eds.) (1980) *Deux pèlerinages au XIXe siècle: Ars et Paray-le-Monial,* Paris: Beauchesne.
——. and Julia, D. (eds.) (2000) *Pèlerins et pèlerinages dans l'Europe moderne. Actes du colloque de l'Institut universitaire européen et de l'Ecole française de Rome. Rome, 4–5 juin 1993,* Rome: Collection de l'École française de Rome.
——. Fabre, P.-A. and Julia, D. (2000) *Rendre ses voeux. Les identités pèlerines dans l'Europe moderne. XVIe–XVIIIe siècles,* Paris: Editions de l'École des Hautes Études en Sciences Sociales.
Bowman, G. (2011) 'The two deaths of Basem Rishmawi: identity constructions and reconstructions in a Muslim-Christian Palestinian community', *Identities: Global Studies in Culture and Power,* 8/11: 47–81.
Bowman, M. (1993) 'Drawn to Glastonbury', in I. Reader and T. Walter (eds.) *Pilgrimage in Popular Culture,* London: Macmillan.
——. (2000) 'More of the same? Christianity, vernacular religion and alternative spirituality in Glastonbury', in M. Bowman and S. Sutcliffe S (eds.) *Beyond New Age,* Edinburgh: Edinburgh University Press.
Brunet, S. (2001) *Les Prêtres des montagnes. La vie, la mort, la foi dans les Pyrénées centrales sous l'Ancien Régime. Val d'Aran et diocèse de Comminges,* Aspet: Universatim Pyrégraph.
——. and Lemaître, N. (eds.) (2005) *Clergés, Communautés et Familles des Montagnes d'Europe; Actes du colloque 'Religion et montagnes', Tarbes, 30 mai-2 juin 2002,* Paris: Publications de la Sorbonne.
Charuty, G. (1985) *Le Couvent des fous. L'internement et ses usages en Languedoc aux XIXe et XXe siècles,* Paris: Flammarion.
——. (1997) *Folie, mariage et mort. Pratiques chrétiennes de la folie en Europe occidentale,* Paris: Le Seuil.
——. (2001) 'Du catholicisme méridional à l'anthropologie des sociétés chrétiennes', in D. Albera, A. Blok and C. Bromberger (eds.) *L'anthropologie de la Méditerranée,* Paris: Maisonneuve et Larose.

Christian, W., Jr. (1981) *Local Religion in Sixteenth Century Spain*, Princeton, NJ: Princeton University Press.

——. (1972) *Person and God in a Spanish Valley* (rev. edition in 1989), Princeton, NJ: Princeton University Press.

——. (1992) *Moving Crucifixes in Modern Spain*, Princeton, NJ: Princeton University Press.

——. (1996) *Visionaries: The Spanish Republic and the Reign of Christ*, Berkeley, CA: University of California Press.

Claverie, E. (2003) *Les guerres de la Vierge. Une anthropologie des apparitions*, Paris: Gallimard.

——. and Fedele, A. (2014) 'Introduction: uncertainty in vernacular religion', *Social Compass*, 61 (4): 497–510.

Coleman, S. (2013) 'Ritual remains: studying contemporary pilgrimage', in J. Boddy and M. Lambek (eds.) *A Companion to the Anthropology of Religion*, London: Wiley Blackwell.

Davie, G. and Hervieu-Léger, D. (eds.) (1996) *Identités religieuses en Europe*, Paris: La Découverte.

Dupront, A. (1958) 'Lourdes. Perspectives d'une sociologie du sacré', *La Table ronde*, 125: 74–96, republished in 1987: 340–365.

——. (1973) 'Sacralités de Rocamadour' in *Colloque de Rocamadour 1973. Saint Louis pèlerin et le pèlerinage de Rocamadour au XIIIe siècle*, Boissor: Cat-Impr, republished in 1987: 315–339.

——. (1985) 'Pèlerinages et lieux sacrés' in *Encyclopaedia Universalis*, Paris, republished in 1987: 366–415.

——. (1987) *Du sacré. Croisades et pèlerinages. Images et langages*, Paris: Gallimard.

Durkheim, É. (1912) *Les formes élémentaires de la vie religieuse*, Paris: Alcan.

Eade, J. (1991) 'Order and power at Lourdes: Lay helpers and the organization of a pilgrimage shrine', in Eade and Sallnow, op. cit.

——. (1992) 'Pilgrimage and tourism at Lourdes, France', *Annals of Tourism Research*, 19 (1): 18–32.

——. (2012) 'Pilgrimage, the Assumptionists and Catholic evangelisation in a changing Europe: Lourdes and Plovdiv', *Cargo. Journal for Social/Cultural Anthropology*, 10 (1–2): 29–46.

——. and Sallnow, M. (1991) *Contesting the Sacred: The Anthropology of Christian Pilgrimage*, London and New York: Routledge.

Fabre, D. (1986a) 'Le sauvage en personne', *Terrain*, 6: 6–18.

——. (1986b) 'La voie des oiseaux. Sur quelques récits d'apprentissage', *L'Homme*, 26 (3): 7–40.

——. (2005) 'Limites non frontières du Sauvage', *L'Homme*, 175–176: 427–444.

Fedele, A. (2009) 'From Christian religion to feminist spirituality: Mary Magdalene pilgrimages to La Sainte-Baume, France', *Culture and Religion*, 10 (3): 243–261.

——. (2012) 'Gender, sexuality and religious critique among Mary Magdalene pilgrims in Southern France', in W. Jansen and C. Notermans (eds.) *Gender, Nation and Religious Diversity in European Pilgrimage*, Farnham, UK, and Burlington, VT: Ashgate.

——. (2013) *Looking for Mary Magdalene: Alternative Pilgrimage and Ritual Creativity to Catholic Shrines in France*, Oxford and New York: Oxford University Press.

——. (2014) 'Energy and transformation in alternative pilgrimages to Catholic shrines: deconstructing the tourist/pilgrim divide', *Journal of Tourism and Cultural Change*, 12: 150–165.

Frazer, J. (1890) *The Golden Bough: A Study in Comparative Religion*, London: Macmillan.

Frey, N. (1998) *Pilgrim Stories: On and Off the Way to Santiago,* Berkeley and Los Angeles: University of California Press.

Froeschlé-Chopard, M.-H. (1994) *Espace et Sacré en Provence (XVIe–XXe siècle). Cultes, images, confréries,* Paris: Cerf.

———. (ed.) (2002) *Itinéraires pèlerins de l'ancienne Provence,* Marseille: La Thune.

Hasluck, F. (1929) *Christianity and Islam Under the Sultans,* Oxford: Oxford University Press.

Hayden, R. (2002) 'Antagonistic tolerance: competitive sharing of religious sites in South Asia and the Balkans', *Current Anthropology,* 43: 205–231.

Hertz, R. (1913) 'Saint Besse. Étude d'un culte alpestre', *Revue de l'histoire des religions,* 67: 115–180.

———. (2009) 'Saint Besse. Study of an Alpine Cult', in M. Mauss, H. Hubert and R. Hertz, *Saints, Heroes, Myths, and Rites. Classical Durkheiminian Studies of Religion and Society,* Boulder and London: Paradigm Publishers.

———. (2014) *Œuvres publiées,* Paris: Classiques Garnier.

Hervieu-Léger, D. (1973) *De la mission à la protestation: l'évolution des étudiants chrétiens en France (1965–1970),* Paris: Éditions du Cerf.

———. (1993) *La religion pour mémoire,* Paris: Éditions du Cerf. (Translated as [2000] *Religion as a Chain of Memory,* New Brunswick, NJ: Rutgers University Press.)

———. (1999) *Le pèlerin et le converti. La religion en mouvement,* Paris: Flammarion.

———. and Hervieu, B. (1983) *Des Communautés pour les temps difficiles: Néo-Ruraux ou nouveaux moines,* Paris: Le Centurion.

Hubert, H. and Mauss, M. (1899) 'Essai sur la nature et la fonction du sacrifice', *Année sociologique,* II: 29–138.

Isnart, C. (2008) *Saints légionnaires des Alpes du sud. Ethnologie d'une sainteté locale,* Paris: Éditions de la Maison des Sciences de l'Homme.

———. (2009) 'Recent papers about Robert Hertz and St. Besse', *Etnográfica,* 13/1, available at http://etnografica.revues.org/1277; DOI: 10.4000/etnografica.1277 (last accessed 20 July 20 2010).

———. (2014a) 'Introduction: Robert Hertz', in *Œuvres publiées,* Paris: Classiques Garnier.

———. (2014b) 'Changing the face of Catholicism in a tourist context. Ritual dynamic, heritage care and the rhetoric of tourism transformation in a religious minority', *Journal of Tourism and Cultural Change,* 11: 133–149.

Jansen, W. and Notermans, C. (eds.) (2012) *Gender, Nation and Religious Diversity in European Pilgrimage,* Farnham, UK, and Burlington, VT: Ashgate.

Julia, D. (2008) 'Riflessioni finali', in S. Gajano and F. Scorza Barcellona (eds.) *Lo spazio del santuario. Un osservatorio per la storia di Roma e del Lazio,* Rome: Editions Viella.

Kozlowski, V. (2008) 'Victimes ou bourreaux ? Les Ukrainiens gréco-catholiques et l' « Holodomor »', *Terrain,* 51: 62–77.

MacClancy, J. (1994) 'The construction of anthropological genealogies: Robert Hertz, Victor Turner and the study of pilgrimage', *Journal of the Anthropological Society of Oxford,* 25 (1): 31–40.

———. and Parkin, R. (1997) 'Revitalization or continuity in European ritual? The case of San Bessu', *Journal of the Royal Anthropological Institute,* 3: 61–78.

Parkin, R. (1996) *The Dark Side of Humanity: The Work of Robert Hertz and its Legacy,* Amsterdam: Harwood Academic Publishers.

Pénicaud, M. (2011) 'L'«hétérotopie» des Sept Dormants en Bretagne', *Archives de sciences sociales des religions,* 155: 131–148.

Piette, A. (2003) *Le fait religieux. Une théorie de la religion ordinaire,* Paris: Economica.

192 Anna Fedele and Cyril Isnart

Poujeau, A. (2014) *Des monastères en partage. Sainteté et pouvoir chez les chrétiens de Syrie,* Nanterre: Société d'ethnologie.

Puccio-Den, D. (2009) *Les théâtres de « Maures et Chrétiens ». Conflits politiques et dispositifs de réconciliation (Espagne, Sicile. XVIIe–XXIe siècle),* Turnhout: Éditions Brepols.

Saintyves, P. (1907) *Les saints successeurs des dieux. Essais de mythologie chrétienne,* Paris: Noury.

Sébillot, P. (1905) *Le Folk-Lore de France. La mer et les eaux,* Paris: Guilemoto.

Sibeud, E. (2004) 'Un ethnographe face à la colonisation. Arnold Van Gennep en Algérie (1911–1912)', *Revue d'Histoire des Sciences Humaines,* 10: 79–103, available at DOI: 10.3917/rhsh.010.0079 (last accessed 2 March 2008).

Turner, V. and Turner, E. (1978) *Image and Pilgrimage in Christian Culture: Anthropological Perspectives,* New York: Columbia University Press.

Van Gennep, A. (1909) *Les rites de passage,* Paris: Nourry.

———. (1913) *En Algérie,* Paris: Mercure de France.

———. (1973) 'Cultes liturgiques et cultes populaires', in *Cultes populaires des saints en Savoie,* Paris: G.-P. Maisonneuve et Larose.

Verdier, Y. (1974) *Façon de dire, façon de faire,* Paris: Gallimard.

Zapponi, E. (2011) *Marcher vers Compostelle: Ethnographie d'une pratique pèlerine,* Paris: L'Harmattan.

Contributors

Dionigi Albera is Director of Research in the CNRS and leads the Institute of Mediterranean, European and Comparative Ethnology at the University of Aix-Marseille. His research interests and publications focus on anthropological theories concerning complex societies and the mixing of religious devotional beliefs and practices, especially in the context of shared pilgrimage shrines. Publications include (edited with M. Couroucli 2012), *Sharing Sacred Spaces in the Mediterranean: Christians, Muslims and Jews at Shrines and Sanctuaries* (Indiana University Press, 2012).

Gábor Barna is Professor and Head of the Department of Ethnology and Cultural Anthropology, Szeged University, Hungary, and Head of the MTA-SZTE Research Group of the Study of Religious Culture. Within the field of religion he studies, in particular, pilgrimages, religious movements, lay confraternities/societies, individual roles in religious life, religious objects, civil religion and the relationship between power/politics and religion. In the field of folkloristics he studies narratives, feasts and rites, national feasts and secular rituals. He also writes about identities; cultural contact; the history of his discipline; and its institutions in Europe, Hungary and especially East-Central Europe. His relevant publications include *Búcsújárók* [Pilgrims: Contacts and Interferences Between the Hungarian and European Religious Cultures] (Lucidus, 2001), *Ethnology of Religion. Chapters from the European History of a Discipline* (Akadémiai Kiadó, 2004) and *Saints, Feasts, Pilgrimages, Confraternities: Selected Papers* (Szeged University, 2014).

Noga Collins-Kreiner is Senior Lecturer in the Department of Geography and Environmental Studies at the University of Haifa, Israel, and a member of the University of Haifa's Centre for Tourism, Pilgrimage and Recreation Research. Her main research interests are pilgrimage and religious tourism development and management, as well as cultural and heritage tourism. She is also a resource editor of the *Annals of Tourism Research* and has published widely on the topic of tourism including *Christian Tourism to the Holy Land: Pilgrimage During Security Crisis* (Ashgate, 2006).

194   *Contributors*

John Eade is Professor of Sociology and Anthropology at the University of Roehampton; Research Fellow at the Department for the Study of Religion, University of Toronto; and co-founder of the Routledge Religion, Travel and Tourism series. His research interests and publications focus on the anthropology of pilgrimage, global migration and urban ethnicity. Relevant publications include (edited with M. Sallnow) *Contesting the Sacred: The Anthropology of Pilgrimage* (Routledge, 1991), (edited with S. Coleman) *Reframing Pilgrimage* (Routledge, 2004) and (edited with M. Katić), *Pilgrimage, Politics and Place-Making in Eastern Europe* (Ashgate, 2014).

Helmut Eberhart is Associate Professor at the Institute of European Ethnology and Cultural Anthropology at the University of Graz. Over the past twenty years his scientific supervision has especially focussed on the history of the subject, the history of piety and research on pilgrimage, particularly with regard to current trends. The other main areas of his research focus on structural changes in rural areas since 1945 and on museums and exhibitions. Publications include 'Compensation as a Culture Determining Fact' in H. Eberhart et al. (ed.), *Migration, Minorities, Compensation. Issues of Cultural Identity in Europe* (Coimbra Group Office, 2001); 'Pilgrimage as an Example for "the Past in the Present"' (with J. Barkhoff) in F. Mugnaini, P. Ó. Héalaí and T. Thompson (eds.), *The Past in the Present: A Multidisciplinary Approach* (Catania, 2006); and 'Introduction' in J. Barkhoff and H. Eberhart (eds.), *Networking Across Borders and Frontiers* (Peter Lang, 2009).

Anne Fedele is an anthropologist whose research focusses on the intersections of gender and religion with a particular emphasis on corporeality, sexuality and ritual creativity. She holds a PhD in Social and Cultural Anthropology from the École des Hautes Études en Sciences Sociales (Paris) and the Universidad Autónoma de Barcelona. Currently, she is a research fellow at the CRIA-Lisbon University Institute. Her publications include *El camino de María Magdalene* (RBA, 2008); *Looking for Mary Magdalene: Alternative Pilgrimage and Ritual Creativity at Catholic Shrines in France* (Oxford University Press, 2012); and the co-edited volume *Encounters of Body and Soul in Contemporary Religious Practices: Anthropological Reflections* (Berghahn Books, 2011) and *Gender and Power in Contemporary Spirituality: Ethnographic Approaches* (Routledge, 2013).

Cyril Isnart is Research Fellow at the CNRS (IDEMEC, Aix-Marseille University). His work focusses on religion, music and heritage making in Southern Europe (France, Portugal, Greece). He published his first monograph in 2008, *Saints légionnaires des Alpes du sud* (Maison des Sciences de l'Homme) and various papers in international journals. He has also co-edited two issues of *Ethnologie Française* (Presses Universitaires de France, 2013) and *Civilisations* (2012, Brussels) and recently edited the collected works of Robert Hertz (*Oeuvres publiés*, Classiques Garnier, 2014).

Nimrod Luz is Senior Lecturer at the Department of Sociology and Anthropology, Western Galilee College, Israel. His research interests and publications concern the multiple and reflexive relations among society, culture (politics) and the built environment of the Middle East, past and present. Since 2000 he has been engaged in a project that examines the socio-spatial and political aspects of pilgrimage to sacred Palestinian sites as part of various transformations in Palestinian communities in Israel and against the backdrop of Islamic resurgence worldwide. His latest book is *The Mamluk City in the Middle East: History, Culture and the Urban Landscape* (Cambridge University Press, 2014).

Anna Niedźwiedź is a cultural anthropologist teaching at the Institute of Ethnology and Cultural Anthopology at Jagiellonian University in Kraków. She is the author of articles and books concerning the phenomenon of Polish Catholicism and Marian cult in Poland. One of her publications is a book titled *The Image and the Figure: Our Lady of Częstochowa in Polish Culture and Popular Religion* (Jagiellonian University Press, 2010). Her other research projects deal with the symbolic dimension of urban space and visual anthropology. Since 2009 she has been conducting ethnographic field research in Ghana, focussed on lived religion among members of Catholic communities there. Currently she is working on a book based on this research.

Ian Reader is Professor of Religious Studies at Lancaster University, where he has taught undergraduate and postgraduate courses on pilgrimage. He spent several years working in Japan and has researched and travelled widely there. Among his main publications on pilgrimage are *Making Pilgrimages: Meaning and Practice in Shikoku* (University of Hawaii Press, 2005), *Pilgrimage in the Marketplace* (Routledge, 2013), a co-edited volume *Pilgrimage in the Japanese Tradition* (as a special edition of the *Japanese Journal of Religious Studies*, 1997) and several journal articles and book chapters, including a chapter on Japanese online pilgrimages in a book he co-edited on *Japanese Religions on the Internet* (Routledge, 2011).

Stella Rock is a Senior Research Fellow at Baylor University, Keston Center for Religion, Politics and Society. Her research focuses on Russian Orthodoxy, in particular popular faith and the relationship between religious and national identity; the historiography of Russia; and the relationship between religion, prejudice and conflict. Her publications include the 2007 single-authored book *Popular Religion in Russia: 'Double Belief'*

196 *Contributors*

and the Making of an Academic Myth (Routledge Studies in the History of Russia and Eastern Europe), the co-edited 2012 volume *Nationalist Myths and Modern Media: Contested Identities in the Age of Globalisation* (I. B. Tauris) and 'Introduction: Religion, Prejudice and Conflict in the Modern World', in *Patterns of Prejudice* (Taylor & Francis, 2004).

Elena Zapponi is an anthropologist whose research focusses on the reinvention of tradition. Currently she is researching the valorisation of ethno-anthropological material and immaterial heritage (Università di Roma, La Sapienza). As an assistant researcher in anthropology of religion, University of Rome, La Sapienza, her recent publications and work focus on the evolution of santería in Cuba and on syncretic and anti-syncretic politics of identity. Her PhD dissertation was published as part of the Harmattan series *Religions in Questions*, and she obtained the Award of the French Association of Social Sciences of Religions (AFSR) Paris for the publication *Marcher vers Compostelle. Ethnographie d'une pratique pèlerine* (AFSR-Harmattan).

Index

Aachen 99, 100, 102
Abbruzzese, S. 164, 166
academic: disciplines 23, 165; French-Italian connections 179
accommodation 72, 87, 100
Africa: 16; North 135, 140, 145, 146, 147; West 5
Agadjanian, A. and K. Russele 51
agricultural: calendar 82; processions 175
agriculture: customs 174
Albera, D. xi, 1–22, 162, 166, 171, 185–7, 193; and A. Blok and C. Bromberger 167, 188, 189; and M. Couroucli 187, 188; and B. Fliche 186, 188; and M. Tozy 186, 188
Algeria 12, 175, 177, 186
Ambros, B. 32, 42, 45
America(s): 3, 11, 16, 77, 161, 166 n. 4, 179, 188 n. 2; North 2, 9, 12, 14; South 9
American: anthropologist 5, 86; Catholicism 53; national parks 8; sociologist 77
Andree, R. 115, 128
Angelini, P. 156, 167
Anglophone: academia 50; anthropologists 2, 177; disciplinary traditions 1; hegemony 1, 11; literary production 1, 79; linguistic traditions 1; pilgrimage studies 2, 6, 7, 11 *passim*, 28, 34, 51, 97, 185; publishers/publications 1, 9, 14, 107, 160; readers 1, 2; research 1, 11, 166, 179, 180; scholars/scholarship 1, 9, 11, 15, 16, 127, 179, 188; social science 7, 8, 11; universities 1, 10, 16; world 35, 166, 166 n. 6

animals 70, 77
anthropologists 2, 3, 5, 10, 51, 57, 62, 77, 80, 107, 159, 163–5, 171, 188; Anglophone 2
French 176 *passim*; Polish 89
anthropology 6, 8, 10 *passim*, 17 n. 4, 23, 28, 39, 41, 49, 52, 53, 58, 71, 90 n. 2, 143, 146, 147, 153, 158, 177, 179, 185, 186; Anglophone 2, 177; cultural 104, 120; interpretive 161; Italian 12, 155, 162; of experience 88, 165; of pilgrimage 51, 145, 162; of religion 78, 88, 145, 157, 179; of tourism 160; post-Soviet 50, 51, 163; Polish 80; visual 156, 157, 159–60
anticlerical 49, 106, 154
Apolito, P. 161
apparitions 75, 82, 103, 161, 162, 179, 183
aristocracy 27, 174
Asakawa, Y. 40, 41, 43 n. 3
ascetics 24, 29, 32, 36
Asia 4; Asia Pacific 9; South Asia 9, 11; South-East Asia 16
Assion, P. 118, 120, 121, 127 n. 2
Aubin-Boltanski, E. 12, 184
Augé, M. 162
authenticity 54, 55, 63
authorities: 106, 139, 146; ecclesiastical 182, 183; feudal 40; local 137; Palestinian 184; political 183; Prussian 75; Soviet 48; temple 40

Badone, E. xi, 6, 121, 123, 143, 165, 179; and S. Roseman 9, 143, 185, 187
Baiburin, A., C. Kelly and N. Vakhtin 50, 51

198 *Index*

Balińskim M. 73
Bálint, S. 14, 97, 98, 104; and G. Barna
102, 103, 104
Balkans 183, 186
Balogh, A. 95, 96
Bango, J. 104
banners 48, 86, 98
baptism 97, 174
Bar, D. 146
Baraniecka-Olszewska, K. 88
Barlay, T. 99
Barna, G. xi, 15, 74, 95 *passim*, 114,
118, 193
Baroque 73, 97, 101, 102, 103, 161
Bartha, E. 103
Baumer, I. 116, 121, 123
Bausinger 116, 118
Bavaria 97, 117, 128 n. 10
Beitl, K. 114
Belarus 74
beliefs 15, 27, 78, 81, 83, 115, 146,
161, 162, 164, 175, 185; folk 1,
29; local 28, 30, 153, 155, 156;
pagan 49; peasant 77; popular
153, 155, 165; religious 2, 12, 29,
40, 71, 89, 125, 154, 157, 186
believers 53, 55, 56 *passim*, 135,
165, 173; Jewish 175; lay 52;
Orthodox 102; post-Soviet 53
belonging 30, 35, 50, 140, 154, 184
Ben-Ari, E. and Y. Bilu 140, 143, 145
Beneskovo-Sabkova, M. 53
Berger-Künzli, D. 118
Bethlehem x, 137, 144
Bhardwaj, S. and G. Rinschede 2, 107
Bilska-Wodecka, E. and I. Soljan 86
Bilu, Y. 138, 143, 145, 146
Birinyi, J. 99
Blackwell, R. 7
Bliem, G. 126
Boesche Gajano, S. and L. Scaraffia
179
Boissevain, K. xi, 12, 184
Boltanski, L. 182, 183; and L. Thévenot
183
bonds: communal 79, 89; organic 79;
national-religious 86; social 61
Bonomi, E. 98
books: 7, 11, 73, 103, 104, 118, 154,
185
borders ix; disciplinary 9; feudal 25;
national 9, 64 n. 277, 106, 107,
187; regional 14; religious 186,
187

Boutry, P. 11, 179, 188 n. 4; and
D. Julia 179; and P.-A. Fabre
and D. Julia 179
Bowman, G. 1, 9, 186
Bowman, M. xi, 6, 63 n. 1, 121, 123,
187
boundaries 2, 14, 16, 50, 117; disci-
plinary 1, 2, 7, 172, 179; fuzzy
51; linguistic 2, 179; national
9, 10; religious 9; regional 152;
sacred 47; traditional 165
Branthomme, H. 11
Britain 12, 123, 153, 160, 185
Brown, P. 11
Brückner, W. 115, 116, 117 n. 2, 120,
121, 127 n. 2
Brunet, S. 179; and N. Lemaître 179
Buddhism 11, 23, 27, 30, 32, 125, 134
Buddhist Studies 23, 25
Burgio, G. 163
buses 38, 48, 54 *passim*, 87, 91 n. 15,
105, 108, 183

Calabria 159 *passim*
camino 9, 10, 40, 162
Canta, C. 163
Carpathian Basin 99, 106
Carpitella, D. 156, 159, 160
Catholicism: Greek 63, 72, 74, 103,
185; Maronite 184; Roman
10, 12, 15, 53, 69 *passim*, 95
passim, 106–7, 115, 119, 122
passim, 155, 157, 162, 163,
166 n. 4, 175, 176, 178, 180,
182, 185 *passim*
Catholic pilgrimage 11, 47, 61, 63, 69,
72, 87 *passim*, 105, 118, 127,
152 *passim*, 162, 175, 187
century: eighteenth 55, 69, 102, 103,
182; fifteenth 101, 157; nineteenth 11, 14, 24, 43 n. 6, 48,
49, 63, 69 *passim*, 83, 85, 89,
95, 96, 105, 115, 137, 152, 153,
161 *passim*, 173, 177, 179, 188
n. 1; seventeenth 74, 96, 102,
103; twelth 25, 27; twentieth 2,
15, 28, 29, 42 n. 1, 43 n. 7, 48,
52, 53, 74, 77 *passim*, 91 n. 6,
97, 100 *passim*, 120, 121, 137,
140, 171 *passim*, 187, 188 n. 1;
twenty-first 39, 188 n. 1
chapels 57, 58, 74, 98, 103, 108,
174
charisma 28, 60, 161

charismatic: and inspirational figures 28, 32, 56, 60, 140, 161, 165; proselytisers 28
Charuty, G. 162, 171, 181–2, 187; and C. Severi 162
Chélini, J. 11
Chernetsov, A. 49
Chichibu 34, 37
China 4, 16
Chistiakov, P. 52, 53
Christensen, K. 54
Christian, W. Jr. 18, 162, 179
Chulos, C. 49, 58, 59
Christy, A. 23, 28, 29, 32, 43 n. 7
Cinquin, M. 179
Cipriani, R. 163, 164
Cirese, M. 154 *passim*, 166 n. 1
class(es): middle 105, 152, 157; marginal 156; peasant 83; social 157; subaltern 158
Claverie, E. 12, 162, 171, 182 *passim*; and A. Fedele 184
Clemente, P. 159
clergy 48, 50, 53 *passim*, 72, 73, 86
clienteles 23, 27, 37, 39, 41
Cocchiara, G. 153
Coleman, S. xi, 3, 7, 8, 10, 12, 59, 187; and J. Eade 7, 9, 59, 143; and J. Elsner 7, 135
Collins-Kreiner, N. 6, 134 *passim*
Cologne 99, 100
communication 1, 10, 14; social 157; with the sacred 105
Communist: party 155; period 89; phraseology 83; regimes 15, 89, 99, 101
communitas 3–7, 14, 17 n. 2, 40, 50, 60–1, 70, 79, 124, 184
communities 51, 64 n. 2; Arab 137; face-to-face 2; imagined 152; Latin and Greek Catholic 102; Jewish 105, 135, 137, 147; kenotic 61; local 30, 98, 159, 165, 184; Mediterranean 185; migrant 165; monastic 58; of pilgrims 60; Orthodox 107; parish 106; religious 106; scholastic 24
community 8, 60, 79, 88, 89, 97, 100, 106, 108, 108 n. 1, 118, 120, 124, 126, 127, 154, 176, 177; Catholic 186; festive 157; Greek Catholic 185; ideal 184; local 158; of believers 135; Orthodox

47, 50, 57; Peruvian 5; pilgrim 38, 40, 96; scholastic 21
compensation theory 118–20, 126
competition 39, 55, 165, 177
consciousness: historical 54; miraculous 82
contestation 6–7, 12, 137, 156
contradictions 6, 50
control: ecclesiastical 55, 56, 60, 161, 178, 182; gates 35; government 25; Israel 138; pastoral 52; political 76; space and time 154
Corso, R. 155
costumes 72, 98, 115, 153, 156
counter-Reformation 96
critique 117, 179 *passim*; of communitas 4–6; Luther 124; of 'popular culture' 159
crosses 48, 50, 98, 108
Crusades 11, 115, 177
Csíksomlyó/Şumuleu 99, 106, 108
culture 8, 83, 108, 119, 143, 146, 147, 152, 188 n. 2; Christian 3, 10; colonial 155; consumerist 156; contemporary 83; death 161; ethnic 39; 'exotic' 155; folk 83, 91 n. 13, 118, 155; gap 158; hegemonic 158; Italian 155, 160; linguistic 13, 39; Japanese 15, 28, 29, 32; local 30, 32; local rural 51, 55, 61; 'magico-religious' 155, 157, 159; material 63, 97, 104, 115; non-European 188 n. 1; Orthodox 80; peasant religious 78 *passim*; peasant 49, 173; pilgrimage 23, 25, 42, 61; Polish folk 71, 77, 82, 83; popular 91 n. 13, 127, 155, 158, 159, 166 n. 1; 'primitive' 155; religious 88, 91 n. 10, 98, 119; resistance 155; Russian folk 49, 50; Russian religious 49, 50; Sicilian folk 154; sorrow 156; Soviet 51; subaltern 155, 158, 161, 166 n. 3; superstitious 154; traditional 120, 157; urban 116; village 50; 'Writing Culture' 161
cultural: activities 96; anthropology 51, 104; arena 37; assets 119; autonomy 4; backgrounds 3, 163; belonging 35; change 140; code 58, 145; compensation 118; conditions 95; context 63, 85, 116, 161; cross-cultural 4, 13;

200 *Index*

debates 23; diversity 9; everyday items 115; evolutionism 173; forms 119; foundations 15; gap 159; geography 143; heritage 41, 49, 126, 152, 153, 158, 159; heroes 144; historians 77, 78; history 99, 101, 114; impact on space 147; meanings 83, 143, 147; mechanisms 83; patterns 85; phenomena 115, 116; practices 60, 173; property 52; region 39; renewal 118; revolution 156; science 119, 123; settings 6; shift 47; shortcomings 119; sphere 24; structures 85; survival 117, 153, 157; tourism 107; traditions 97, 153; trends 29, 143; 'turn' 7

cult(s): ancestors 175; Black Madonna of Częstochowa 102; Christianised 173; connections 97, 98; Europe 102; gender 145, 184; generalised and rigid 178; healing fountains 173, 174; healing saints 178; Hungary 98; images 80, 83, 85, 103; interreligious 186; Italian 153; Jewish 140, 145; Jewish female saints 145; Kōbō Daishi 25; Ksenia 56; Lourdes 178; Margaret of Hungary 100, 101; Marian 95, 154, 178; mixed 186; model of 173; non-Christian 127; objects 103; Orthodox 80; Padre Pio 165; pilgrimage 6, 25, 173; Polish Catholics 80; popular faith 27; regional 5; relics 164; rigid and generalised 172; saints 100, 164, 165; shrine 96, 154; St. Besse 176, 177; St. Expedito 163; St. Mary 85; St. Patrick 78; Tunisia 184; Virgin Mary 154

Czachowski, H. 82
Czarnowski, S. 14, 78–83, 88, 91 n. 12
Czechoslovakia 192, 106
Częstochowa 69 *passim*, 91 n. 5, 100, 102, 108

Dal': lexicographer and folklorist 48
Dám, I. 98, 121, 127 n. 2
Darwin, C. 153
Davie, G. 180
Davies, J. 2
Daxelmüller, C. 123
de Busser, C. 89

de Certeau, M. 162
Dei, F. 159
de Martino, E. 12, 154 *passim*
devotion(s): aristocratic 174; books 73, 74; calendrical 57; Catholic literature 74; changes 162, 164, 179; clerical 172, 174, 183, 187; communal 48, 57; Curé d'Ars 179; folk 175, 184; gender 175; holy men 140; images 114; itineraries 162; Kōbō Daishi 33; lived religion 154; local 152, 163; Marian 80, 85, 96, 98, 102, 152, 183; Mary Magdalene 185; object 56, 96, 153; pagan 173; peasants 173; pictures 97, 103, 104; pilgrimage 27, 96, 97, 157; pilgrims 158, 174; popular 154, 155, 157, 162; practices 74, 98; regional 5; religious 102, 179; saint 152, 156; sanctuaries 74, 174; spontaneous 172, 187; subaltern culture 155; Syria 184; tradition 95; variability 175; writings 73

dialogue: between research traditions 2, 9, 10, 16, 51, 161, 181, 185; interreligious 128 n. 10, 187
diaspora 137, 185
Digance, J. 6, 143
di Gianni, L. 159, 160
di Giovanni, E. 163
disasters—natural 97
discourses 51, 53, 73, 74, 185; anthropological and sociological 77, 82, 88; colonial 79; competing 6, 55, 143, 183; everyday 122; media 114, 161; public and academic 121; religious and political 184; secular nationalist 14
disease 37, 157
divine assistance: personal appeals for 57, 59
divinities 171, 173, 174
Dixon, S. 50
Dobos, I. 105
documentaries 99, 157, 159, 160
Dodge, M. and R. Kitchen 8
dominant religious traditions or groups 14, 15, 30, 140
Dore, G. 155
Dubisch, J. 7, 13, 32, 48, 124; and M. Winkelman 9
Duijzings, G. 6

Dupront, A. 11, 14, 160, 162, 171, 172, 177 *passim*, 187, 188 n. 4
Durand, J.-Y. 50, 51
Durkheim, E. 3, 61, 172, 175–77, 184
dwelling and crossing 7

Eade, J. xi, 1 *passim*, 59, 143, 179; and M. Sallnow 7, 9, 55, 107, 123, 143, 183, 184, 187; and M. Katić 1, 7, 9, 10, 15
Eberhart, H. 97, 114 *passim*, 128 n. 4; and Ponisch 118; and Fell 120
ecclesiastical: authorities 182, 183; centre 55; control 55, 60; experiences 178; hierarchy 55; institutions 52; objects 57; pilgrimage services 55; policy 54; publications 56; representatives 55; traditions 53; unity 61
economic: changes 39, 41, 97, 159, 161; context 24, 27, 35, 36, 37, 95, 157; crisis 163; development 34, 35; growth 29; interests 10; processes 7; structure 36
economic studies 23, 35, 36, 37, 41, 90 n. 2
Ederer, B. 122
egalitarian 60
Eickelman, D. 4; and R. Piscatori 2
Eliade, M. 83, 91 n. 14
Eliav, Y. 136
emotional 8, 70, 119; description 76; ecstasies 61; experiences 121; needs 118, 119; rituals 78
emotions 70, 80, 162
empathy 29, 71
energy 63, 185
Engelstein, L. 50
English as a medium of scientific communication 1–2, 10–14, 23–4, 32, 42, 43 n. 6, 64, 105, 121, 125, 143, 162, 166, 176, 179–80
environment 8, 108; concerns 117; contested 55; pollution 117; religious 48; shrine 47
epidemics 97
equality 60
Eretz Israel 135, 137, 138, 141
Esposito, V. 157
ethnic: composition 91 n. 6; cultures 39; focus 28; frontiers 2, 50; groups 50, 80, 146; identities 51, 80; links 103; minorities 9; pilgrimage 163; practices 32; shrine 80

ethnicity 7
ethnographers 49, 50, 57, 70–1, 76–7, 171, 181
ethnographic: account 162; analyses 89; approaches 153, 156, 161, 162, 186; case studies 82; contexts 4; data 89, 182, 186; descriptions 70, 71, 173, 176; details 175; discussions 177; experiences 70; facts 176; filmmakers 159; humanism 156; literature 152; material 39, 73, 89; movies 159; museums 114; perspective 162; regions 72; research 12, 70, 81, 160; sources 77; study 158; synthesis 176; terms 39; work 160, 173
ethnography 49, 52, 58, 71, 173, 174, 182; Algeria 175; E. Clavérie 182, 184; folk 15, 28; France 174; pilgrimage 181, 182; state 50
ethnology i, 10, 13, 15, 156; applied 155; European 116, 120, 125–7; French 104; Hungary 96 *passim*; Italian 156; Japanese 24; local 29; 'native' 15, 16, 28 *passim*; Polish 82 *passim*; Soviet 155
ethnomusicology 71, 156
ethnos 50, 153
Eurasia 13, 15, 16
European Ethnology 116, 120, 125, 126, 127
European Union 10, 122
everyday: attitude 138; cultural items 115; discourse 122; life 5, 50, 108, 116, 118, 152, 156; Orthodoxy 51; pilgrimages 122; social relations 5; structures 60
everyday life 5, 50, 103, 108, 116, 118, 152, 156
evolution(ism) 77, 115, 153, 166 n. 5, 173, 175
exchange 10, 16, 90, 123, 161
experience: anthropology of 88, 165

Fabre, D. 162, 182
Fabre, P.-A. 11, 162, 179
Fadeeva, L. 53
Faeta, F. 156, 160
fairs 56, 98, 181
family: holiday 157
Farbaky, P. and S. Serfozo 102
Fasching, M.-K. 104

202   Index

Fatima 161, 162
Fattorini, E. 154, 164
Fedele, A. 6, 162, 171 *passim*
feelings 81, 177; human universal 178;
  national 76; of communitas 4,
  60, 61; of inconsistency 78; of
  solidarity 79; of spontaneity 87;
  patriotic 75; personal 71;
  religious 179, 187
Feldman, J. 136, 142, 143
Ferrarotti, F. 163
festivals: 99, 102; Italian 153, 157, 159;
  Jewish 105, 134; religious 30,
  76; saints 157; shrine 98
feudal 25, 34, 35, 40, 91 n. 13
fieldwork 4, 29, 39, 51, 57–8, 145,
  161, 172, 176–7, 179
Filicheva, O. 55
film 98, 99, 159; art 99; documentary
  99; festival 160; makers 12, 99,
  159, 160
Finkelstein, I. and N. Silberman 136
Finucane, R. 2
First World War 99, 154, 177
flags 75, 79
Fliche, B. 186
flows: economic 35, 36; knowledge and
  ideas 1, 9, 10, 165
folk 50, 72, 83, 89, 91 n. 13, 153, 166
  n. 1, 173, 177, 178; beliefs and
  practices i, 27, 29, 30, 175, 181,
  184; culture 49, 50, 71, 77, 82,
  83, 91 n. 13, 118, 154, 155,
  157; customs 15, 75, 175; ethnography 28; gestures 172; ideas
  41; faith 32; legends 72; levels
  41; medicine 98; mysticism 83;
  nation 155; Orthodoxy 58; protest 154; religion 28, 31, 43 n. 8,
  48 *passim*, 82, 85, 174; religiosity 15, 82, 85, 91 n. 13; rivalry
  180; songs 75; 118; studies i,
  xi, 15, 16, 23, 24, 28 *passim*,
  41, 57, 114 *passim*, 153 *passim*,
  161; tales 30; tradition 30, 153,
  174; type 83, 85, 88, 89
folklore 10, 15, 23, 25, 29, 30, 40,
  48 *passim*, 71 *passim*, 89, 96,
  96, 103, 105, 114 *passim*, 138,
  139, 144, 145, 152 *passim*, 171
  passim
folklorists 48, 49, 51, 57, 71, 77,
  114, 159, 171, 177, 181,
  182, 188

France XI, 2, 11–15, 118, 153, 160,
  162, 164–5, 171 *passim*, 182,
  184
Franciscan 97, 102
Frank, A. 115
Frauhammer, K. 105
Freeze, G. 53
French: and German sources 1; and
  Italian research 11–12, 161,
  179, 181; and Italian institutions
  152; anthropologists 176, 182,
  188; approaches 171, 172, 187;
  ethnology 104; folklorists 188;
  homeland 185; language 23, 42
  n. 1, 78, 162, 165; pilgrims 183;
  religious historians 188; research
  15, 160, 172–3, 178–79, 182,
  187, 188 n. 1; scholars 30, 171,
  180, 187; sociologists 176, 180;
  sociology of religion 162; universities 162
Frey, N. 10, 143, 162, 187
Fridrich, A. 74
Froeschlé-Chopard, M.-H. 179
frontiers: ethnic 2; geographical 2;
  religious 186
funerals 76, 88, 181

Gaál, K. 97, 98
Gabriel, R. 121, 122
Gadamer, H.-G. 81
Gajano, S. 165, 179
Galbraith, M. 86–7
Galilee 137, 139, 140
Gallini, C. 12, 156 *passim*, 165; and
  F. Faeta 156
Gandin, M. 157, 159–60
gaps 1, 14, 16, 73, 88, 155, 158, 159,
  160
gender 7, 37, 58, 79, 175, 184, 187;
  cultural 143; experience 182;
  hagio 137; historical 143; identity 182; social construction of
  182
geography; 13, 42, 136; of pilgrimages
  91 n. 16; religious 91 n. 16;
  social 41
Geramb, V. 115
German-speaking countries 2, 16, 114
  passim; Europe 114 *passim*;
  European ethnology 127; folklore studies 125, 127 n. 1;
  humanities 126; pilgrimage
  research 121, 126, 127 n. 1;

social sciences 126; sociology 125, 127; universities 10; world 116
Germany i, 15, 91 n. 6, 115, 118
Gerndt, H. 116, 117, 123
Gietrzwałd 75, 91 n. 6
Glässer, N. 105, 106
Gleszer, N. 105
global: analysis 9; approach 9, 16; arena 12; competition between universities 165; dominance of English 1; exchange of ideas I; *lingua franca* 14; market 10; medium of communication 1; migration 9, 127; travel 138; trends 15, 142; world 159
globalisation 7; academic 16
god 47, 63, 97, 117, 124, 135, 136, 137; Mother of 56, 117
goddess 185
gods 27, 33, 35
Gohl, Ő. 102
Gonzalez, R. 10; and J. Medina 10
Gorai, S. 27, 30, 43 n. 5
Gothóni, R. 48
Grabner, E. 114
Grabowski, A. 73
Gramsci, A. 155, 158
graves 63, 76, 100, 138, 146
Graz 114, 120
Greek Orthodox 186
Greene, H. 58
Grimaldi, R. 163
Grodziska, K. 76
Gromyko, M. 49, 50
Gugitz, G. 114
guidebooks 37, 42 n. 1, 74

Hahn, M. 97
Halbwachs, M. 175
Hann, C. 1, 10; and H. Goltz 10, 53, 62, 89
Harmening, D. 118
Harvolk, H. 114
Harris, A. 8, 10
Harris, T. 123
Hasluck, F. 186
Hayami, T. 25, 27
Hayden, R. 186
healing 12; bodily 82, 181; Dupront 178; energy 185; fountains 173; functionalist interpretation 175; images 82; Lourdes 158; miraculous 27, 72, 102, 158, 161;

pilgrimages 175; processions 175; place 57; requests 139; saints 178; spiritual 82; water 98
Heiser, P. 114
Herberich-Marx, G. 118
Hermkens, A.-K., W. Jansen and C. Notermans 1, 6, 9
Hertz, R. 5, 12, 14, 171, 172, 175–7, 187, 188 n. 2
Hervieu-Léger, D. 162, 171
Heteny, J. 105
Hinduism 4, 11, 125, 134
Hinonishi, S. 25
historians: 2, 8, 11, 37, 52, 73, 100, 114, 164, 171; art 80, 101, 103, 104, 106; cultural 77; economic 35, 36; festivals 102; Italian 165; of religion 25, 177, 188; pilgrimage 34, 171; Polish literature 69; social 35
Hofauer, H. 126
holy: authentic copies 82; Buddhist 25; Church of the Holy Sepulchre 63; comparative research 63; devotees 60; direct contact with 58; energy 63; events 48; figures 23, 25, 33, 36, 41, 63, 80; ground 63; Holy Crown 96; Holy Diana 123; Holy Family 72; Holy Land 82, 100, 102, 105, 135 *passim*, 143; Holy Stairs 102; icons 60; image 75, 80, 82, 83; Jerusalem 147; Jewish cities 137; Jewish sites 143, 145, 146; man 97, 105, 140; migrating 60; objects 50, 56, 58, 60, 61, 80, 82; people 50, 58, 59, 60; physical contact with 62; physical manifestation of 48; pilgrimage 48; pilgrims 63; places 25, 27, 47, 48, 52 *passim*, 64 n. 4, 82, 123; relics 60; search for 135; spring 106; wandering men 25; water 62; wells 103, 106; years 100, 102
Hoppál, M. 99
Hoshino, E. 4, 17 n. 2, 24, 31, 33, 39–41, 43 n. 3; and Y. Asakawa 40, 41, 43 n. 3
Howard, D. 2
Hubert, H. 175, 188 n. 2; and M. Mauss 176, 188 n. 2
Hugger, P. 114
Huhn, U. 53

204 *Index*

Hungary i, 1, 14, 15, 74, 91 n. 8, 95 *passim*
Hyndman-Rizk, N. 1, 9

identity 35, 88; ethnic 50; gender 182; homeland 158; Hungarian 106; individual 152; Israeli 135; Japanese 23, 28, 29, 41, 42; local 152, 159; national 159, 184; Orthodox 50, 59, 63; pilgrimage 79, 109; Polish 74, 89; politics 159; quest for 162; religious 50, 51; Russian 50; shrines 80, 85; Soviet 50; studies 89
images 71, 73, 74, 80–2, 89, 91 n. 12, 105; apparitions of 82; copies of 82; cult of 80, 83, 85, 103, 114; devotional 114; *ex-voto* 118; Marian 74; miraculous 80–82; mystics 78; perception of 82; votive 98
individuals 6, 49, 51, 55, 56, 59, 60, 63, 79, 107, 115, 118, 124, 182
Ingold, T. 8
Ise 25, 33, 35, 36
Islam 11, 64 n. 2, 125, 134, 145, 186
Isnart, C. 171 *passim*
Israel 2, 13, 15, 134 *passim*
István, A. 105
Italy i, 2, 11, 12, 14, 152 *passim*, 181, 182, 185
itineraries 2, 12, 16, 27, 35, 162, 179
Ivakhiv, A. 6

Jackowski, A. 6, 75, 91 n. 16; and I. Soljan 85, 86
Jakacka-Mikulska, K. 70
Janosi, G. 103
Janotta, C. 118
Jansen, W. 89; and Hermkens and C. Notermans 1, 9; and C. Notermans 6, 187
Japan i, 1, 4, 9, 13, 15, 16, 23 *passim*
Jasna Góra 57, 69 *passim*, 85, 86
Jerusalem 48, 82, 105, 115, 134 *passim*
Jews: Orthodox 105 *passim*, 138, 147; Reform 105
John Paul II 85, 90
Jordánszky, E. 96
Josephson, J. 23
journeys 13, 50, 59, 64 n. 2; believers 173; critical 185; pilgrim 115, 126; processional 35; rites of

passage 185; sacred 164; spiritual 27, 28
Juhász, G. 97, 99
Julia, D. 11, 162, 177, 178, 179
Jung, C. 178

Kalwaria Pacławska 72
Kalwaria Zebrzydowska 74, 87, 88
Kaneko, S. 30
Kannon 25, 27, 33, 34
Kaufman, S. 7, 9
Kawa, M. 70
Kirichenko, O. 50
Kirill, Metropolit 56
Kiss, I. 102
Knott, K. 8
knowledge 42, 74, 104, 177, 179, 186; exchange of 90; flows of 10, 165; folk 50; Italian ethnological studies 162; liturgical 55; popular 155; scientific 72; secular sites 143; sources of 32
Kojima, H. 33
Kolberg, O. 71–3, 77, 90 n. 4
Korff, G. 115, 121, 128 n. 2
Kormina, J. 51 *passim*; and A. Panchenko and S. Shtyrkov 51; and S. Shtyrkov 56
Korpics, M. 107
Kościuszko, T. 76
Kozlowski, V. 185
Kouamé, N. 30, 42 n. 1
Kraków 74, 76, 85–7, 90, 91 n. 7 and n. 8
Kramer, K. 115, 118
Krech, V. 120
Kretzenbacher, L. 114
Kriss, R. 114; and H. Kriss-Heinrich 114
Kriss-Rettenbeck, L. 114, 115; and G. Möhler 117
Kromer, H. 118
Kurrat, C. 114

Ladner, G. 2
LaFleur, W. 4, 17 n. 2
Łagiewniki 88
Lambert, Y. 162
landscape 7, 76; academic 175; (re)Christianising 54; ethnoanthropology 153; holy figure 59; information about 70; Israeli 145; local 58; mystical dimensions 31; national research 158;

perceptions of 31; and pilgrims 8; pilgrimage 47; remote 75; (re)sacralised 25, 47; sacred 103; shared 88; spatial 103; spiritual transformation 31; travel 60

language 1, 12, 14, 24, 128 n. 5, 166; barrier 42; English 11, 23, 24; French 23; issue 41; films 159; Italian 165; Latin 95; pilgrims 108; Polish 75; priesthood 95; religious 75; Russian 47; scholarly 71; studies 43 n. 3; Western 30

Lanternari, V. 156, 166 n. 3

Latour, B. 182

leaders: charismatic 165; festivals 102; Franciscans 102; Israel 142; Jesuits 102; Jewish 138; lay 53; of new religions 28; pilgrimage 38, 97, 185; Polish ethnology 83; spiritual 55

legends 23, 24, 32, 71, 105, 153; folk 72, 73; itinerant religious figures 29; local 28; Margaret of Hungary 100; of origins 81; pilgrimage 31, 36; shrines 103

Leitner, M. 126

Łepkowski, J. 73

Levin, E. 49

Lévi-Strauss, C. 182

Licheń 88

Limor 134, 137

Lithuania 71, 74, 90 n. 3, 91 n. 6

Lohse, B. 124, 128 n. 8

Lombardi Satriani, L. 161

Lorenzer, A. 119

Loreto 98, 100

Lourdes 3, 7 passim, 108, 158, 161, 162, 177–9, 185, 187

Lubańska and Ładykowska 62

Lübbe, H. 119

Luehrmann, S. 50

Luther, Martin 124, 128 n. 6

Luzzatto, S. 154

MacClancy, J. 12, 176

Macioti, M. 163, 164

McKevitt, C. 166 n. 6

Maddrell, A. 7, 8

Maeda, T. 30, 37, 38

magic(al): attitudes 77; folk culture 157, 159; Israel 145; Italy 155; rituals 159; world conception 156

magicians 161

Mantegazza, P. 153

Margry, P. 1, 6, 7, 9, 143

Máriapócs 103

Máriaradna 97, 105, 106

Mariazell 100, 102, 104, 108, 120–2, 127, 128 n. 4 and n. 11

Markus, R. 136

market: Church 56; economic 35; globalised 10; Hebrew readers 144; Kraków 86; pilgrimage 36, 39; religious 119; tourist/pilgrimage 35

Marquardt, O. 7, 9, 119

Marx, E. 2

Marxism 6, 15, 82

Mary Magdalene 162, 184, 185

Massignon, L. 187

material 32, 39, 58; artefacts 126; conduits of the divine 63; culture 63, 97, 104, 115; ethnographic 39, 70, 73, 75, 89; folklore 77; objects 8, 116; pictures 81; pilgrimage 177; preservation 32; qualitative 39; religion 15, 97; religious rituals 89; Russian-language 47; textual 9, 31, 71, 103; votive 115

Matsuzaki, K. 30

Mauss, M. 61, 78, 175, 176, 188 n. 2

Mayeur-Jaouen, C. 12

meaning(s) 8, 115; cultural 143, 147; ecclesiastical control 55; images 83; implicational 3; local 176; local holy places 57; nuances of 32; pilgrimage 124, 147; post-secular 120; quest for 119; social 143, 147; spiritual guides 119; structures 61; study of 126; suffering 115; Zionists 142

Mecca 4, 5, 134

Mediterranean 162, 179, 185–7

Medjugorje 63, 182, 183

Mehes, I. 103

Messerschmidt, D. and J. Sharma 4

Mester, J. 99

Mickiewicz, A. 75, 76

Middle Ages 100–2, 108, 117 n. 1, 118

migration: global labour 9, 127; Italy 163; Sephardic Jews 135, 146; transnational 163

Mihályfi, E. 104

Millerowa, E. and A. Skrukwa 71

Mingozzi, G. 159, 160

206 Index

miracle(s) 161, 173; books 103, 118; icons 57; industry 161; Judaism 140; Lourdes 158; objects 57; phenomenological dimension 158; pilgrimage 36; records 97; shrines 74, 103; stories 31, 53, 103; trivial 118

Mitrokhin, N. 58

Miyake, H. 25, 27, 43 n. 5

modernity 15, 32, 49, 58, 106, 134, 135; secular 14, 126

Mohay, T. 107

monasteries 47, 48, 52, 56, 58, 60, 184

Móra, F. 99

Mori, M. 39–41, 43 n. 7

Móricz, Z. 99

Morinis, A. 2, 4, 9, 11

Morocco 4, 140, 186

Moroz, A. 54, 59

Moscow: Patriarchate 48, 56, 57

movement(s) 30, 43 n. 6, 47, 48, 57, 59, 60, 62, 142, 147, 172, 180, 183; esoteric and spiritual 121; goddess spirituality 185; Filipino Catholic transnational 163; mystical 79; pilgrimage 124; political and ideological 14; religious 166 n. 3; Solidarity 85, 86

Munich 116, 128 n. 10

Murray, M. and G. Graham 10

museum(s): 32, 47, 64 n. 3, 75, 116, 117, 119, 120, 128 n. 10, 157; ethnographic 114; local 126; regional 120, 126

music 72, 95, 102, 156

Muslims 175, 184, 186, 187

mystical 30, 31: affinity 70; experiences 78; line of defence 98; movements 79

mysticism: individual 77, 78; peasant 78

mystics 79; Christian 78; Jewish 140

mythologisation: of nation 75; of past 138; of sites 141

mythology: Hungarian 96; Polish national 83

myths 35, 83; charter 53; foundational of modern Israel 142; of nation 155

Naletova, I. 48, 54, 56, 57, 59, 61

Naquin, S. and Y. Chün-Fang 4, 11

narratives: and restoration 53; anthropology 53; individual 53; insti-

tutional 53; locals 55; marginalised 145; of desecration and destruction 53, 54; oral 53, 54; personal 53; pilgrims 53, 55, 116, 185; Russian academics 55, 57; Russian folklore studies 53; shrine guardians 55

nation 15, 75, 79, 153; building 154; emerging 15; European 75; folk foundations 155; German 124; Italian 155; modern 34; myth 75, 83; new 15; Palestine 184

national: bibliography 161; boundaries 1, 9, 10, 187; character 163; conferences 9; costumes 115; cultural heritage 49; development 42; discourses 74; economic structure 36; ethos 145; feeling 76; folk studies 153; funding 9; heroes 76, 78; history 42, 75, 140, 152, 154, holidays 142; icon 138; identity 29, 42, 74, 89, 106, 159, 184; ideology 76; jubilees 100; Kraków 76; levels 127; life 184; Marian cults 154; memorabilia 75; memory 141, 142; monasteries 58; multiconfessional 50; museum 75, 117, 157; networks: 9, parks 8; 142, past 75, 76; pilgrimage 30, 69, 75, 76, 85, 104, 142, 144; pilgrims 75, 76; politics 35, 54, 155; publishing 9; religion 107, 135, 138, 141, 164; religious bonds 86; research 158; resurrection 141; rural customs 154; Russian 50; shrine 74, 79, 107; sites 141, 142; soul 154; structures of knowledge 1; struggle 137; survival 106; traditions i, 13, 75, 154, 166 n. 2; universities 9; uprising 91 n. 7

nationalism 15, 135, 165; Jewish 142; Polish 15, 69; and dominant religious groups 15

nationalist(s): discourse 14; secular 14; theory 142

nationhood: modern concept of 74

nation-state(s) 134; Israeli 135, 138; modern 23; new 106; secular 14

nature 77, 108; and people 83; and society 8; culture 8; healing 175

Németh, L. 99

Netherlands, The 10, 91 n. 6

Neville, G. 2
Niedźwiedź, A. 14, 69 *passim*
Nolan, M. and S. Nolan 2, 47
Notermans, C. 6, 9; and Jansen 187
Numata, K. 28

obstacles 1, 14, 16, 56, 82, 184
Oda, M. 34
Olszewski, D. 71, 72, 75, 91 n. 6
oral: circulation 73; folk songs 71; narratives 53, 54; traditions 24, 31
Orbán, A. 99
Orikuchi, S. 29
Orosz, I. 97
Orsi, R. 53, 63
Osada, K. 37, 40; and M. Sakata and M. Seki 38, 43 n. 9
Otto, R. 178

Pace, E. 154, 163
pagan: beliefs 49; Christianity 155, 173; clerical responses 50; communities 64 n. 2; deities 185; pilgrimage 55; practices 49, 173; religion 107, 173; survivals 49, 51, 58
paganism 174; European 172
Padre Pio 160, 165
Palermo 153, 154, 163
Panchenko, A. 49, 51 *passim*
Paris 75, 78, 164, 185
parish 48, 56, 86, 108; communities 106; feasts 79; holy image 83; life 56, 57; pilgrimages 85, 86; Roman Catholic 72, 96; Russian Orthodox 60; towns 61
parishioners 30, 56, 86
Parkin, R. 176
Pásztor, L. 100–2
Pauline order 70, 72, 102
peasants: emancipation 74, 89; European 173; folk 91 n. 13; holy images 80; Italy 156; Japan 36; mystical experience 78, 79; nineteenth century 83; pilgrimages 76 *passim*; Polish 70 *passim*; popular rituals 173; religion 15, 77, 78, 91 n. 11; shrines 74
Pelkmans, M. 52
Pénicaud, M. 187
peregrination 59, 83, 84
performances 4, 98, 154, 182
Petersen, A, M. Vasquez and P. Williams 9

Pfaffenberger, B. 2, 4
Phenomenological: approach 8, 11, 83, 126; dimension 158
Piette, A. 162, 183
piety 120, 124, 125, 128 n. 2; German-speaking Europe 120; Marian-centred 82; votive pictures 115
pilgrim(s) 28, 48; academic research 52; accessing information 50; Anglican 63; attitudes 40, 85, 180; 'authentic copies' 82; badges 101, 102; bags 104; banners 86; bricolage 181; bus trips 54, 60, 105; cleansing desecrated ground 54; clerical guidance 55; Communist regime 15, 89, 99, 106; communitas 4, 60; community 38; Compostela 162; contemporary 53; controls 35; conversation 70; crisis networks 58; cryptic encounter 178, 181; Częstochowa 72; detachment 61; devotion 173; diverse backgrounds 3, 5, 61, 108, 163; divine grace 63; ecclesiastical representatives 55; ecstasy 61; everyday life 116; Fascist regime 154, 155; female 38; folk orientations 40; finance 56; foot 41, 86, 87; gender 182; God's help 117; Greek Catholic 72; health 56; healing 82, 181; Hervieu-Léger 180; history 54; house 100; Hungarian 100 *passim*; icon 57; images 82; individualism 61; infrastructures 36, 37, 56; interaction with locals 40; Jerusalem 137; Jewish 136 *passim*; journeys 115, 126; Kōbō Daishi 33; Kolberg 71–72; landscape 8; liminal social status 60; liturgy 55; local 69; local support 86, 87; lodges 31; Lourdes 178; markets 36; Mecca 4, 5; medieval tour 116; memoirs 52; miracle 82; monasteries 58; motives 108, 139; musealisation 119; Muslim 162; *namolennost'* 63; narratives 53, 55; 'national' 75; North Africa 140; numbers 36, 37, 38, 44, 142; palmer 47; passports 102; path 117; 'pathways' 74; peasants 70; performances 4; personal experiences 3; petitions 118; *pilgern*

208 *Index*

122, 123; pilgrim 60; practices 53, 103, 181; prayer 86; procession 124; 'professional' 174; Protestant 63; provenance 30, 37; regime 60; religious 60; religious experience 63; Reymont 69–71; Roman Catholic 63, 72; Russian 48; sanctifying space 63; saint 61, 108; Shikoku 30 *passim*; shrines 58, 59, 140; sites 63; *sobornost* 61; social strata 76, 101; solitude 61; songs 104; spiritual atmosphere 56; support structures 31, 42 n. 1; teenaged 86; the 'holy' 63; Tokugawa 35; Tokugawa period 37; trauma 54; travel 59, 89, 105; urban shrine 55; worker 58, 61
Pinna, F. 156
Pitrè, G. 14, 153–4, 161, 166 n. 2
political: academic disciplines 143; authorities 183; bodies 126; change 14, 27, 69, 85, 86, 137, 140; claims for territory 152; concerns 117; conditions 95; cultural heritage 152; De Martino 155; dimensions 89; discourse 184; fervour 155; flows of knowledge 10; generation 155; hierarchies 40; imagined communities 152; interests 10; Israel 135, 137 *passim*; local factors 34; manoeuvring 177; meaning 143, 147; mobilisation 135; movements 14; Padre Pio 165; pilgrimage 134, 144, 184; power 139; processes 7, 89, 142, 147; protests 86; relations 95; religion 139, 176; resistance 85; St. Besse 176; structure 139; support 27, 152; system 104; tensions 183; trends 143; worlds 15
Poniatowski, J. 76
Ponisch, G. 116, 118, 121
Poplavskaia, K. 50, 52
Posony, E. 100
Post, P. 7, 107, 119, 128 n. 3
post-modern 9, 60, 61
post-Soviet 47 *passim*
Poujeau, A. 184
Prawer, J. 137
prayer 74, 75, 87, 97, 106, 158; pilgrimage 86; pilgrims 97; votive objects 102

Presley, Elvis 123, 128 n. 5
Prettenthaler-Ziegerhofer, A. 122
Protestant: Hungarians 106; Northern Europe 124; pilgrims 63, 91 n. 6; Santiago 125
Protestantism 77, 95, 123, 185; Luther 124; pilgrimage 124, 127, 128 n. 10
Provence 162, 179, 186
Prussia 69, 75, 90 n. 3
psychological: anthropologist 145; Dupront 178; pilgrimage 97, 157; religious experience 178
Pusztai, B. 105, 107

Raj, R. and N. Morpeth 6
Reader, I. 4, 6, 7, 9, 13, 17, 17 n. 2 and n. 5, 23 *passim*, 97; and Swanson 13
Rech, G. 164
Reformation 97, 102
Reiner, E. 137; and O. Limor and M. Frankel 134
religion 10, 14, 28, 35, 40, 43 n. 6, 77, 79, 117, 120, 127, 134, 135; ancient 173; anthropology of 10, 77, 78, 80, 88, 145, 158, 172, 179; civil 148; collective forms of 78; communal dimension of 88; concept of 77; contemporary 2, 179, 180; definitions of 9; De Martino 156 *passim*; dominant 140; Eliade 83; ethnographic research 160; ethnology 82 *passim*; experiencing 171; feminist spirituality 185; folk 28, 31, 43 n. 8, 82, 85, 91 n. 13, 174; folklore 77; folk-type 83, 89; French sciences of 172, 173, 183; generations 180; historians of 25, 156, 157, 177; historical 3, 10; institutional 10, 15, 180, 181, 184, 187; Japanese 23 *passim*; Jewish 148; lived 89, 154, 157, 165, 182; localisation of 120; and magic 77; material 15; movement 180; and the nation 15; new 166 n. 3; pagan 173; and pilgrimage 36, 89, 90; place 88; political dimensions of 176; popular 82, 152, 156, 157, 164, 174, 179; power 88, 184; secular 154; senses 119; sociology of 77, 145, 158, 162, 175, 177, 180;

Index 209

studies of 29, 160, 171, 180; and tourism 36, 42 n. 2; vernacular 179; of villagers 78; world 2, 134

Reymont, W. 14, 69–71, 85, 90 n. 2, 91 n. 15

Rhodes 186, 187

Ricci, A. 160

Rinschede, G. 6; and J. Bhardwaj 2, 107

Rite: and pilgrimage 87; Eastern 102; external regulation 162; Jewish 105; rebbe dynasties 106; religious 98; shrines 99

rites of passage 2, 171, 174, 175, 181, 185; *see also* A. van Gennep

Ritter, J. 119

ritual(s) 5, 72, 82, 119, 134, 156, 185; abortion 174; activities 2, 173, 174; ancient 156; archaic 159; behaviour 4; bizarre 173; charismatic operators 161; Christianised 174; clergy 30; and conflict 2, 142; consumerism 157; De Martino 155 *passim*; drama 107; efficacy 181; elements 186; Elvis Presley 123; experimentation 187; failure 181; formalised and decorous 138; forms 173; fountains 174; gender 175; Hertz 176; image of Our Lady of Częstochowa 83; invented 83; life cycle 174; lived 175; magico-religious 155, 159; male initiation 182; marriage 182; metaphorical and physical levels 136; miraculous images 81; mortification 181; mountains 27; movement 59; North African Jews 146; objects 156; Orthodox 186; pagan 173; participation 187; peasants 173; performance 137, 176; personal adaptation 175; pilgrimage 12, 173, 174, 182; popular 173; practices 54, 186; processes 7; processions 30; religious 70, 78, 88, 89, 154, 157, 172; ritualism 82; S. Italy 155 *passim*; sacred 82, 157; saints 148; shrines 184; social structure 182; structural divisions 3; survival of 176; symbolic reorganisation 161; symbols 3; syncretism 186; system 182;

traditional 12, 157, 159; V. and E. Turner 3 *passim*, 123; van Gennep 12, 172; walking 59

Robson, R. 58

Rock, S. 15, 47 *passim*, 80, 83

Rogers, D. 51, 54, 63 n. 1, 64 n. 4; and C. Verdery 62

Röhricht, R. 115

Roma 95, 98, 163

Romania 100, 105, 106; Hungarian minority 107; Orthodox 106–7

Romano, F. 161

Rome 76, 100, 102, 104, 108, 108 n. 2, 124, 134, 157, 162, 163, 166 n. 4, 179

Rossi, A. 12, 156–7, 160

Rousselet, K. 54, 64 n. 2; and A. Agadjanian 52

routes 99; anthropology 88 *passim*; Buddhist 9; Częstochowa 85–87; Kalwaria Zebrzydowska 87–88; new 85, 106; pilgrimage 9, 27, 33 *passim*, 72, 106, 108, 122, 125, 127; procession 47; revival of 9; Roman Catholicism 10; sacralisation 9; Santiago de Compostela 8, 127; Shikoku 33; shrines 59, 97, 108; traditional 127

Russian Orthodox: culture 80; icons 80; Russian 83, 102, 104; Russian pilgrimages 80

sacred: accessing 57; apparition 178; boundaries 47; centre 43 n. 6, 100, 135, 137; communication with 105; contestation 6, 10, 123; Durkheim 172, 176; figures 32; geographies 23, 27, 31, 142; goal 48; Hertz 176; history 63; images 178; journeys 64 n. 2, 154, 164; landscape 103; map 137; objects 71, 82, 85; officially 143; perception of 178; pilgrimage 36, 142; place 3, 9, 13, 46, 53, 55, 64 n. 2, 80, 82, 85, 88, 97, 106, 108 n. 1, 135, 140, 144, 184; prayers 63; profane binary 3, 8, 98, 123, 183; representation of 178; return of 158; rituals 82, 157; routes 108; sites 4, 75, 136, 138, 146, 147, 177–9, 183; space 55, 58, 103, 146, 147, 162; springs 47, 98; supernatural

210   *Index*

178; territory 59; transition to 59; wells 97, 98
Saikoku 25, 33 *passim*
Saintyves, P. 173
Sakata, M. 37, 40; K. Osada, M. Sakata and M. Seki 38, 43 n. 9
Sallnow, M. 2, 5, 6
Samson, J. 89
sanctuaries 11, 74, 152, 157, 174, 184; *see also* urban
Santiago de Compostela 8, 9, 40, 99, 100, 125–7, 134, 154, 162, 164, 181
Sasson, A. 146
Satō, H. 30, 37, 39
Saucken, P. von 164
Sax, W. 9
Scharfe, M. 117–19; and M. Schmolze and G. Chubert 117, 123
Schmidt, L. 114, 116
Schön, D. 105
Schram, F. 104
Schreiber, G. 97, 103, 118
Schuh, B. 118
Schützeichel, R. 125
Sébillot, P. 172 *passim*, 187
Sekerdej, K., A. Pasieka and M. Warat 88; and A. Pasieka 88, 89
secular: Austrian Social Democratic Party 122, 127; courts 108; debates 62, De Martino 156; discourses 143; feast-day 105; ideology 141; Lady Diana 123; modernity 14, 126, 141; nationalism 142, 145; nationalists 14; nation-states 14; pilgrimage 6, 107, 122, 123, 135, 141, 143; post-secular 60, 120; ritual operators 161; ritual walking 59; sites 143; Soviet 52; state 51; world 3, 15, 123
secularisation: communal engagement 106; Hervieu-Léger 180; model 145; paradigm 2; perspective 105; processes 145; religous phenomena 125; Soviet 61; spiritual phenomena 125; theory 145
Seki, M. 37, 38, 43 n. 9
self: assurance 11; authentic 127; conscious 71; critical 71; discovery 40; Polish social sciences 71; quest for 125; reliant 16; religion 120
Serb: Orthodox Church 106

Sered, S. 137, 138, 140, 143, 145
Shevarenkova, M. 59
Shchepanskaia, T. 57–9
Shtyrkov, S. 50, 51, 56
Shultz, J. 39
Sibeud, E. 175
Shevzov, V. 50, 64 n. 4
Shields, R. 8
Shikoku 4, 25, 26, 30 *passim*
Shinjō, T. 24, 25, 30, 31, 35 *passim*
Shinno, T. 24, 25, 27, 31, 32, 34, 43 n. 8
shrines: aristocracy 27; atmosphere of 98, 108; Christian 9, 11; concept of 96; contested 55; copies 82; cryptic 178; custodians 103; dark Madonna 185; denominational links 103; desecrated 47; devotional literature 73, 74; economic life of 164; ethnic links 103; Eucharistic 101; emergence of 100, 103; ethnology 104; European 2; folklore 55, 105; folk religiosity 82; functioning of 100; Greek Catholic 74; hierarchy of 58; histories 73, 74, 96, 105, 108; holy persons 58; identity-building 85; Italian folk studies 153; Jewish 105, 140 *passim*; journeys to 13, 14, 25, 50; Kolberg 71; Kumano 33; large 74; local 51, 54, 55, 58, 60, 72, 103, 135; Lourdes 179; Marian 72, 74, 80, 99, 102, 164, 177, 179; Middle Ages 102; minor 139; miracles 103; motivations 103; museums 119; network 100; newest Polish 88; non-Christian 127; northern Russia 58, 59; old 165 *passim*; Partitions (Poland) 74; Passion 72; peasants 74; pictures 81; pilgrimage 3, 9, 10, 35, 69, 71, 73, 87, 99, 104, 105, 108, 115, 139, 181, 186, 187; popular 87, 97, 99, 139, 141; processions 98; regional 80, 102, 108; religious majority 186; roads 103; Roman Catholic 74, 152 *passim*; royal saints 100; rural 55, 57, 58; Russian Orthodox 47, 64 n. 2; shared 16, 162, 186, 187; Shinto 25, 27, 33, 35; small 73, 165; social life of 164, 165;

Index 211

spirituality 97; springs 98; Syria 184; therapeutic qualities 12; thriving 72; Transylvania 106; unofficial 57; urban(ised) 3, 5, 55; village 51; votive objects 98, 103, 115; well 98

Sibireva, O. 51

Signorelli, A. 156

Simeoni, P. 166 n. 5

society 8, 146, 184; consumer 199; cultural shortcomings 119; emotional needs 119; European 2; isolated 157; Israeli 143, 145; Japanese 35; Jewish 135, 138, 140, 142, 148 n. 1; modern 120, 145; multicultural 165; pastoral 157; peasant 182; pilgrims 182; poorer sections of 38; postindustrial 120; post-Soviet 50; reintegration into 61; ritual 182; rural 2, 29; Russian 49; secularised 181; spiritual shortcomings 119; strata 25, 76, 79; urban 119

Soeffner, H. 124

Sokolovskiy, S. 50

Solomon, N. 134

space 16, 48, 62 passim, 89, 162; controlling 154, 178; cultural impacts 147; desecrated 54; investigation 155; memory 106; ontological 5; public 88; reclaiming 54; religious controversy 187; sacred 3, 55, 58, 146, 147, 162; sanctification 63, 147, 148; symbolic 157, 161; utopian 156

spiritual: atmosphere 56; benefits 29; Compostela 162; considerations 152; developments 121; elevation 79; effusion 177; entities 27; experience 162; figure 29; finding the self 120; gifts 58; guides 119; healing 82; higher realms 25; inner life 79; journeys 27, 28, 31; leaders 55; lives 53; longings for 120; master 105; movements 121; phenomena 125; pilgrimages 6, 72; post-modernity 9; processes 7; shortcomings 119; symbols 137; wanderer 30

spirituality 117, 125, 128 n. 11, 162; feminist 185; individualised 152; Israel 145; Mary Magdalene 162; movement 185; peasant 79;

research 125; Russian Orthodox 61; shrines 97

Starnawski, J. 69

St. Besse 5, 12, 176, 177

St. Donato 160, 181

Stomma, L. 82, 83

Stausberg, M. 6, 126

structures: behavioural 85; classificatory 34; cult of images 83; cultural 85; economic 35; everyday 60; folklore 23; holy places 57; infrastructures 35, 36, 38; institutional 2, 3; meaning 61; mental 85; narratives 53; of national knowledge production 1, 9; pilgrimage 23, 34, 36, 38, 86, 95; religious 23, 27 passim, 41; religious thought 178; routes 108; social 41; spatial 34, 103; support 27, 31, 36

Sumption, J. 2

Sutcliffe, S. and M. Bowman 121

Swatos, W. 7

Switzerland 114, 118, 188 n. 5

symbolic: analysis 83; anthropology 156; expression 106; Jerusalem 136; Kraków 76; passing through 27; Polish history 76; practices 156; reorganisation 161; spaces 157, 161; strategy 163; systems 153, 154, 160, 181, 182; transcendent universe 161; visible actions 121

symbols 7, 80, 119; metaphysical 137; Palestine 184; religious 75, 82; ritual 3; Roman Catholic 70; saints 184; spiritual 137; subgroup 79

Syria 184, 186

Szabo, M. and I. Zombori 105

Szakály, I. 99

Szamosi, J. 104

Szeged: 97, 105; university 104, 105

Szendrey, Á. 96

Szilárdfy, Z. 102, 103; and G. Tuskes and E. Knapp 103

Szőts, I. 99

Takeda, A. 30

Tari, J. 99

Tenishev, N. 49, 58

text 6, 9, 31, 71; anthropologists 159; biblical 136; canonised 136; Czarnowski 78; Di Gianni 160;

212 *Index*

documentaries 159; Dupront 177; Durkheim 175, 176; hagiographic 176; Hertz 172, 176; Hervieu-Léger 180; inter-religious relationships 186; nineteenth century 73 *passim*; original 77, 128 n. 6; representation 160; twentieth century 77 *passim*; van Gennep 2

Thévenot, L. 182; and Boltanski 183

Thomas, W. and F. Znaniecki 77–8, 90 n. 4, n. 9 and n. 14

Thrift, N. 8

time(s) 9, 63, 162; baptism 174; conditions 95; control 154; crisis 48, 58; decline 36; free 60; harvest 156; Hertz 177; misfortune 58; modern 28, 42 n. 1, 179; pilgrimage 70, 117; Polish social sciences 71; premodern 42 n. 1; Reymont 91 n. 15; shrines 50; sickness 58; timeless 160, Tokugawa 36

Timothy, D. and D. Olsen 6

Tishkov 49, 51, 52

Tokarska-Bakir, J. 81, 91 n. 12

Tokugawa period 25, 34–7

Tokyo 34, 35

Tomasi, L. 7

Tomicki, R. 82, 83, 91 n. 14

tourism 158; anthropology of 160; cultural 107; and faith 164; heritage 54, 106; industry 152; Japan 36; offices 107; operators 126; and pilgrimage 6, 7, 11, 17 n. 3, 36, 107, 126, 127, 143, 147, 152; religion 42 n. 2; religious 36, 99, 106–7; research 143, 146

tradition(s) 29, 49, 50; academic i, 2, 11, 12, 23, 57, 162; Anglo-Saxon 160; Buddhism 25, 32–33, 40; Christian 10, 48, 136, 137; community building 89; cultural 97, 153; cultural survival 153; devotional 95, 96; devotional literature 73; disciplinary 1, 2, 13, 15, 16, 173; dominant faith 30; Europe 13; European ethnology 126; folk 30, 153, 164; folk culture 118; folk knowledge 50; folkore studies 63, 126, 127 n. 1, 153, 181; French research 160, 161, 162, 171 *passim*; holy place 59; Hungarian 104; iden-

tity studies 89; Italian research 161, 162, 179, 181; Japanese 39; Jewish 105, 136, 138, 147; linguistic 1, 13; literary 95; local 30, 32; local conditions 55; Marian 95; meaning 61; and modernity 15; mountains 27; multilayered 53; Muslim 137, 186; national 13, 75, 154; non-Christian 9; oral 24, 31; parishes 105, 108; philology 63; pilgrimage 24, 25, 28, 40, 48, 104, 106, 124, 138, 143, 147, 152, 161, 182; pilgrimage research 11, 114, 171; Polish 88; popular 153, 155–58, 164, 166 n. 1 and 2; processions 48; Pure Land 30; regional 153, 161; reinvention 165; religious 2, 16, 23, 28, 29, 39, 42, 164, 179; rituals 12, 59; Roman Catholic 124; rural 159; Russian Orthodox 47, 48, 50, 60, 61, 63; Shugendō 28; social 147; worldviews 78

traditional: attire 81; authentic 158; boundaries 165; cult of images 83; culture 120, 159; ethnic groups 146; focus on Roman Catholic pilgrimage 89; folk 83; folk culture 77, 82, 83, 118; groups of pilgrims 124; local life 152, 154; peasantry 155; perpetuation of pilgrimage 104; pilgrim route 122; pilgrimage 122, 124, 135, 154, 157; pilgrimage route 127; religion 148; rituals 12, 88, 155, 157, 159, 161; societies 91 n. 13, 145; ways of life 119

transnational 53; migration 163, 166 n. 4; movement 163; processes 89; relationships 88; shrine 106

Tuchschaden, K. 114

Turner, V. 2–7, 10 *passim*, 17 n. 2, 40, 43 n. 3, 50, 60, 61, 70, 107, 124, 160, 171, 174, 184; and E. Turner 123, 177

Tüskés, G. 96, 103; and E. Knapp 103; Z. Szilardfy, G. Tuskes and E. Knapp 103

typologies 5, 34; of pilgrimage 32, 163

Tweed, T. 7, 8, 10

Index   213

Ukraine 64 n. 4, 74, 147, 185
universal: analytical approach 42;
cyptic process 178; folk-type
religiosity 85; human feelings
178; humanity 3; model of pilgrimage 13; pilgrimage 10, 24,
42, 48, 163; religious thought
178; Western agendas 24
universities 1; Anglophone 10, 16;
French 162; German-speaking
10; global competition 165;
national 9; Polish 77, 78
Urbach, E. 136
urban: culture 116; religiosity 57;
religious practices 51, 61; sanctuaries 184; society 119; Temple
Mount 136; *see* shrines
urbanisation 14, 32, 118, 126

Vajkai, A. 98
van Gennep, A. 2, 12, 14, 171 *passim*,
187
Vasquez, M. 9; and M. Marquardt 7;
and A. Petersen and P. Williams
9
veneration 57 *passim*; distance 56;
Eastern Christianity 47; holy
objects 50, 52, 61; Hungarian
saints 96, 100, 105; icons 48;
Jewish saints 138, 145; local
level 52; Marian 64 n. 4, 83;
mass 54; mountain 27; of popular figures 79; people 50; sacred
places 106; spiritual masters 105
Vedernikova, N. 59
Verdier, Y. 182
village(s) 5, 29, 37, 57, 84, 85; affiliation 79; culture 50; Czarnowski
78–79; Gietrzwałd 75; Italy 87,
161; Kolberg 71; Lebanon 184;
local disputes 183; pilgrimage
87, 154; Polish 78; Reymont 70;
shrines 51
villager(s): Polish 91 n. 10; and regional
group 79

Vindis-Rösler, L. 125, 126, 128 n. 11
Vinogradov, V. 52, 55
Vorhad, M. 99
votive: churches 104; images 96, 98,
103, 105; objects 58, 98, 102,
104, 115; offerings 114–16, 126;
pictures 114–15; records 126;
statues 126; tablets 114
vows 97, 108 n. 1, 178, 179; health
174; to the saint 175
Vukonic, B. 6

Wanner, C. 62
war: and revolution 114; Cold War
51; First World War 99, 154,
177; interwar period 83; Second
World War 82, 98, 114, 152,
155, 159, 164; Six Days War
138
Warsaw 69, 73, 78, 85, 90 n. 1
water 72, 86, 173, 178; healing power
98; holy 62; sacred well 97
Werbner, R. 5
Weyl, C. 48
Wiebel-Fanderl, O. 114
Wilson, S. 176
Wincenty, P. 76
Witkowska, A. 74
women 36, 81, 144; history of 160;
Jewish 175; peasant pilgrimage
50; religious and symbolic prac-
tices 156; social position of 156
Worobec, C. 50, 58, 63 n. 1, 64 n. 4
Wynn, M. 63

Yamaori, T. 30
Yamashita, S., J. Bosco and J. Eades 1
Yanagita, K. 29
Yamba, B. 5

Zacher, C. 2
Zapponi, E. 152 *passim*, 181
Ziejka, F. 75, 76, 90 n. 1
Zola, E. 158
Zowczak, M. 77